THE ARTISTS IN PERSPECTIVE SERIES

H. W. Janson, general editor

The ARTISTS IN PERSPECTIVE *series presents individual illustrated volumes of interpretive essays on the most significant painters, sculptors, architects, and genres of world art.*

Each volume provides an understanding of art and artists through both esthetic and cultural evaluations.

PETER SERENYI, editor of this volume, is presently Associate Professor of Architectural History at Northeastern University in Boston. A specialist in the fields of modern architecture and city planning, he has published several articles on Le Corbusier.

LE CORBUSIER
in Perspective

Edited by

PETER SERENYI

A SPECTRUM BOOK

Prentice-Hall, Inc., Englewood Cliffs, New Jersey

Library of Congress Cataloging in Publication Data

Serenyi, Peter, 1931–   comp.
  Le Corbusier in perspective.

  (Artists in perspective series) (A Spectrum Book)
  Bibliography: p.
  1. Jeanneret-Gris, Charles Edouard, 1887–1965.
I. Title.
NA1053.J4S47   720′.92′4   74–22451
ISBN 0–13–527291–2
ISBN 0–13–527283–1 pbk.

© 1975 BY PRENTICE-HALL, INC.
ENGLEWOOD CLIFFS, NEW JERSEY

A SPECTRUM BOOK

1 2 3 4 5 6 7 8 9 10

Printed in the United States of America

PRENTICE-HALL INTERNATIONAL, INC. (LONDON)
PRENTICE-HALL OF AUSTRALIA PTY., LTD. (SYDNEY)
PRENTICE-HALL OF CANADA, LTD. (TORONTO)
PRENTICE-HALL OF INDIA PRIVATE LIMITED (NEW DELHI)
PRENTICE-HALL OF JAPAN, INC. (TOKYO)

To Agnes

CONTENTS

PREFACE

No single historian or critic can fully explore a mind as rich and complex as Le Corbusier's, and no single monograph can give the full flavor of the responses he elicited over the past decades. Hence, a sampling of the writings of the most spirited contemporary critics and selections from significant historical evaluations may provide the best tool for a better understanding of the nature and meaning of his art.

This volume has a dual purpose: it offers a range of critical writings on Le Corbusier from the earliest to the most recent, and it shows the development of his work, from its beginnings to its culmination, through the eyes of some of the most perceptive critics and historians in the field. Yet completeness is far from what is being attempted here. Only two aspects of his multifarious activities—the most significant to be sure—have been singled out for inclusion: architecture and city planning. It must be remembered that Le Corbusier was also a painter, sculptor, furniture and tapestry designer, and author of over forty books and innumerable articles.

The purpose of the bibliography is not to duplicate but rather to complement those already in existence, of which the three most outstanding were compiled by C. L. Ragghianti, Maurice Besset, and Jean Petit. In 1963 Ragghianti published a catalogue that accompanied the exhibition of Le Corbusier's works in the Palazzo Strozzi in Florence. This catalogue contains the most complete bibliography of critical and historical works on Le Corbusier published in Italy between 1921 and 1962. In his book *Who was Le Corbusier?* (New York, 1968), Maurice Besset offers a remarkably complete list of books, exhibition catalogues and special issues of journals devoted to Le Corbusier. Jean Petit's *Le Corbusier lui-même* (Geneva, 1970) contains the first extensive list of articles about the architect published in journals and newspapers.

A book of this nature can only be made possible with the help of many. First, I owe a note of thanks to the authors and copyright owners without whose cooperation this volume could not have been realized. The invaluable help given by George Baird, H. Allen Brooks, George R. Collins, William Curtis, Kenneth Frampton, Eduard Sekler, as well as H. W. Janson, the editor of this series, is deeply appreciated. Among the many libraries that were used, the Frances Loeb Library of the Harvard Graduate School of Design stands out. Its rich holdings and its ever helpful staff made my work easier.

The English rendering of Karel Teige's article is based on translations made by Karel Kovanda and two students of George Baird: Elisabeth and Ladislav Holovsky. Hildegarde Hunt von Laue undertook the difficult task of translating the articles by Sigfried Giedion, Cornelius Gurlitt, Steen Eiler Rasmussen, and Paul Westheim. All translations were edited by my wife and myself. My wife translated the articles by Marcello Piacentini, Maximilien Gauthier, and Waldemar George, and spent countless hours editing the entire manuscript. Her support helped make this book possible, and it is to her that it is dedicated.

LE CORBUSIER

in Perspective

INTRODUCTION[1]

During his long creative life Le Corbusier responded primarily to emerging tendencies rather than to the circumstances of a given moment. He gave form to a life pattern in the making rather than to one already in existence. No wonder therefore that especially during the early phase of his career there were only a select few who could discern the nature and significance of his ideas. These critics were by no means always positively inclined toward Le Corbusier's vision, but they comprehended his diagnosis of the contemporary situation and could foresee the implications of his responses.

When Le Corbusier exhibited his seminal projects at the *Salon d'Automne* of 1922—a mass-production house (Maison Citrohan), a new kind of apartment house (Immeubles Villas) and A Contemporary City for Three Million Inhabitants (Une Ville Contemporaine)—he provoked a wide range of reactions in the journals and newspapers of Paris. The idea of living in mass-produced houses, or in apartment houses with roof-top recreational facilities, or in cities dissected by highways disturbed contemporary sensibilities. Hence, Waldemar George's evaluation of Le Corbusier's city published shortly after the exhibition seems remarkably balanced and foresighted. He admired the Ville's responsiveness to the ills of the modern metropolis and hailed the rational order underlying its plan. He recognized that the Ville was not simply an abstract diagram but rather a city plan related to certain key features that characterize Paris: straight avenues, uniform apartment blocks and large parks. This view was shared by some other noted French critics such as Raymond Cogniat and Maurice Raynal.[2] Valuing the plan's rationality, clarity and functional fitness, the French were more receptive to the Ville than most foreign critics, who had in fact very little good to say about it.

However, it was not at the *Salon d'Automne* of 1922 that Le Cor-

---

[1] All works mentioned in the Introduction are included either in the text or in the bibliography unless otherwise indicated.
[2] For Raynal's evaluation, see "La Cité contemporaine de Le Corbusier," *Les Feuilles Libres*, 4, No. 30 (1922), 407–11.

1

busier's seminal projects were first made public. They had already been published in *L'Esprit Nouveau,* a periodical he founded in 1920. His article, "The Engineer's Aesthetic: Mass-Production Houses," appeared in October, 1921, and it is to this piece that Marcello Piacentini addresses himself. His brief evaluation succinctly states the major objections that have been raised by many critics since the 1920s to the impersonal, stand-ardized, machine-processed architecture Le Corbusier proposed to initi-ate. Yet Piacentini, an architect who had himself designed progressivistic middle-class housing during the 1910s, stopped short of a mere dismissal of Le Corbusier's ideas. He recommended instead a fusion between the personal and the impersonal, the vernacular and the international, the old and the new. This is precisely the road Le Corbusier began to follow from 1930 onward, culminating in such later works as the Maisons Jaoul of 1952–56 (Fig. 21). The stylistic change that prompted James Stirling to say in 1954, "frequently accused of being 'internationalist,' Le Corbusier is actually the most regional of architects," must have pleased Piacentini.

Notwithstanding his admiration for the engineer and his advocacy of mass-production houses, Le Corbusier did not wish to replace architec-ture with engineering or artistic expression with mere functionalism. The first critic to dwell on this theme was Paul Westheim. Basing his observa-tions primarily on articles published in *L'Esprit Nouveau,* he noted in 1922 that Le Corbusier "wants to create as an artist from a pre-conceived notion of form" and instead of pursuing transitory purposes as the engi-neer, he is seeking "eternal values."

The ideas presented in *L'Esprit Nouveau* and at the *Salon d'Au-tomne* of 1922 were initially tested in a small villa Le Corbusier built near Paris in Vaucresson during the following year. There the gap between theory and practice became quickly apparent to him.[3] In 1923 he was offered an even more challenging opportunity to test theory against prac-tical requirements by Raoul La Roche, a Swiss banker, and by the artist's brother, Albert Jeanneret, a musician.[4] Because the needs of his clients were rather complex, the prototypal Maison Citrohan could not simply be transferred from Le Corbusier's atelier to the site on the square du Doc-teur-Blanche in Paris. But as if to prove that the double-storied living room of the Maison Citrohan is an eminently flexible idea, Le Corbusier transformed it in the La Roche house into the most imaginative entrance hall he had ever conceived. Sigfried Giedion rightly compares it to the interiors of certain Baroque chapels (Fig. 9).

The International Exhibition of Decorative Arts held in Paris in 1925 offered Le Corbusier another opportunity to disseminate his ideas. There he erected the Esprit Nouveau pavilion, a model of one unit of the Villa-Apartment Blocks (Immeubles Villas) of 1922 (Fig. 8). In it he ex-hibited the Voisin plan of Paris, named after Gabriel Voisin, the auto-

---

[3] Le Corbusier, *Oeuvre complète, 1910–1929* (Zurich: Les Editions Girsberger, 1960), p. 48.
[4] This double house is now the "Fondation Le Corbusier," the chief research center for Le Corbusier studies.

mobile manufacturer who supported it financially. The Voisin plan was the direct application to the center of Paris of ideas first proposed in the Ville Contemporaine (Fig. 7). The plan called for the demolition of some key sections of the inner city and the erection of a commercial center and a residential district. Although the former would have replaced a largely dilapidated area, the latter was to occupy some of the choicest parts of the city bounded by the Avenue Gabriel and the Rue de Rivoli on the south and the district surrounding the Boulevard Haussmann toward the north.[5] For her losses Le Corbusier offered Paris steel and glass office towers placed in the midst of greenery, apartment superblocks surrounded by parks and a railroad station topped by a landing platform for airplanes. Moreover, he proposed the building of two highways running east to west and north to south, connecting the outskirts of the city with its inner core. As in the Ville Contemporaine, Le Corbusier addressed himself in the Voisin plan to what he considered the four most urgent needs of Paris: apartment houses, parks, office buildings and highways.[6] His solution called not for piecemeal cure but surgery. In 1922 Le Corbusier used the plan for A Contemporary City as a guise to introduce his proposals for the rebuilding of Paris, whereas in 1925 he overtly applied these ideas to the center of the French capital. This taxed the tolerance of even his most avid admirers, not to mention the added ammunition it provided for his enemies.

The strongest opposition from abroad came primarily from the Germanic countries, and to a lesser extent from England. One of his most outspoken critics was the Swiss architect, Alexander von Senger, who, in his *Krisis der Architektur* (1928) became Le Corbusier's fiercest antagonist. In it he called the architect's large-scale projects communistic and his executed buildings mechanistic. Yet the most literate outcry came from the pen of Cornelius Gurlitt, the eminent historian of architecture. His article was occasioned by the appearance of the German translation of *Urbanisme* in 1929. In trying to assess the book in general and the Voisin plan in particular, Gurlitt wonders whether Le Corbusier was indeed serious in offering such drastic proposals, or whether he meant to be ironic. In England Trystan Edwards considered the Ville as an oversimplified solution to the complex problems of the big city, and S. D. Adshead lamented the fact that Le Corbusier was unconcerned about man's unique needs and idiosyncracies. But today the ideas embodied in the Ville Contemporaine and the Voisin plan are, for better or worse, the realities of many large cities. Scores of fine buildings are gutted to provide space for steel and glass skyscrapers, and many residential districts are leveled to make way for highways—just as Le Corbusier had proposed. Yet Stanislaus von Moos rightly poses the question of whether we

---

[5] For a comparison of the Voisin plan with the corresponding area of Paris, see Le Corbusier, *The City of Tomorrow* (Cambridge, Mass.: The M.I.T. Press, 1971), p. 278 and p. 275.

[6] These were codified in the Athens Charter of 1933 as habitation, leisure, work and traffic.

should "use him as a scapegoat for current urban diseases." The author's probing evaluation places the Ville and the Voisin plan in a historical context and links them to the realities of the present.

The late 1920s mark the appearance of the most stimulating criticism written not only by conservative critics such as Gurlitt and Edwards but also by such progressives as Karel Teige. As an exponent of pragmatic utilitarianism, this Czech architect-critic singled out Le Corbusier's Mundaneum, a plan for a world center of learning and understanding, as his chief target of attack. Planned in 1928 for a site north of Geneva facing the lake, the Mundaneum [Fig. 17] was an architectural response to ideas formulated by Paul Otlet, the secretary of the "Union des Associations internationales" of Brussels. Otlet's aim was to promote international understanding through peace and progress founded on broad humanitarian ideals. Le Corbusier responded to this programme by conceiving a world center inspired by the ideal plans of École des Beaux Arts competition entries.[7] Its quasi-academic plan and its seemingly historicist buildings elicited hostile reactions in the progressivistic architectural circles of the late 1920s. Teige's critique articulates most succinctly the views of Marxist materialists and those of the exponents of the *Neue Sachlichkeit* (New Objectivity), largely prevalent in Germany, Holland, Czechoslovakia and Hungary.[8] His denunciation of monumentality, aestheticism and a commitment to "elevated ideas" in architecture foreshadows the attitudes of progressivistic architects and city planners of today.

The extent to which Le Corbusier took the young Czech architect's criticism to heart can be seen in his direct response published in Teige's journal, *Stavba* in 1929, and later reprinted in the April, 1933 issue of *L'Architecture d'Aujourd'hui*, entitled "Défense de l'architecture." Here, as well as in his book *Précisions*, also published in 1929, he defends the Mundaneum as a manifestation of machine-like functionalism and poetic imagination. Like so many of Le Corbusier's creations, the Mundaneum is a fusion of the past and the present, the temporal and the eternal, of history and modernity.

Exponents or defenders of the organic-structural approach to architecture mostly prevalent in Germany and the United States also attacked Le Corbusier for his formalism and commitment to geometry. In 1931, for example, Walter Curt Behrendt took issue with Le Corbusier's "academicism" and upheld Frank Lloyd Wright's organic-structural style.[9] He called the architecture of the former learned and that of the

---

[7] Cf. Paul Otlet and Le Corbusier, *Mundaneum*, Brussels, 1928. For an important visual and ideological source of the Mundaneum, see Hendrik Christian Andersen and Ernest M. Hébrard, *Creation of a World Centre of Communication*, Paris, 1913. The authors sent a copy of this book to Otlet, who in turn refers to Andersen's project on page 28 of *Mundaneum*.

[8] For a comparison of the idealist and utilitarian approaches to architecture as exemplified by the League of Nations competition entries of Le Corbusier and Hannes Meyer, see Kenneth Frampton's article referred to in the bibliography.

[9] The original version of Behrendt's essay reprinted here from his *Modern Building* had already appeared in the November, 1931 issue of *Kunst und Künstler*. How-

latter authentic and natural. Behrendt's incisive observation of 1931 that "Le Corbusier's art is revolutionary without being new and Wright's art is new without being revolutionary" was echoed in the writings of many later critics. In fact, his comparison of the two most original architects of this century was followed by those of many later authors such as Kantorovich (1942), Stillman (1948), Troedsson (1951), Cordier (1971) and Fishman (1974).

However, not every early critic of Le Corbusier censured him for his commitment to geometry and eternal values. We have seen that as early as 1922 Paul Westheim recognized this as a positive part of the architect's work. He in fact argued that Le Corbusier valued geometry not for its own sake but rather for the sake of a "higher will to form." Six years later the foremost American historian of modern architecture, Henry-Russell Hitchcock, presented the first serious interpretation on this side of the Atlantic of the theoretical basis that underlies Le Corbusier's work. Writing in *The Architectural Record* of 1928, Hitchcock rightly emphasized the fact that for the "New Pioneers," referring to Oud, Gropius and particularly Le Corbusier, "engineering is not . . . the whole of architecture" but is instead the "spiritual" which for them is the "true architectural problem." This view of Le Corbusier's art and thought reached an early culmination in the writings of Colin Rowe. A student of Wittkower and Hitchcock, he was the first to recognize how deeply and in what manner Le Corbusier was indebted to the past. He discovered that Palladio, one of the most honored masters of the Academies, was also Le Corbusier's mentor. Owing to the pioneering work of Rowe, the implications of Le Corbusier's desire expressed in a letter to Rex Martienssen in 1939 "to build a villa in the spirit of Palladio's villas" becomes fully comprehensible.[10]

The years between 1922 and 1930 represent the most active period in Le Corbusier's mid-career. Although his plans for cities remained on paper, he was able to find a few private clients who understood his vision. They came from two segments of society: the world of art and the world of business. They included the artists Amédée Ozenfant, Albert Jeanneret and Jacques Lipchitz as well as Miestschaninoff, Cook and Planeix, and the businessmen Raoul La Roche, Michael Stein and Pierre Savoye. His clients had two things in common: most of them were outsiders or foreigners living in Paris, as was Le Corbusier, and most of them wanted studio houses. In his previously mentioned article Walter Curt Behrendt first characterized Le Corbusier's dwellings as studio houses best suited for men of the world or businessmen who are constantly on the move, living out of their suitcases, so to speak. Subsequently Reyner Banham

ever, his comparison of Frank Lloyd Wright with Le Corbusier is not included in this anthology.

10 For this unpublished letter of Le Corbusier written to the most eminent architect of South Africa of the 1920s and 1930s, refer to Gilbert Herbert's article in the bibliography. On Wittkower's influence on the architects of the 1950s, see Henry A. Millon's article in the bibliography.

was the first to place Le Corbusier's studio houses in a historical context.[11]

The chapters entitled "The Mechanical Analogy" and "History and Modernity" are brought to a close with the writings of Reyner Banham. The underlying connection between these themes rests on Le Corbusier's belief that houses should be built like ships, airplanes or automobiles, without forgetting, however, "the eternal verities" that must always animate them. The "mechanical analogy" as realized by Le Corbusier is elucidated by Banham in his first essay, while his second offers a spirited description of the Villa Savoye of 1928–31 (Fig. 15). Here Le Corbusier's most unique villa is seen not only as a modern realization of the Virgilian dream, as had first been pointed out by Colin Rowe in the preceding essay, but also as "the home of a fully motorized post-Futurist family."

Le Corbusier could best preserve most of the original characteristics of the prototypal studio house, the Maison Citrohan of 1920–22 (Fig. 6), when no specific client had to be kept in mind. Such was the case when he designed a workers' settlement in 1924 for the industrialist Henri Frugès in Pessac, near Bordeaux (Fig. 10), and in 1927 when he built two houses for the Weissenhofsiedlung in Stuttgart, the site of an international housing exhibition organized by the German Werkbund. The settlement in Pessac had undergone drastic changes since its completion in 1926 (Fig. 11), and the forces that prompted its transformation were investigated by Philippe Boudon. In spite of Le Corbusier's standpoint to the contrary, Boudon argues that the extensive modifications made in the houses of Pessac should be regarded as a positive rather than a negative consequence of the architect's original conception.

To evaluate the "success" or "failure" of Pessac, two questions must be raised. First, did it live up to Le Corbusier's own criterion of good architecture; second, can houses whose owners must reshape them immediately and often entirely at great expense be called successful? Even if Le Corbusier made the "conversion game" possible through his use of a flexible skeletal system, the cost of the "game" made it expensive to play. But more importantly, Le Corbusier believed that good architecture must fulfill certain specific structural, biological, economic, social and psychological requirements. Steen Eiler Rasmussen summed up the problem of Pessac succinctly in 1926: "It is doubtful whether the housing is at all serviceable for the worker population for whom it was intended, since actually it ought to be inhabited by extremely cultivated people." He advised Le Corbusier that "a project like Pessac should be based upon a careful study of the needs and wishes of its future residents." From Brian Brace Taylor's historical evaluation of Pessac we learn that Le Corbusier had carefully studied the history and evolution of workers' housing. Yet like a true Ruskinian he believed that he could shape, indeed elevate, humanity through architecture. Instead of responding to the actual social and psychological needs of working-class people, he tried to

[11] See not only the selection included in Chapter II but also his first article on the subject listed in the bibliography.

redefine those needs in order to bring about a new consciousness. By creating a settlement in Pessac consisting of variations of the Maison Citrohan studio house not unrelated to his Parisian villas, Le Corbusier had hoped that he could transform Frugès' workers into sensitive recipients of his artistic and ethical vision. The fact that he failed to achieve his goal reveals the ineffectualness of architecture as a molder of men. Architecture can express and influence but not transform man's nature and predilections.

Le Corbusier began the introduction to the second volume of his *Oeuvre complète,* covering the early years of his period of "reassessment," which extends from 1930 to 1945, with these words:

> 1929 . . . meant to me, to a certain extent, the end of the first period of investigations. 1930 opened a period of new tasks; it relates to important works, great events in architecture and city planning, to the marvellous epoch of evolving a new machine civilization.

The marked changes that appeared in his art from about 1930 are due to several reasons. The political forces that were at work in Europe at that time, the economic depression of the same years, and his disappointments of the 1920s encouraged Le Corbusier to abandon his solitary approach to large-scale reform in favor of collective action. He joined the Syndicalist movement and became one of its leading propagandists through its organs, *Plans* and *Prélude.* In 1935 he published most of the articles that appeared in these journals in *La Ville Radieuse.* It is to this important theoretical-polemical book that Kenneth Frampton addresses himself in his pioneering article, "The City of Dialectic."

The year 1930 also represents a significant turning point in Le Corbusier's architecture. My paper presented at the second Modern Architecture Symposium held at Columbia University in 1964 and devoted to the decade 1929–39, first drew attention to these changes, notably to his adoption of a more organic-structural approach to architecture.

Between 1942 and 1948, with the help of Gerald Hanning, Elisa Maillard and Jerzy Soltan, Le Corbusier created the Modulor, "a harmonious measure to the human scale," to use his words (Fig. 27). Its antecedents in his own work go back to the "regulating lines" first introduced in the house designed for his parents in 1911.[12] Following the Platonic belief that geometry underlies the structure of the universe, the architect used regulating lines forming various geometrical shapes to establish a harmonious link between his works and the universe. He applied these not only to most of his buildings and city plans until the early 1940s but also to some of his paintings. His urge to create unity in the face of the disunity caused by World War II prompted him to develop the Modulor,

---

12 Cf. Le Corbusier, *The Modulor* (Cambridge, Mass.: Harvard University Press, 1958), pp. 26, 213. For Le Corbusier's reference to a villa designed by Lauweriks, where a forerunner of the regulating lines was used, see Helen Searing's review of N. H. M. Tummers, *J. L. Mathieu Lauweriks* in the *Journal of the Society of Architectural Historians,* XXXII (1937), 255.

a new system of measurement based on man. Its intellectual sources, going back to Pythagoras, are explored illuminatingly by Rudolf Wittkower, and its limitations are concisely summed up by Peter Collins.

The Modulor was first tested in the Unité d'Habitation (Fig. 22), built in Marseilles between 1948 and 1952, during the early years of Le Corbusier's period of "fulfillment." The sources and meaning of this seminal building are discussed in my article, "Le Corbusier, Fourier, and the Monastery of Ema." The Unité was severely condemned by such early critics as F. J. Osborn and Lewis Mumford,[13] but in 1973 Roger Schafer examined it after two decades of use and found that although it is not functioning as the architect had originally planned, the building is "working very well" for those who now live there.

The Unité of Marseilles was followed by such landmarks as the Chapel at Ronchamp of 1950–55, the Jaoul houses of 1952–56, and the Monastery of La Tourette of 1957–60 (Figs. 25, 21, 26). The finest analysis of the Monastery was written by Colin Rowe, while the liveliest criticism of the other buildings came from the pen of James Stirling. Writing even before the Jaoul houses were entirely completed, Stirling found in them disturbingly "little reference to the rational principles" that characterize the architecture of the 1920s as exemplified by the villa at Garches (Fig. 12). This view of Le Corbusier's postwar architecture was widely held in the 1950s, and is echoed in the title of Frederick Gutheim's article, "The New Corbusier." However, in 1958 John M. Jacobus made the incisive observation that the Chapel at Ronchamp, "novel as it is, is really a development (if not an ultimate realization) of ideas concerning the manipulation of space that Le Corbusier has clung to since the early 1920s." He also indicated the applicability of this statement to the architect's other late buildings.

The pilgrimage chapel at Ronchamp elicited admiration for its poetic form but criticism for its content from Stirling for having an "entirely visual appeal," without demanding "intellectual participation . . . from the public." Although he had already suggested that the chapel may indeed have been inspired by the dolmens of Brittany, it was John Alford who, as early as 1958, explored the symbolic significance of this connection. Making a comparison between Ronchamp and a megalithic tomb, Alford argued that the chapel "can best be understood as a symbolic fortress and tomb," and characterized it as a "fortress . . . against death." He also recognized the chapel's visual affinity to a ship, calling it a "ship of life."

Ronchamp may be viewed as the summation of the human predicament, as the ship of life of the transient pilgrim, or as the fortress against death for the weary and restless—a fortress which inevitably becomes his tomb. This interpretation of Ronchamp is reinforced by Alan Colquhoun's sensitive evaluation of the project for the Venice Hospital of 1965, which he views both as a "machine for healing" as well as a necropolis (Fig. 32).

---

[13] Lewis Mumford, "The Sky Line: The Marseille 'Folly,'" *The New Yorker*, XXXIII (October 5, 1957), 76ff.

Le Corbusier's ever present yearning to create a city from zero was fulfilled when he was given the opportunity to design Chandigarh, the capital of the province of Punjab in India (Figs. 28–30). In her eloquent description, Norma Evenson recognizes the city's poetic qualities without losing sight of its shortcomings. Her observation that it lacks "the functional viability of a traditional Indian town" is echoed in the writings of such critics as Hubert Hoffmann and Brent C. Brolin. But the critical essays of Charles Correa and Stanislaus von Moos clearly show that the visual imagery of Chandigarh is indeed related to India's past. The utilization of its underlying principles by younger Indian architects to suit various local needs is discussed by Mulk Raj Anand, the noted editor of the Indian cultural journal, *Marg*. The fact that its poetic forms are imitated and its sociological weaknesses debated the world over reveals the power of Chandigarh's aesthetic and ideological premises. Hence not only the achievements but also the defects of Le Corbusier's city may serve as lessons for the future.

Until his late years Le Corbusier largely suppressed the publication of his early works, and rarely alluded to the richness of his beginnings. The only house built prior to his settling in Paris in late 1916 which he allowed to be published was the Villa Schwob in La Chaux-de-Fonds (Fig. 3). The first critical evaluation of this villa was written by Amédée Ozenfant, under the pseudonym Julien Caron, in the March, 1921 issue of *L'Esprit Nouveau*, after Le Corbusier illustrated it in the previous number of the same journal. Some fragmentary early accounts of his formative years appear in his *L'Art décoratif d'aujourd'hui* and *Almanach d'architecture moderne*, published in 1925 and 1926, respectively, and in the introduction to the first volume of his *Oeuvre complète*, which also includes illustrations of some of his early projects such as the well-known Domino houses (Fig. 4). Shortly before his death in August 1965 Le Corbusier completed editing his account of a decisive trip he undertook to the Balkans and Asia Minor in 1911. It is characteristic that what could have been one of his first books became his last.

In view of Le Corbusier's own attitude toward his early development it should not seem surprising that the first sketch of his formative years appeared only in 1944. As the short excerpt included here shows, Maximilien Gauthier was interested primarily in the architect's life rather than in his art. It was not until 1963 that a brief exposition of his first houses built in Switzerland was published by Etienne Chavanne and Michel Laville, correcting the errors made in *Perspecta 6* just three years before. In his "Mannerism and Modern Architecture" of 1950 Colin Rowe made an initial attempt to place the Villa Schwob in a historical perspective, and in 1968 Stanislaus von Moos published the first critical assessment of Le Corbusier's entire early phase.

The intellectual foundation of Le Corbusier's formative years was studied by Paul Turner, who discovered how deeply the idealistic strain of the architect's thinking was based on his early education. Turner's pioneering study exploring Le Corbusier's initial search for abstract, universal knowledge rooted in Platonic and Pythagorean thought takes us back to the prophetic observation made by Paul Westheim in 1922: "The axes, spheres, and right angles are not there because axes, spheres, and right angles as such were wanted—that would be academicism, that would be an engineer's materialism—they are there as a testimony to a higher will to form, which seeks freedom in law and enduring greatness in obedience to law."

PART ONE / The Formative Years: 1887–1918

Whatever you do, see that you do it!

> MARIE CHARLOTTE AMÉLIE
> JEANNERET-PERRET*

ORIGINS (1944)

Maximilien Gauthier

Le Corbusier is the pseudonym of Charles-Edouard Jeanneret, who was born on October 6, 1887, in La Chaux-de-Fonds, and became a French citizen in 1930. . . . Le Corbusier was the name of one of his grandfathers. . . .

Both his father and grandfather were skillful watch engravers; on his mother's side the Perrets were businessmen and travelers who owned a library, kept horses, and had had their portraits painted by Dajou, one of the court painters of the Empress Eugénie. A respectable background: craftsmen on the one side and solid middle class on the other. . . .

Artistic and high-spirited, Madame Jeanneret was an accomplished musician. Though she was perhaps less intellectually inclined, her powerful example was most instrumental in shaping the course her sons were to follow: one was a musician like herself; the other was to reintroduce to his contemporaries the forgotten idea that architecture is above all poetry, the music of the physical world. Madame Jeanneret's piano has the same relationship to Le Corbusier's aesthetics as the principles of Monsieur Jeanneret have to his discipline as an architect and to his awareness of man's responsibility toward his fellow man. For an artist, this education is at least as important as the study of Latin in a musty school. His father's eldest sister, a deeply religious, self-sacrificing person, lived with the family and embodied the noble traditions which had been maintained through the centuries in the Jura valley.

"Origins" by Maximilien Gauthier. From *Le Corbusier—ou l'architecture au service de l'homme* (Paris: Les Éditions Denoël, 1944), pp. 11, 16–19. Reprinted by permission of the publisher.

---

* W. Boesiger and H. Girsberger, *Le Corbusier 1910–1960* (Zurich: Editions Girsberger, 1960), p. 6.

From the time that he was four years old until he was thirteen, Charles-Edouard Jeanneret acquired a reputation as a hard-working and gifted student in primary and secondary school. He had such a passion and talent for drawing that after classes and on Sundays when he had finished his homework, he was enrolled quite naturally in the Art School of La Chaux-de-Fonds, which had been founded in the nineteenth century as a training school for watch engravers. . . .

Among the professors at the Art School there was one who commanded Charles-Edouard Jeanneret's undivided attention. The son of a local peasant, he was called L'Eplattenier, and he had recently returned from Paris, where he had studied painting at the Ecole des Beaux-Arts. In his "Cours Supérieur de Décoration" he was the only teacher who did not confine himself merely to technique. Because L'Eplattenier's vision extended beyond watchcases, Charles-Edouard Jeanneret was introduced to the fundamental problems of art. He was so fascinated that the distance between the young pupil and the older man quickly diminished. Through L'Eplattenier, who had set up a library in his drawing class, Charles-Edouard Jeanneret's eyes were opened to the masterpieces of the past and he enjoyed studying them. . . .

ORIGINS, YOUTH, TRAVELS (1968)

Stanislaus von Moos

JEANNERET'S FIRST BUILDING

Jeanneret wanted to become a painter. But his teacher insisted: "You will be an architect." At first Jeanneret demurred. In the school's small library there was a copy of Charles Blanc's *Grammaire des arts du dessin*,[1] one of the best-known textbooks of the period, in which architecture was described as the mother of the arts. Jeanneret must have been fascinated by that book, for it is far more than a dry text: it renders the panorama of history in an arresting prose and contains the promise of great things to come. Blanc was decidedly opposed to the conception of an architect as the mere decorator of an engineer's constructions.[2] In the spirit of Viollet-le-Duc and Choisy he proclaimed that the architecture of the future would develop from new construction methods and would be based on a thorough knowledge of the masterpieces of the past, which the nineteenth century had rediscovered. "But the regeneration of our schools can only be accomplished on one condition: if they do not become entrenched in archaeology, in pure imitation of objects, but grasp instead the spirit of things, extracting from the jumble of relics only those great and rare ideas that stand out."[3]

L'Eplattenier contacted the architect René Chapallaz, who had a small studio in Tavannes, and asked him to assist his student in the design and execution of a small house. Before he had persuaded a member of the school board to give the seventeen-year-old Jeanneret the commission to build this small villa. And so Jeanneret's first house took shape

"Origins, Youth, Travels" by Stanislaus von Moos. From *Le Corbusier: Elemente einer Synthese* (Frauenfeld and Stuttgart: Verlag Huber & Co. AG, 1968), pp. 21–24. 47–53. Reprinted by permission of the author and publisher.

[1] Charles Blanc, *Grammaire des arts du dessin*, 4th ed. (Paris: T. Renouard, 1881).
[2] *Ibid.*, p. 68.
[3] *Ibid.*, p. 305.

13

between 1905 and 1906, the Villa Fallet, situated on a slope of the Jura north of the town [Fig. 1]. . . .

In later years Le Corbusier was not particularly keen on including his first house in La Chaux-de-Fonds among his works. There are no pictures of it in his books, and it is seldom mentioned. Yet it is useful to cast a glance at his "youthful sins." [4] The living area and the bedrooms are grouped around an open, two-storied hall, an idea that Jeanneret abandoned in his subsequent efforts, but which nevertheless anticipated his open treatment of the unified two-storied living space with galleries. However, the façade and the decorative detailing are far more interesting than the floor plan. The overall design is characterized by the local *Jugendstil* tradition, intermixed with a specifically Swiss blend of romantic-national style, typical of the early years of the century. It is striking how carefully the detailing was carried out. Jeanneret himself, together with his friends, worked alongside the carpenters. The most ordinary forms received special treatment. For example, in the Villa Fallet the windowpanes are not framed by simple crossbars; they are more like branches on a tree stretching upward. Geometric shapes crop up everywhere, all of them derived from the form of Jura firs—on the iron knocker on the front door, as part of the decorative design on the balcony's iron balustrade, in reliefs on the interior paneling, and in the graffito pattern on the façade. Even the shape of the roof and the metal trim on the upper-story windows seem reminiscent of the outline of a Jura pine.

There is, however, a very significant difference between the naturalism of these architectural decorations and the naturalism in the works of the major contemporary architects of the *Jugendstil* era. However much the works of van de Velde in Belgium and Germany, Guimard in Paris, or Gaudì in Spain varied in style, they still had in common an organic representation of nature. Jeanneret, on the other hand, translated the inspiration of nature into a strict, geometric language. This was obviously a result of L'Eplattenier's teaching. One basic tenet of Le Corbusier's later thought and works was already apparent in his early experiments with form: the synthesis of nature and geometry, the urge to make the structural laws of nature visible and to express them in clear, universal, geometric patterns. This idea pursued him throughout his life; in the *Modulor* it finally developed into a universally applicable system. . . .

---

[4] The first documentation on these early buildings was compiled by two students at the ETH (Zurich): E. Chavanne and M. Laville, "Les premières constructions de Le Corbusier en Suisse" (thesis, ETH, Zurich, n.d.), partly published in *Werk*, 50 (1963), 483–88.

BUILDINGS AND PROJECTS IN
THE STYLE OF BEHRENS
AND HOFFMANN

After his return from the East Jeanneret was busy with more than just teaching. His parents, who had changed apartments frequently, decided to build their own house on the Rue de la Montagne, near the Villa Fallet. Jeanneret designed an unspectacular villa for them in the cultivated style of 1910 [Fig. 2]. The rooms are grouped around a large music room in which Madame Jeanneret gave her piano lessons. A strikingly large window opens toward the south. On the side facing the garden an apsidal wing protrudes. The windows on the second floor are aligned in a horizontal band, somewhat reminiscent of houses designed by Peter Behrens at the time. The hip roof brings to mind the roof of the Villa Ast, designed by Joseph Hoffmann; but it may well be that the inspiration came from a closer source, such as the buildings by René Chapallaz or the villas by Curjel and Moser, which were becoming widely known through the professional journals. In the Villa Favre-Jacot in Le Locle, also built in 1912, there is a similar mixture of ideas borrowed from Hoffmann and Behrens, but rendered in an even more complicated form. . . .

THE DOMINO HOUSES

Shortly after the dissolution of the *Nouvelle Section*[5] there came alarming reports of war ravages in Flanders. In September of 1914 it was not expected that the war would continue; it seemed that the time for rebuilding had arrived. Hence, Jeanneret reduced his chiefly theoretical experiences with reinforced concrete construction methods to the lowest common denominator: he designed a system of two horizontal concrete slabs supported by columns and connected by stairs [Fig. 4]. He believed that the elements of this simple system could be mass-produced. The skeleton could be erected in war-ravaged areas, and it would then be up to the individual owner to supply the missing parts: prefabricated window and wall sections should be made available in order to permit completion of every apartment according to the needs of each dweller.

The skeleton made of steel and supporting reinforced concrete slabs was of course not Le Corbusier's invention. What was new was that the columns were recessed with respect to the outer walls. This made it

[5] [In 1911 the "Cours Supérieur," which was founded by Charles L'Eplattenier in 1906, was expanded into the "Nouvelle Section." Le Corbusier, together with the sculptor Léon Perrin and the interior designer Georges Aubert, joined L'Eplattenier in teaching the newly established curriculum.—ED.]

possible for the exterior walls to be independent from the structural system. Windows could easily go around corners, a possibility that had already been demonstrated by Olbrich in his Wedding Tower in Darmstadt, and Gropius in the Fagus works in Alfeld in 1911. Some of Jeanneret's sketches point in a similar direction.

The numerous variations of the Domino house sketched by the young architect between 1914 and 1915 show above all that he was deeply influenced by Tony Garnier's projects for Lyons.[6] Jeanneret had visited Garnier in 1915 . . . and there is no doubt that his Domino variations reveal a greater kinship with the revolutionary Tony Garnier, the Prix de Rome winner, than with any other contemporary architect. But neither in Flanders nor in Sicily, where a member of Parliament showed some interest, were the Domino houses built. It is typical of Le Corbusier's career that an idea which grew out of a desire to create radically less expensive buildings first found application in a luxurious villa for a businessman.

THE VILLA SCHWOB

In contrast to his earlier buildings, to which Le Corbusier rarely referred, he pointed with pride to the Villa Schwob and even published it in detail in *L'Esprit Nouveau* [Fig. 3].[7] The characteristic elements were already foreshadowed in his father's house: the large center window and the apsidal wings protruding on each side. These wings were now enlarged and arranged symmetrically on two sides, and the center window was stretched over two stories. The inspiration for this house can be traced back partly to Perret, for whom Jeanneret had previously drawn a small villa.

The main room is two stories high; the second floor, which contains the bedrooms, has a gallery that opens toward the living room. . . . The idea of a house consisting essentially of a single "foyer" that extends in different directions and adjoins the bedrooms and the various utility rooms points more to Frank Lloyd Wright than to Perret. Wright, following the publication of his drawings in the Wasmuth edition in 1910, exerted an enormous influence primarily on the Dutch architects of the time. . . . In fact, Jeanneret had read a reprint of a lecture by H. P. Berlage on new American architecture, which had appeared in the *Schweizerische Bauzeitung*.[8] Among the many buildings by Frank Lloyd

[6] Cf. Le Corbusier, *Oeuvre complète 1910–1929* (Zurich: Les Editions Girsberger, 1960), pp. 23–26 and Le Corbusier, *Précisions sur un état présent de l'architecture et l'urbanisme* (Paris: Les Editions G. Crès et Cie., 1930), pp. 92–95.

[7] Julien Caron (pseudonym of Amédée Ozenfant), "Une villa de Le Corbusier, 1916," in *L'Esprit Nouveau*, 6 (1921), 679–704. According to this publication, the interior decoration of this villa is not by Jeanneret. . . .

[8] *Schweizerische Bauzeitung*, 1912, pp. 148–50, 165–67, 178. Plates 33–44. Le Corbusier recalls having seen buildings by Wright in a journal in 1913. Cf. *Oeuvre complète 1910–1929*, p. 10.

Wright illustrated in this journal one was particularly close in spirit to the Villa Schwob: the Thomas P. Hardy house in Racine, Wisconsin, which also had a double-storied living room.[9] However, entirely different from Wright's design were the sculptured cornices that crowned the front and the two apses of the house. By this device the building achieved a compositional climax similar to a Florentine palace. Such cornices are not found in the works of either Perret or Wright but rather they recall Joseph Hoffmann.[10]

With this building Jeanneret brought the chapter "Charles-Edouard Jeanneret, architect" to a close. He succeeded in translating the most contradictory influences of his day into a genuine and personal idiom. The result was a generous, elegant, if somewhat crowded and heterogeneous composition with an air of pretentiousness. It soon became apparent, however, that his development was to proceed in other directions. . . .

[9] The plan with apsidal wings seems to owe something to Wright's Darwin D. Martin house, which was among the works published in the *Schweizerische Bauzeitung*.
[10] See especially the Villa Ast, 1910–11, or the *Villenkolonie* in Kaasgraben, 1912–14, where one finds similar cornices.

THE BEGINNINGS OF LE CORBUSIER'S EDUCATION, 1902–07 (1971)

Paul Turner

. . . This article is part of a study of Le Corbusier based on a hypothesis that his attitude toward architecture was fundamentally intellectual and Idealistic—that is, that for him architecture was above all an expression of ideas and transcendent principles, rather than of those aspects which have been the ostensible concern of most twentieth-century architects, such as function, structural and material integrity, economy, etc. The fact that Le Corbusier himself is associated with many of these latter, strictly "architectural" concerns, and indeed helped to propagandize some of them in his writings, is just one of the apparent paradoxes in Le Corbusier's thought. This article cannot undertake to resolve the larger questions of the nature of Le Corbusier's thinking; but an attempt will be made to show how the groundwork was laid, very early in his life, for the Idealistic beliefs and assumptions which I believe characterize his work throughout his life.

In search of clues to the early development of Le Corbusier, I examined the contents of his personal library, presently at the Fondation Le Corbusier in Paris. By various means it was possible to determine the approximate acquisition dates of most of the books, and thus to arrange them in chronological periods corresponding to the important phases of his development. This article will deal with the earliest of these periods, the youthful years of Jeanneret in La Chaux-de-Fonds, before he left home to travel in 1907 (when he was nineteen), and will concentrate in particular on a book which clearly impressed him a great deal, Henry Provensal's *L'art de demain,* published in 1904.

But before we turn to Jeanneret's library, his early training in La Chaux-de-Fonds may be outlined briefly here. His drawing-teacher L'Eplattenier dominates this period, especially after he became director of the Art School in 1903. Since the age of thirteen, Jeanneret had been learning the traditional local art of watchcase engraving; but L'Eplattenier believed this was a dying trade and, as part of an attempt to broaden the scope of the Art School, seems to have encouraged the boy to set his sights higher. For a while Jeanneret wanted to be a painter, but then L'Eplattenier turned him toward architecture, as part of the "Cours supérieur" he founded in 1906, as a plan to train a whole community of craftsmen embracing all the arts, apparently on the pattern of Victor Prouvé's school in Nancy.[1]

The formal expression taken by these activities at the Art School was a combination of Art Nouveau and other contemporary decorative styles, judging from Jeanneret's surviving drawings of that period, and from his skillfully engraved watchcase which was exhibited at the Turin decorative arts exposition in 1902. This watchcase is distinguished by a peculiar juxtaposition of two designs—one an abstract design of over-lapping rectangles, the other a curvilinear design of flowers and a bumble-bee—which reveal two different sources, one French and the other Germanic. The flower-and-bee design must have been inspired by a series of Art Nouveau watchcases designed by René Lalique, also with flower and insect motifs, which had been published in 1901 in a periodical to which the Art School subscribed.[2] Le Corbusier later recalled that Lalique, Gallé, and Guimard were among his favorite designers in these early years, and admitted his admiration for French Art Nouveau.[3] But the other, abstract part of Jeanneret's watchcase reflects a more sober style in Germany and Austria (whose decorative arts were also represented in periodicals in the Art School), in which surfaces were treated as thin overlapping planes,[4] and may have been inspired even more directly by Hermann Obrist's strikingly cubic piece of sculpture which was illustrated in *Die Kunst* in 1900.[5]

In retrospect, the rectilinear "Germanic" style seems much more prophetic of Jeanneret's later development. Yet L'Eplattenier was not so much interested in teaching his students "styles" as an underlying attitude toward nature and art. As Le Corbusier later recalled, "My teacher had said: 'Only nature inspires, is real, and is capable of serving as the basis for a work of art. But don't imitate nature the way landscape painters do, who only show its appearance. Ponder its cause, its form, its vital

---

[1] Charles L'Eplattenier *et al.*, *Un mouvement d'art à La Chaux-de-Fonds* (La Chaux-de-Fonds: Imprimerie Georges Dubois, 1914), p. 25; and Gauthier, *Le Corbusier* (Paris: Les Éditions Denoël, 1944), p. 18f.

[2] *Art et Décoration*, IX (January 1901), 37–40. . . .

[3] Gauthier, *Le Corbusier*, 26. Le Corbusier also mentions Rodin, and two lesser-known figures whose work was not strictly Art Nouveau, Rupert Carabin and Jean Carriès.

[4] Examples of this style of overlapping planes can be found around 1900 and 1901 in the interior decoration of Peter Behrens and others. Magazines which illustrated this work, and to which the Art School subscribed, include *Die Kunst, Deutsche Kunst und Dekoration,* and *The Studio.* (See, for example, a door designed by Behrens, in *The Studio*, XXIV [1901], 26.)

[5] *Die Kunst,* II (1900), 178–79.

development and synthesize it by creating *ornaments.*' He had a heightened conception of ornament, which he viewed as a microcosm." [6] On one level, this can be seen as a call for understanding the organic structure of natural forms, and this is surely part of what L'Eplattenier meant. But in the light of Jeanneret's reading at this time (some of which we know L'Eplattenier suggested to him), we shall see that there was probably a deeper meaning as well—a Platonic conviction that one must penetrate beneath the superficial appearance of nature and seek out the ideal, universal reality. Each form thus idealized by the artist would become a "microcosm" of the divine Idea.

A more mundane and specific goal of L'Eplattenier's teaching was to lay a groundwork, with his "Cours Supérieur," for a regional Jura art style to be inspired partly by local plant and animal forms—related to a theory of his that all the great periods of art had been based on similar local forms (such as the lotus in Egypt and the acanthus in Greece).[7] These ideas may have come partly from Ruskin and Owen Jones . . . but they also simply reveal L'Eplattenier's deep love of nature and the Jura region, a love which Jeanneret's father also possessed to a very high degree, and which thus surrounded the boy. This spirit of Jura regionalism is reflected in the first house which Jeanneret designed [Fig. 1], apparently in 1906, for a local citizen named Fallet—with its rough stone lower walls, its steep roofs with deep overhanging eaves supported by wooden brackets, and its stucco upper surfaces painted with decorative motifs based on the pine tree.

But more significant for Jeanneret's development than this regionalist spirit was L'Eplattenier's introduction to him of the world of books and ideas: ". . . Through L'Eplattenier, who had set up a library in his drawing class, Charles-Edouard Jeanneret's eyes were opened to the masterpieces of the past, and he enjoyed studying them." [8] Of these books in L'Eplattenier's drawing class, Le Corbusier later specifically mentioned only Ruskin, Owen Jones's *Grammar of Ornament*, and Eugène Grasset's *Méthode de composition ornementale.*[9] Formally, Jones's book was probably the most influential of these on Jeanneret. Many of its more abstract plates are similar in spirit to the designs done by Jeanneret in L'Eplattenier's class, and these designs follow a number of Jones's "Propositions"—for example, that natural forms should always be stylized and conventionalized before being used as ornament.[10] As for Ruskin, Le

[6] Le Corbusier, *L'art décoratif d'aujourd'hui* (Paris: Les Editions Crès et Cie., 1925), p. 198.

[7] *Ibid.* . . .

[8] Gauthier, *Le Corbusier*, p. 19.

[9] Jones's book is mentioned by Le Corbusier in *Le Corbusier* (Paris: Editions Vincent, Fréal & Cie., 1960), 24; and Grasset's book is mentioned in Gauthier, *Le Corbusier*, p. 27.

[10] "Proposition 13," *The Grammar of Ornament* (London: B. Quaritch, 1910), p. 6. . . .

Corbusier recalled that he and L'Eplattenier "admired Ruskin passionately. . . ." [11]

JEANNERET'S EARLY READING

There are about a dozen books in Le Corbusier's library which seem to date from this early period in La Chaux-de-Fonds. Only three of them are actually inscribed with the year Jeanneret acquired them. Four more can be dated because they contain Jeanneret's signature of this period. And several others contain clues of one sort or another linking them to these early years. Luckily, the books which are of most interest to this study are among those whose acquisition dates can be pin-pointed most precisely.

The earliest of these datable books contain little or no art theory per se; but they do suggest that Jeanneret's early training was by no means divorced from the climate of academic French art instruction. For example, Eugène Müntz's *Raphaël* was given to the boy by his parents in 1902. The author, who was librarian of the Ecole des Beaux-Arts, expresses the typical academic reverence for the Italian High Renaissance, for example in stating that Bramante and Raphael are "the greatest of modern architects and . . . the greatest of modern painters." [12] And the next year, when Jeanneret was sixteen, a prize-book was given to him by the Art School—Maxime Collignon's *Mythologie figurée de la Grèce*—which was part of a teaching series published by the Ecole des Beaux-Arts, and like Müntz's book expresses academic assumptions without ever specifically discussing theory. It is a kind of textbook of Greek mythology for art students, describing the standard ways each god was represented in antiquity, and illustrated by line-drawings. Inherent is the concept of classical "norms," standard ways of designing which are to be assimilated by the student and then applied to new problems. Jeanneret seems to have sensed this message, for he did a sketch (left in the pages of the book), which transformed a Greek coin illustrated in the work into a decorative device picturing a pine tree, that ubiquitous Jura motif of these years—thus showing his interest in Classical formats, and a feeling that the new Jura regionalism could be linked to a larger tradition. Furthermore, years later Le Corbusier returned to this book, reread part of it, and made some annotations; he apparently was trying to identify the expressive meaning of certain colors, and went back to this childhood text to see how they had been used in antiquity. This is typical. Many of Jeanneret's early books show similar evidence that he later returned

---

[11] . . . Le Corbusier's recollection of this brief passage is found in Gauthier, *Le Corbusier*, p. 19. . . .

[12] From the English edition of Eugène Müntz, *Raphaël* (London: Chapman and Hall Ltd., 1882), p. 1.

to them in search of specific information—a good indication of Le Corbusier's serious attitude toward books and ideas.

The most intriguing book dating from this early period in Le Corbusier's library is Henry Provensal's *L'art de demain* (Paris, Perrin, 1904). It contains a La Chaux-de-Fonds bookstore label; Jeanneret's signatures in it are pre-1907; and there are markings by him in the text typical of this early period. Unlike the books mentioned above, this is a theoretical work; indeed it is almost wholly devoted to art theory and general philosophical questions. It may well have been the first such book Jeanneret read, and in any case he seems to have been greatly impressed by its ideas, some of which reappear later almost unchanged in the architectural theory of Le Corbusier. Furthermore, as we shall see later, this book may have been suggested to Jeanneret by L'Eplattenier and have reflected some of his own ideas. . . .

Why did Jeanneret read Provensal's book in the first place? The possibility that it was suggested to him by L'Eplattenier is plausible in view of the fact that a similar work in Le Corbusier's library, Edouard Schuré's *Les grands initiés*, was actually inscribed to Jeanneret by L'Eplattenier, having apparently been given as a kind of farewell gift in 1907. Despite the fact that Jeanneret probably did not read this book until he was settled in Paris the next year, its ideas can be outlined briefly here since they must have reflected, to at least some degree, the views of L'Eplattenier himself.

Subtitled *Esquisse de l'histoire secrète des religions*, this work appears to derive from German Idealism as much as did *L'art de demain*, with which it has much in common.[13] But Schuré's hero, rather than being the artist, is the mystical prophet, appearing throughout history in different guises but always bearing the same esoteric truths. Eight of the greatest of these prophets are examined in turn: Rama, Krishna, Hermes, Moses, Orpheus, Pythagoras, Plato, and Jesus. Schuré's main theme, like Provensal's, is the need for the spiritual revival of modern civilization and the rejection of the prevailing Materialism, which Schuré blames on the "positivisme" of Auguste Comte and Herbert Spencer (page xi). In philosophical terms, Schuré differs somewhat from Provensal in his attitude toward material reality; whereas Provensal tended to grant validity to both spirit and matter and emphasized their ideal unity, Schuré views matter in more strictly Platonic terms as merely an inferior reflection of spirit: ". . . Spirit is the only reality. Matter is merely its inferior, changing, ephemeral expression, its dynamism in space and time" (page xx).

Jeanneret was not uninterested in these metaphysical issues. In one of his few annotations in Schuré's book, he associates this spirit-matter dualism with religious doctrines with which he was already familiar; next

---

[13] Edouard Schuré (1841–1929) was a French dramatist and critic who was instrumental in familiarizing the French public with Wagner, and wrote "mystical Wagnerian plays" as well as *Les grands initiés* (first published in 1889), and another book *Précurseurs et révoltés*, 1904. (See *New Century Cyclopedia of Names.*)

to a passage describing the mystical journey of one's soul toward good-
ness or evil, Jeanneret wrote "the Gospels: sin against the Mind." Not
much is known about Jeanneret's early religious training, except that it
was Protestant. But this annotation is thoroughly consistent with the
Calvinist tradition in this part of Switzerland—with its emphasis on the
Gospels ("Evangile") as the source of religious doctrine, and its opposition of two primal forces, Man's innate sinfulness on the one hand,
and God's grace (granted by the Holy Spirit) on the other. The fact
that Jeanneret thought to make this comparison with Schuré's mysticism
suggests that his religious training had not been superficial, and that it
influenced the way he interpreted new ideas. We know that a devoutly
religious maiden aunt lived in the Jeanneret household when Charles-
Edouard and his brother were boys; and also that there was a Jeanneret
family legend that their ancestors had belonged to the heretical mystical
sect in southern France known as Catharism—a sect which Le Corbusier's
library reveals him to have been extremely interested in, especially in
his later years. So Jeanneret's "Evangile" annotation undoubtedly represents a familiarity with religious ideas going back to his earliest training
at home. The Idealism of both Provensal and Schuré would thus have
appeared quite normal and proper to him, and we can better understand
his attraction to their philosophies.

Several specific aspects of *Les grands initiés* may be mentioned here.
One is Schuré's emphasis on an elite—even stronger than in Provensal's
book, since it is naturally basic to the notion of esoteric doctrines and
"initiates." Schuré claims that throughout history certain rare men endowed with extraordinary abilities have been able to penetrate the most
profound spiritual mysteries, enter the realm of the Initiated, and as a
result acquire "a practically limitless strength, a radiant and creative
magic." [14] Of all the great Initiates of the past, according to Schuré, the
one most relevant to modern Man was Pythagoras, whose "esprit scientifique" was closest to "l'esprit moderne" (page 431). Like Provensal,
Schuré means "scientifique" not to refer to empirical activity, but to quite
the opposite: to abstract, *a priori* thought, and in the specific case of
Pythagoras, mystical numerology. Jeanneret seems to have been particularly interested in the chapter on Pythagoras, and all of his markings
and annotations are found in it. Schuré's descriptions of Pythagorean
numerology often call to mind Le Corbusier's "Modulor" system, for
example when Schuré describes it as a system unfolding mathematically
from simple divine numbers: "Pythagoras took the teaching of numbers
much further. In each one he discerned a principle, a law, an active force
of the universe. He said that the essential principles are contained, however, in the first four numbers, because by adding them or multiplying
them one finds all the others." [15]

Another interesting aspect is the emphasis that Schuré places on

[14] Page 437. This, and all subsequent page references, are to the 1960 Librairie Aca-
démique Perrin edition of the book, rather than to Jeanneret's own copy.
[15] Page 393. See also page 331. . . .

the youthful voyages of Pythagoras, his years spent in traveling to all the ancient centers of learning in search of the knowledge which would allow him to become one of the Initiated (pages 326–65). When he was given this book in 1907, Jeanneret was embarking on his own voyage of discovery. Was L'Eplattenier perhaps thinking of this parallel when he presented him with the book? In any case, Jeanneret himself thought of his travels in very much the same spirit as that of Schuré—as a heroic search for knowledge, and specifically for abstract, universal knowledge. Le Corbusier later recalled this youthful search for "Truth," as well as the inevitable periods of despair which accompany such quests: "Searching for truth in the Libraries. Books. Countless books. Where is the beginning? Those hours spent in the libraries perusing books in search of truth! And suddenly you fall into a hole. It is dark, and you don't understand anything anymore." [16]

This remarkable dedication to the discovery of abstract knowledge is equally apparent in annotations made by Jeanneret in Paris the next year—such as his inscription in one book that he was buying it "in order to *learn,* for *knowing* I can create." [17] This reveals the extent to which he had absorbed the Idealism of Provensal and Schuré. Architecture for him was not the mastery of technical skills or the solving of specific problems, but simply the knowledge of "la vérité" which would then allow him to "create."

In June, 1907, Jeanneret left La Chaux-de-Fonds and began a period of wandering which was to lead him through Italy, then to Vienna, and in the following year to Paris. There he was to meet and work for Auguste Perret, the most progressive representative at that time of the French tradition of "Architectural Rationalism"—the attitude that architecture ought to be primarily a logical expression of the structural, material, and social forces which produce it in any given time and locale. Perret was to influence Jeanneret in a number of ways; but the essential spirit of his Rationalism was to have little effect on Jeanneret's deeply-rooted Idealism, which would shape Le Corbusier's thinking throughout his career. From his "Dom-Ino" system of 1914, and his "Purist" forms and utopian urbanism of the 1920s, to his sculptural architecture and obsession with the "Modulor" in his later years, Le Corbusier's work was to be characterized most essentially by a search for generalization, universality, and absolute formal truths which would put Man in touch with a harmony underlying nature—a divine "axis," as he called it, which "leads us to assume a unity of direction in the universe, and to admit a single will at its source." [18]

Jeanneret's own library reveals that even in his earliest years in La Chaux-de-Fonds, his training was pervaded by a spirit of philosophical Idealism, and that this had many special influences on his thinking. Henry

[16] *L'art décoratif d'aujourd'hui,* p. 201.
[17] This was Viollet-le-Duc's *Dictionnaire raisonné de l'architecture française,* which Jeanneret bought in August, 1908. . . .
[18] . . . Le Corbusier, *Vers une architecture* (Paris: Editions Vincent, Fréal et Cie., 1958), pp. 165 and 170.

Provensal's vision of a new art uniting matter and spirit, his deductive notion of "science," his definitions of architecture as a cubic play of volumes, and his challenge to discover formal "harmonic rapports"; and Edouard Schuré's descriptions of Pythagorean numerology and of a priestly elite of Initiates charged with the revelation of truth—these were not isolated ideas but integral parts of an Idealistic world-view, for which the true aim of art was the expression not of material but of spiritual forces. Jeanneret himself seems to have associated this Idealism with his own Protestant upbringing; and even his teacher L'Eplattenier encouraged this thinking, as shown by his gift of *Les grands initiés* to his favorite student. In sum, all of the important forces in the education of the young Jeanneret conspired to inculcate in him a very special notion of the nature and role of art.

The house is a machine for living. . . . As to beauty, this is always present when you have proportion. . . .

LE CORBUSIER*

LE CORBUSIER'S "THE ENGINEER'S AESTHETIC: MASS-PRODUCTION HOUSES" (1922)

Marcello Piacentini

Le Corbusier declares that . . . the state of mind for building mass-production houses, the state of mind for living in mass-production houses, the state of mind for conceiving mass-production houses is lacking. Specialization has hardly touched the field of home construction—there are neither factories nor specialized technicians. . . .

The prime consequences of industrial evolution in building appear at this fundamental stage: the substitution of artificial materials for natural materials, of homogeneous, standardized products tested in the laboratory for heterogeneous substances of undetermined composition. Standardized materials are to be substituted for the natural, infinitely variable materials. . . .

Nothing is ready, but everything can be done. In the next twenty years industry will have coordinated its standardized materials, and technical progress will have perfected the methods of rational construction. Social and financial planning will solve the housing problem, and construction sites will no longer be haphazard breeding places of chaos and confusion, but run scientifically on a large scale.

Inevitable social evolution will have transformed the relationship between landlord and tenant, and will have modified the concept of the dwelling. Cities will be planned instead of being chaotic. A house will no longer be a formidable structure flaunting its age, a sign of wealth:

"Le Corbusier's 'The Engineer's Aesthetic: Mass-Production Houses'" by Marcello Piacentini. From *Architettura e Arti Decorative*, II (1922), pp. 220–23.

* Le Corbusier, *Towards a New Architecture* (London: The Architectural Press, 1946), pp. 100, 223.

it will be a tool, just as the automobile is becoming a tool. The house will no longer be an archaic entity heavily rooted in the ground by deep foundations, an ancient symbol of the cult of the family and of the race.

If we erase all rigid notions of the house from our hearts and minds and look at the question from a critical and objective point of view, we will inevitably arrive at the "house-tool," the mass-production house within everyone's reach, incomparably healthier than the old (even morally) and imbued with the beauty of the working tools of our daily lives. . . .

Thus did Le Corbusier-Saugnier launch his ideas of universal, anti-regional architecture. Many of his conclusions are profound and wise. Undoubtedly one cannot think of each house today as a personal dream. The concept of a system, of a method must necessarily intervene. However, houses must not become uniform all over the world for this reason. Also, the acclaimed superiority of *standardized materials* is not always valid; many times local materials are more readily available, easier to use and cheaper.

The problem is strikingly timely. It involves, basically, resolving the debate between impersonal, international, standardized architecture and localized, vernacular architecture. The former is a typical by-product of our times responding directly to changed technical processes and even more so to the changed social order, while the latter is tied to the past.

But then, are the two tendencies really antithetical? Is it really logical to speak of an architecture which is mathematically new, scientifically adapted to today's materials and customs, and of an old architecture which is no longer adequate for us, to be cast into the attic among the broken and unusable furniture? Is there really this distance, this clear separation between old and new? . . .

Le Corbusier-Saugnier offers us numerous examples of mass-production houses designed by him and by the widely noted architect Perret. Theirs could be called an architecture of cubes and cylinders, which has already been tried by the Dutch, by some Americans, and by Joseph Hoffmann. . . . These examples are not unimpressive, though they seem to be rather less audacious than the underlying theory. This fact should prove, as I said previously, that this conflict between the new and the old does not exist for all practical purposes, and that it is possible to arrive at a vision of a *sane architecture* which will be neither old nor new but simply *true*—not through a spirit of compromise at all costs, but through logic and the realistic evaluation of materials and needs.

ARCHITECTURE IN FRANCE:
LE CORBUSIER-SAUGNIER (1922)

Paul Westheim

The general impression of architecture in France—insofar as one can form a picture after a few weeks' stay there—is still that there are no efforts comparable to our so-called "New German" architectural movement, even though small groups are occasionally organized, such as the one recently formed by Dervaux, Leon, Bayard, and a few others, who call themselves simply "Quelques architectes." The explanation is perhaps that all building in France, even in the worst period, between 1870 and 1914, remained firmly rooted in tradition. There was no sensational unrest which, after all, is what produced the new German movement. In France one had, and continued to have, the support of convention. This was in many ways a safeguard. Architecture could not decline so completely as in Germany into an individualism made even worse by the parvenu minds of official and unofficial builders. This individualism could never operate with such lack of restraint in France. Perhaps people were less concerned with the architectonic aspects. They had no objection to having a house built just like the neighbors' to the right and left and in the way in which they had been built before. It is also possible that the builders and architects were still dominated by a traditional discipline. With a sense of tact and propriety which they had never wholly lost, people arranged themselves in rows of houses along the street. The "uniform block-front," which Walter Curt Behrendt's book once preached to us as a necessary reform, was not only the plan for the single show-piece of the Rue de Rivoli, but also seems to have unconsciously determined the whole layout of Paris. In precisely this respect Paris is still the most splendid example of the character that a creatively conceived city plan can offer. Things did not run wild there as they did with us. And it is therefore also natural that a countermovement to lead the way out of that wild confusion could not have the same force that united all

"Architecture in France: Le Corbusier-Saugnier" by Paul Westheim. From *Wasmuths Monatshefte für Baukunst*, VII (1922), pp. 69, 71–73. Copyright Verlag Ernst Wasmuth Tübingen. Reprinted by permission of the publisher.

enlightened minds among us. It is true that, when the Art Nouveau movement started, there were also a number of architects in France who strove
to introduce into architecture what was already called the "spirit of the
glass and iron age." The warehouses of Sédille and Binet are the best
known examples. Various houses and interiors of this sort have sprung up,
especially on the newer boulevards in the suburbs. But none of these,
we can say with confidence, passed beyond the Art Nouveau stage. Nor
was the movement widespread; it continues to be swallowed up by that
conventional tradition. Now, however, the time seems to have come when
this convention is nothing but pure convention, no longer having the
strength to live and to grow, and when it comes more and more into
conflict with the needs and the very essence of contemporary life. This
situation seems to have released forces of opposition whose representative
could be said to be Le Corbusier-Saugnier. He cannot actually be called
the leader of a movement: Le Corbusier-Saugnier has the qualities of a
leader to an especially large degree, but there is not yet a movement, in
France at least.

Nor has he found large scale opportunity to realize his ideas in
practice. This may be related also to the fact that there is even less opportunity at present for a young architect in France than here. Business
is bad, there is a constantly increasing economic crisis. . . . So it is
wholly understandable that for the few existing opportunities—not to
speak of the official ones—no one seeks an architect who does not correspond to the customary type and who seems disinclined to abandon any
of these notions of reform. . . .

Le Corbusier-Saugnier regards a house as a machine for living (he
cites a modern ship's cabin as the most perfect example of this), a chair
as a machine for sitting. "Wash-stands are machines for washing. Twyford
created them." It is the engineers who understand today how to heat, to
ventilate, to illuminate. For this is the age of construction. Such ideas are
not new to us in Germany. Twenty years ago van de Velde already
pointed out the logic, beauty, and appropriateness of machine forms. And
his call did not go unheeded. We should also remember Loos, whose
article "Ornament and Crime" has, by the way, recently been reprinted
in *L'Esprit Nouveau*. We can be said to have already passed through this
stage of unbounded enthusiasm for machine forms. We have also readily
faced up to this problem. Technological beauty is no longer unappre-
ciated by us. But this has perhaps also led to the fact that we are no
longer so completely deceived as to its conditions and limitations. The
comment of the Russian, Mesnil, about this movement, which is supported
in Russia by Tatlin, does not sound strange to our ears. "This fanatic
admiration of the machine is a thoroughly 'futuristic' trait and derives
directly from the post-industrial civilization which was produced by
capitalism in its last stage of development and of which materialism, in
the nonphilosophic sense, is the result. The Italian Futurists are much
more logical than Tatlin in allying themselves with nationalist imperialism
and in loving war for war's sake. The pyrotechnic poetry of Marinetti is
in complete accord with the quintessence of Tatlin's machines."

Poelzig recently set forth another point of view in a lecture, that of the architect as artist. He argued that all purely technological creations serve a purely practical human need. . . . They attain an unambiguous, thoroughly satisfying, even completely organic form, but they disappear again when they no longer satisfy the practical need. They are superseded by forms which serve new purposes. . . . None of these things, not even the technological constructions, are planned for eternity. They were conceived to serve transitory purposes; they are ephemera in the life of the world:

> Everything technological, each purely technological form, is temporary; man destroys it ruthlessly when it no longer serves his ends. But the art form is eternal and is not destroyed without detriment. With it a part of beauty disappears from the world. It comes from love, not from the calculating mind; its roots reach into the eternal, whereas the technologist, as he himself says proudly, must stand with both feet on the ground and fit into the world. This is not to criticize the ethics of the technologist or the engineer; we must merely establish the boundaries of his field. His ethics are on the contrary far greater than those of most artists, because he effaces himself behind his work and anonymously creates things of value, impelled by the spirit of the times.

Le Corbusier-Saugnier is not unfamiliar with this development in Germany, which he knows, by the way, from firsthand observation. He believes, however, that the ideas were at once watered-down in Germany and that a certain class of architects—our arts and crafts architects— arrived at hybrid forms. At the AEG buildings,[1] for example, the practicality of the engineer turned into a sort of sham. Once again, as is undeniable, people were radical in theory but middle-of-the-road in practice. It would scarcely be worthwhile to go so thoroughly into this train of thought, if Le Corbusier-Saugnier wanted merely to propagate the machine form anew. But only a superficial view can interpret him—as has already occurred—as wanting to substitute the engineer for the architect. He is enthusiastic about what the engineer accomplishes, about his lack of prejudice and of preconditioning, but he wants more. And this "more" is the decisive point. Beyond the simple demand for functionalism he is governed also by an aesthetic attitude:

> "When something," he says, almost in agreement with Poelzig, "fulfills a need, it is not beautiful; it satisfies a whole part of our mind, the first, the one without which higher satisfactions are not possible. Let us reestablish the sequence. Architecture has another meaning and other purposes besides addressing itself to construction, and responding to needs (needs implying here utility, comfort and practical enjoyment). ARCHITECTURE is the supreme art which attains Platonic grandeur, mathematical order, speculation and perception of harmony through proportional relationships."

[1] [German General Electric Company Buildings in Moabit, near Berlin, by Peter Behrens: 1909–1911.—ED.]

In other words, he rises above the level of pure functionalism. He remains by no means satisfied with that which the engineer logically develops as a technological necessity. He wants to create, to create as an artist from a preconceived notion of form. The engineer has reached the standard of excellence in his construction when he has found the most concise, useful, and economical solution for a particular purpose. He thinks of the purpose, and the form results by itself. He then immediately and unhesitatingly abandons this form again, for the sake of a new purpose. Le Corbusier, on the other hand, wants architecture, wants the shaped form, wants the same thing as the cubist painter, who relies upon *esprit,* logic, and adherence to the laws of mathematics: the grand harmony of elementary values of form. He admires the way the engineer poses the problem correctly, figures it out practically and logically, does not hesitate to unload the ballast of convention, and as a matter of course ruthlessly eliminates every element of form which is solely the result of traditional outlook and of the law of inertia. He holds him up as a model to encourage the architect to cast off false ballasts and rid his construction of obsolete and alien elements. Le Corbusier-Saugnier discards ornament, the canon of beauty of a former age which has now become a cliché, and demands contemporaneity, originality of formation, and, like Cézanne, professes faith in the "vérités de la géometrie," not for the sake of geometry itself but rather for the sake of eternal values. There is a standard of excellence, of course. Architecture, too, must strive toward this. It too must rise to the pinnacle of its potential. It, too, must pose the problem correctly. But in the last analysis his creed is: "Architecture is plastic formation, it is spiritual speculation, and it is higher mathematics. Architecture is a fine art. The standard which is imposed upon us by the law of selection, is a social and economic necessity. But harmony is a state of conformity with the norms of our universe. Beauty reigns; it is a pure human creation; it is the necessary 'extra' for those alone who have an exalted soul." The axes, spheres, and right angles are not there because axes, spheres, and right angles as such were wanted— that would be academicism, that would be an engineer's materialism— they are there as testimony to a higher will to form, which seeks freedom in law and enduring greatness in obedience to law. . . .

THE NEW HOUSE (1926)

Sigfried Giedion

Today one can build factories but not houses. There are two reasons to begin with. Houses are burdened down by tradition and prejudice, both of which inhibit 'the power of architectural creation; of course there is also the resistance of the occupants. But in addition, the technological and social conditions for which the truly good architect creates today have not been attained either. We can recognize the architectural genius of our time by the greatness of his visionary power, which must as always soar on wings in order to foresee the new human habitat made from modern materials.

The technological conditions have not yet been attained because, with the possible exception of the English metal frame houses, there are as yet no factories for houses producing standardized windows, doors and walls for the architect's disposal. Present techniques of mass production indicate that they can be standardized. The social conditions have not yet been reached either because today's clientele, the rich middle class, is still wholly inclined toward complicated individual needs, such as an abundance of furniture and a sequence of fragmented rooms—the very opposite of the standardization and simplification wanted by the architecture of the future. In all countries the laboratories of the "new spirit" will have enough to do in the next ten years if they are to find a way of transforming the cumbersome, costly house into a practical tool, "as the automobile is becoming a tool," to use Le Corbusier's words. In other words, industrialized mass production with ready-made parts assembled on the spot! To be sure, the desire to create a style will facilitate the task.

The new house is as lean and spare as possible, as empty as possible. The new house is planned for sociability. But absolutely no ostentation! When translated into form it means: the interiors of all new houses are grouped around one big room, to which the others are joined, often

"The New House" by Sigfried Giedion. From *Das Kunstblatt*, X, no. 4 (1926), pp. 153–57. Copyright Akademische Verlagsgesellschaft Athenaion, Potsdam. Reprinted by permission of the publisher.

without intervening walls. There are no other large rooms besides the big room. Dining rooms, bedrooms, and work rooms should be as carefully designed as ships' cabins. Even dining rooms are small, because people are no longer accustomed to gastronomical feasts on a large scale. The house contains a minimum of equipment: few partitions, few doors, few rugs, few pictures, few curtains; little furniture, as much of it built in as possible; recessed lighting, the smallest possible lighting fixtures; the utmost reduction of all plastic detail in favor of the room itself! Every detail is calculated most exactly. Empty spaces are avoided, therefore attics are eliminated, but the surface of the roof is utilized. Economy, conciseness, construction reign!

The immediate sources are ships, railroad cars, airplane cabins. Why? Because in all of these it is not the walls but the framework that is load-bearing, hence the partitions are only thin insulators. Today one desires light partitions because the house is free-floating, as it were, and is carried by only a few interior supports. Its exterior should also emphasize this sense of lightness. That is why the self-consciously modern cube-like houses, which look as bulky as frozen lumps of dough, are unspeakably repulsive! Lightness! . . .

To conclude, the demand arises for admitting as much light as possible so that a studiolike brightness results. As one formerly could not do without ivy or grape-clad arbors, which formed another cell within the enclosure of the garden, so the new house cannot do without the roof garden. There one faces the sky directly in an architectonic setting, making it possible to live among the treetops. Moreover, interior partitions are largely eliminated. . . . Hence, the individual rooms of the ground floor are not divided by doors and walls, but rather by appropriate placing of the furniture. In the 1890s while Germany was going through the third or fourth Rococo period, in America Frank Lloyd Wright had already formulated the classic solutions for the new house. This is where the impetus of the whole movement of modern architecture begins, and gains new significance by fusing the central room of the house more closely with the others not only on one floor level, but on two. We have all grown up in individual rooms. Many of us need seclusion for rest or thinking. The next generation will perhaps be astonished by this. This is already becoming evident in the formulations of the new architecture. In a word, the meaning of the new architecture is penetration! Penetration from without to within, from within to without, from above to below.

As an example, let us consider Le Corbusier's house for the collector La Roche, in the Paris suburb of Auteuil. It is a double house, the left wing of which is owned by M. La Roche. The problem of the new house has not only been posed here for the first time but also carried out with architectural imagination. For the way in which the cool concrete walls, alive in themselves, are divided, cut up and dispersed in order to allow new room compartmentalizations has only been known, in a wholly different context, in some Baroque chapels. When one steps into this hall [Fig. 9] one feels at once in touch with all parts of the house. In the wall to the right a black staircase appears between the great cutout sections, and to the left can be seen a second flight of stairs with its lightly suspended landing. To the right one sees the living quarters composed of small rooms. To the left is the art gallery. As one goes up and down the stairs, the vistas change, with a continuous succession of intersections and bridges. The new statics, which had been thought possible only through the use of overhanging slabs of concrete, are realized here by spatial vision alone.

One should not confuse the big room with the hall of upper middle-class houses. The stairs are not plastic monsters which rip the room apart. Like the furniture, they are recessed as much as possible. The steps swing into the room from behind the large sections of the wall, without weighing it down by their bulk. Moreover, one should not confuse the big room with the ordinary hall, since Le Corbusier had planned his houses to be as one-celled as possible from the very beginning. He has, to be sure, come a long way, artistically speaking, from connecting the different levels of space by spiral stairs, as in his *Vers une Architecture* (the chapter "Mass-Production Houses"), to his solution in Auteuil. His Esprit Nouveau Pavilion at the Paris Exhibition of 1925 reveals the same thought process. There the big room actually comprises the whole house, with the exception of the sports area and the sleeping cabins. A few pieces of furniture placed diagonally divide the room into its separate functions. Over it stretches the typical space-bridge, whose open, low rooms are in touch with the ones below. In the La Roche house the study is stretched out like the bridge of a ship, making it possible to see in all directions. Connecting the rooms in a vertical direction and welding the floor levels together is precisely the point where the French-Swiss Le Corbusier forges ahead into new territory beyond the architectural range of Frank Lloyd Wright.

The exterior of the La Roche house is also a high point among the houses realized by Le Corbusier so far. It is conspicuously quiet. And like his books, it is unostentatious. Le Corbusier will someday be counted among the classicists of the movement. The lower row of windows reminds one of the disciplined design of an express train, and the upper unframed windows can be compared to those found on the deck structure of a ship of the Canadian Pacific Company which appears in one of Le Corbusier's books.[1] . . . With the La Roche house the leap from perception to actual creation has succeeded.

[1] [*L'art décoratif d'aujourd'hui* (Paris: Crès, 1925), p. 187.—ED.]

PROGRESSIVE BUILDING
IN PARIS: 1918–1928 (1960)

Reyner Banham

. . . The bulk of Modern architecture in Paris in the Twenties consisted of one particular *maison-type*, the studio-house, twisted out of recognition by random or personal factors. Thus the pure studio-type appears far more frequently in Le Corbusier's projects than in his built work, and André Lurçat, the most prolific builder of studios, only on one occasion approximates really closely to the type, in a house in Boulogne-sur-Seine, late in the decade. Yet, if the type was obscured, it was never absent from architects' thoughts for long, and often coloured their designs for buildings with quite different functions. The existence of the type dates back to the previous century, when it could often be found in its pure form of a long, narrow house, its dimensions fixed by the normal dimensions of a Paris building plot. Since it was usually hard up against other buildings on either side, its windows were all on the ends, those on the more northerly end usually being amalgamated into one single expanse of glass, often two stories high and spreading from wall to wall to light the studio.

The two-storey studio can also be taken as a given feature, often with a storage or sleeping balcony across the back of it, reached by a spiral stair or cat ladder, especially where studios were stacked up in multi-storey blocks, as they are at the foot of Montmartre. In these cases any other necessary rooms were usually at the back of the studio, but in single-studio houses they were more often underneath. The difficulty of spanning the width of the studio with beams strong enough to support further rooms on top was one of the main factors in planning the accommodation this way up, but even when reinforced concrete had obviated this difficulty, this arrangement remains the custom—though Perret, for instance, inverts it in the Orloff house, and has a ground-floor studio. The other form of section, with the smaller rooms behind the

"Progressive building in Paris: 1918–1928" and "Vers une Architecture." From Reyner Banham, *Theory and Design in the First Machine Age* (New York: Frederick A. Praeger, Inc., 1960), pp. 217–19, 221–22. Copyright The Architectural Press, London, 1960. Reprinted by permission of the author and publishers.

studio, was the particular preference of Le Corbusier, who continued to use the long narrow plan with double-height studio and sleeping balcony even in his designs of the Fifties (as the flats at Marseilles) even in buildings that were not studio-houses (where the high room becomes a living room) and even in buildings that were not on long narrow sites (as the single house at Weissenhof) and did not need to have their fenestration confined to their end-walls.

There was a sharp divergence in the way in which architects faced the problem of the studio-house façade. The north-light window gives on to the street much more often than a statistical average would lead one to expect, and thus has to share the elevation with an entrance, probably garage doors and one or more small windows. Perret and his followers employ a strongly accentuated exposed frame, and distribute the various openings within it in such a way as to create at least an illusion of symmetry. The others, Mallet-Stevens, Lurçat, Le Corbusier and their followers, who were responsible for something like four studios out of every five in the Twenties, exploit the difference in size and function of the openings to create an asymmetrical pattern of holes pierced in a flat white surface,[1] on which an all-over rendering has been spread to obliterate the distinction between support and load, frame and fill.

For this they could plead the support of tradition—not the tradition of the professional architects, but that of the vernacular buildings of the Paris region, for the city still affords many examples of unpretentious utilitarian buildings, with windows of various sizes set asymmetrically in white-rendered walls. Attention had been drawn to such buildings by the paintings of Utrillo, which take them as their prime subject-matter, and by the Cubo-Futurist magazine *Sic* which exhorted its readers in 1916

> Aimons la maison neuve
> Aimons la maison blanche

which, judging from the elaborate surface finishes preferred by professional architects of the period, can only refer to whitewashed vernacular buildings.

But Le Corbusier, at least, had other reasons for admiring white-washed architecture, reasons that seem to be involved with his own experiences as a painter, and his theories about the beauty of banality. In reviewing the architectural section of the *Salon d'Automne* of 1922 in *L'Esprit Nouveau* he wrote, complaining of a preoccupation with *de luxe* materials.

> If the house is entirely white, the design of things stands out without possible transgression, the volumes of things appear clearly, the colour of things is explicit.

---

[1] In the Rue du Belvedere, Boulogne-sur-Seine, and in the villa Seurat, off the Rue de la Tombe-Issoire, the Perret solution and that favoured by the younger Modernists can be found almost next door to one another.

So far, he could be a painter extolling the virtues of working on a white ground, but he pursues the theme to the point where whitewash becomes a sort of *couleur-type,* with folkloristic overtones.

> Whitewash is absolute; on it, everything stands out, inscribes itself absolutely; it is sincere and loyal. Whitewash is the riches of poor and rich, of all men—just as bread, milk and water are the riches of the slave and the king.

Thus, the vernacular architecture of Paris provokes him to reflections that reach deeply into his experience and theories, but it also provokes him to conceive something more specific: the project for the *Maison Citrohan* [Fig. 6]. This simple house is almost a pure *studio-type,* but he provides for it a derivation as characteristically unexpected as it is deeply indebted to the authority of the vernacular[2]

> We were eating in a little cabbie's restaurant in the middle of Paris. There was a bar (zinc), the kitchen at the back, a garret-floor divides the height of the premises in two, the front opens directly on the street. Simplification of source of illumination—just one big bay at each end; two lateral bearing walls, a flat roof on top; a veritable box that could usefully become a house.

while the fenestration of *Maison Citrohan,* like that of the bulk of the studio-houses standing in Paris at that time (1920), drew on another vernacular tradition.

> We had observed that the glazing of factories in the Paris suburbs let light in and kept thieves out without any difficult joinery. And was very attractive aesthetically, judiciously used.

But *Citrohan* is an admitted pun on *Citroën,* and raises a problem that can only be discussed in the context of Le Corbusier's first book over that famous signature, *Vers une Architecture. . . .*

As has been said, the invented name *Citrohan* was a conscious pun

to avoid saying "Citroën." In other words, a house like a car

a concept that introduces two other important lines of thought besides those that have already been discussed in connection with this project. On the one hand there was the cut-to-the-bone aesthetic of *"Outillage,"* of equipment as against furniture; on the other hand was the dream of a

2 This is wisdom after the event, not a contemporary record of his feelings, and did not appear in print until Volume I of the *Oeuvre Complète,* p. 31. [Le Corbusier, *Oeuvre complète, 1910–1929* (Zurich: Les Editions Girsberger, 1956).] The windows in question had tall narrow panes which can still be found on older industrial buildings all over the Paris area, as well as on the electricity sub-stations built in the early Twenties.

mass-produced *maison-type,* and in 1919, when the basic form of the *Maison Citrohan* was taking shape in his mind, this dream appeared to be on the point of realisation. The Voisin Company, at the termination of its war-time aircraft contracts (like other aircraft companies after the Second World War) tried to keep its plant occupied by breaking into the housing business. At least two prototypes of the *Maison Voisin* were built, one plain, one fancy, and neither of them very distinguished architecturally, though they present the technical peculiarity (presumably derived from aircraft practice) that their roof-trusses span the longer dimension of the rectangular plan, not the shorter, and the gables, in consequence, are on the sides, not the ends of the house.

Le Corbusier himself will not admit to any part in their design, but his description of them[3] shows that they lay very close to his own ideas.

> Up till now it seemed that a house must be heavily attached to the soil, by the depth of its foundations, the weight of its thick walls. . . . It is no trick that the *Maison Voisin* is one of the first to mark the exact reversal of this conception. The science of building has evolved in a shattering manner in recent times. The art of building has struck root firmly in science.
>
> The statement of the problem by itself indicated the means of realisation, powerfully affirming the immense revolution on which architecture has embarked. When the art of building is modified to such an extent, established aesthetics of construction are automatically over-thrown.

Thus far, Choisy up-to-date. Next, having posed the problem of post-War building in terms of a shortage of skilled labour overwhelmed by an almost unlimited demand for houses, he adopts a more Futurist tone.

> . . . Impossible to wait on the slow collaboration of the successive efforts of excavator, mason, carpenter, joiner, tiler, plumber . . . *houses must go up all of a piece, made by machine tools in a factory, assembled as Ford assembles cars, on moving conveyor belts.*
>
> Meanwhile, aviation was achieving prodigies of serial production. An aeroplane is a little house that can fly and resist the storm.
>
> It is in aircraft factories that the soldier-architects have decided to build their houses; they decided to build this house like an aircraft, with the same structural methods, lightweight framing, metal bracers, tubular supports.

A house built like an aeroplane would be a very fair realisation of the kind of architecture that Sant'Elia had demanded, built of light-weight replacements for brick, stone and wood, and a knowledge of Saint'Elia's views probably lies at the back of the enthusiastic tone of this passage, but his concluding remarks seem to return to his desire for simplicity and normality; he appears to specify for this house an *habitant-type.*

[3] The account of the Voisin house will be found in *L'Esprit Nouveau,* no. 2 (1920), 211.

These lightweight houses, supple and strong as car-bodies or airframes, are ingenious in plan: they offer the comforts a wise man might demand. To inhabit such houses one needs the mind of a sage, animated by *L'Esprit Nouveau*. A generation is coming to birth that will know how to live in *Maisons Voisin.* . . .

Today I am accused of being a revolutionary. Yet I confess to having had only one master: the past; and only one discipline: the study of the past.

LE CORBUSIER*

THE MUNDANEUM (1929)

Karel Teige

. . . A detailed study of Le Corbusier's and Pierre Jeanneret's impressive project of the Mundaneum [Fig. 17] will reveal all those qualities of Le Corbusier's work that earned him the admiration and respect of an international audience and guaranteed him a leading position in the history of modern architecture. We recognize these qualities in the Mundaneum's system of order and more particularly in the many well-designed details, as well as in the architecture of individual buildings, especially in the superb design of the University with its amphitheatrical, superimposed classrooms and spacious lecture hall.

In contrast, the general concept . . . evokes a curious impression of the past. For example, the World Museum is shaped like a pyramid, which is functionally unwarranted, with rooms in a spiral arrangement, offering more space for more recent periods. The price for this is a dark inner hall, . . . difficult access from the top along the lengthy path of ramps and the barely adequate elevators. Moreover, exhibition spaces are illuminated by longitudinal windows with no regard for the compass points. In general the Mundaneum recalls Egyptian or rather Mexican religious architecture. An axonometric view of the entire plan creates the impression of an aerial photograph of some ancient ruin of Egypt, Babylonia, Assyria or Mexico of the Mayas or the Aztecs. . . .

What is it that makes Le Corbusier's Mundaneum nonmodern and backward-looking? What is the reason behind this architectural mistake and fallacy? In our view, the first and foremost cause of this mistake is the very program, the idea and theory of the Mundaneum, which is not alive,

---

"The Mundaneum" by Karel Teige. From *Stavba*, 7 (1928–29), pp. 151–55.

---

* Le Corbusier, *Précisions sur un état présent de l'architecture et de l'urbanisme* (Paris: Editions Vincent, Fréal & Cie., 1960), p. 34.

and was not born out of a vibrant, felt need. It is the fruit of very abstract and rarified speculation about the nature of intellectual societies within the League of Nations. The Mundaneum will not be realized in this form precisely for this reason. . . .

This is not the place to offer a detailed study of the ideological program of the Mundaneum, but I shall try to analyze it as an architectural project. It is an oft-repeated and confirmed experience that architectural solutions based on ideologically fuzzy, falsely constructed, or generally stillborn problems and projects never result in works of a clear and pure nature. Programs that leave the architect guessing can never be realized by more than half-baked compromises and hence they always lead to misunderstandings. Modern architecture was not born of abstract speculation but from an actual need dictated by life itself and not by the academies or officialdom. It is the real necessities of life that engender programs for factories, bridges, railway stations, office buildings, workers' housing, schools, hospitals, hotels and apartments. A fundamental understanding and shaping of these problems brought about modern architecture. . . . Monumental and votive architecture, architecture as a memorial to anyone and anything, to revolutions and liberations, all those contemporary triumphal arches, ceremonial halls, tombs, palaces and châteaux result in monsters. Examples of both positive, that is concrete and utilitarian architecture, and of negative, that is metaphysical and monumental architecture, clearly indicate that today an architect will not succeed if he does not respond to the actual needs of social and economic life. The task and the territory of modern architecture is in the scientific design of constructions, rationally and exactly defined. Seeking to solve metaphysical, abstractly speculative tasks artistically in a monumental composition is the wrong approach, the dangers of which are exemplified by the Mundaneum.

The fallacy of Le Corbusier's Mundaneum is one of monumentality, though of a different, less brutal nature than the Germanic monumentality of architectural megalomania: it is the error of "The Palace." This danger manifested itself already in Le Corbusier's *Une Maison–Un Palais*: the definition of the house as a palace, as a machine for living endowed with a certain dignity, architectonic potential and harmony. Le Corbusier's theories suffer when as clear and tangible a concept as "a machine for living" is devalued by vague attributes of dignity, harmony, architectonic potential—a possible cover-up for all kinds of aestheticism and academicism. (Reviewing the above mentioned book in *Stavba*, Vol. 7, No. 6, p. 95, I noted that the house-palace idea might lead to severe mistakes, and to the neglect of physical and concrete needs for more or less fictitious ones). The Mundaneum, in its glaring historicism and academicism, reveals that in the modern world *architecture as an art* is impossible.

Furthermore, the Mundaneum highlights the failure of those aesthetic and formalistic theories of Le Corbusier which we have always opposed from the constructivist viewpoint: the theory of the Golden Section, of geometric proportionality, in short, all *a priori* aesthetic formulae deduced from a formalistic perception of historical styles. . . . Though they appreciate the importance of practical and utilitarian requirements, both Wagner and Le Corbusier view the ultimate goal of architecture— the queen of the arts according to them—to be the creation of a temple or a sanctuary. Poelzig wants to build "for the dear Lord"; that is where architecture begins for him. Meanwhile Gustave Eiffel, despite the doubts of all aesthetes, believes he will equal Phidias, and prefers to be a great engineer of the present rather than a craftsman of the past. In this century of machine civilization—a period of lean years for "art" and monumental architecture—the intention of creating art instead of houses, monuments instead of schools leads to hybrid forms and deprives works of the natural and modern beauty which is characteristic of functionally perfect objects.

Measure the sides of the rectangle forming the Mundaneum's esplanade and you will find its proportions based on the Golden Section. Moreover, all other proportions within this rectangle are also in strict accordance with the Golden Section in order to achieve a monumental unity and harmonious proportionality. In the World Museum a rational orientation of the windows of the exhibition hall with respect to daylight has been sacrificed to numerical and astronomical symbolism. The entire Mundaneum is ordered by the major axes which intersect at the top of the Museum pyramid, and these axes also conform to the Golden Section. . . . Thus the Mundaneum is . . . a project born not from a factual and rational analysis of a program (for its program could hardly sustain such an analysis and such a solution), but from an *a priori* aesthetic and abstract speculation, based on historical clichés. It represents not a solution, realization, or construction, but a composition. Composition: this word best expresses the entire architectural blunder of the Mundaneum.

Hannes Meyer proclaimed: "All things in this world are a product of the formula: function times economy. But these things are not works of art. All art is composition and hence contrary to utility. All life is function and thus nonartistic. The idea of a 'composition of a dock' sounds ludicrous. Then how is a city plan or a plan for a house created? Is it composition or function? Art or life?"

The Mundaneum is a composition, a manifestation of ideological and metaphysical concepts. This creative metaphysics, devoted to "supreme things," "things of the spirit," and to "the divine mission of architecture," cares little for the practical, utilitarian approach. A rectangular esplanade created according to the Golden Section, the main axes of communication also controlled by the Golden Section, a pyramid marking the four corners of the world in a symbolic and monumental manner (the enormous mass of the Museum is to perform a function otherwise accomplished by a pocket compass)—all this reveals the architect's work to be based on *a priori* aesthetic speculations rather than on an analysis of actual conditions. . . . Life of course is neither symmetrical nor triangular, neither star-shaped nor based on the Golden Section. For example, when Le Corbusier lengthened the side of the Vaucresson villa's main façade by adding two small nonbearing slabs in order to satisfy the "regulating lines," he followed Leon Battista Alberti (*De re aedificatoria*) who calculated the dimensions of the windows from the proportions of the façade irrespective of their purpose, and came to describe staircases as elements of chaos in the harmony of construction.

We see more and more clearly that architecture as "art" cannot rid itself of the constraints of antiquarianism. It remains in the tradition of Michelangelo. It looks back to the architecture of the past for formal schemes. It uses the Golden Section and other recipes for composition, and draws these proportions on small reproductions with lines so thick that reality might differ from these proportions by several meters. Thus one may prove how perfectly the façade of Notre Dame follows harmonious proportions, but what if the street level is considerably higher today than when the façade was originally built? [1] Architecture as an art believes that its mission begins where construction ends, that is, after the rational solution of the engineer. It aspires to eternity while the engineer serves the present. . . .

The opinion prevails that in order to create dignified architecture, a functional solution requires something extra. This "extra" however might serve a purpose and emphasize functionalism, in which case it is purposeful and functional and hence not an extra. But it might also hinder it, in which case it is a defect; or it neither helps nor hinders and thus is superfluous and useless, and therefore likewise a defect. The criterion of functionalism, the only reliable criterion of quality in architectural design, has led modern architecture to do away with mammoth bodies of monumentality and to cultivate its brains: *instead of monuments, architecture creates instruments.* Aesthetic intervention in utilitarian design, including architecture, leads inevitably to an imperfect object. It obscures the utilitarian aspect and considers practical values such as comfort, warmth, stability to be necessary sacrifices which people should make for cultural tradition. It has been proven that objects which combine practical functionalism with an autocratic artistic form compromise one or the other, and most frequently both. Only when the architect's work is governed by the requirements of practical life, as opposed to ideological-metaphysical-aesthetic intentions, does the tendency toward art cease.

I am dealing with the Mundaneum in detail because I believe that this work, created by the first and foremost representative of modern architecture, can serve as a warning both to its author and to modern architecture. The Mundaneum is a fiasco of aesthetic theories and traditionalist superstitions, and it reveals fully the danger of the slogan "House-Palace": the danger of a utilitarian architecture with an artistic superstructure and dominant. The way from here leads to the sphere of full-fledged academicism and classicism, or else back to well-grounded reality: to the starting point described exactly by the motto that "a house is a machine for living," and in the direction of scientific, technical, industrialized architecture. Between these two poles there is room only for misguided and compromised solutions.

[1] [The foregoing is a veiled attack on Le Corbusier's *Vers une Architecture,* especially on the chapter "Regulating Lines."—ED.]

LE CORBUSIER (1937)

Walter Curt Behrendt

. . . In each of his numerous manifestoes, Le Corbusier explains modern
building as a problem of functional structure. But to draw conclusions
from his practical achievements, he himself seems to be interested not so
much in *building* as a structural problem as in Architecture, which, according to his own definition, is supposed to be "a thing of art, a phenomenon of poetic emotion." Auguste Perret, his teacher, though still
using in his designs the classical detail, already showed more respect for
the structural problems of building, and made an honest attempt towards
an architectural interpretation of modern concrete construction when in
1922 he built the little Church of Notre Dame, Le Raincy, near Paris. And
Eugène Freyssinet, the boldest among the modern building-engineers of
France, in another effort to interpret modern construction, created a new
form when he built the airship shed at Orly, near Paris, in 1916: a para-
bolically curved vault with ribs of thin-shelled concrete pipes, a utilitarian structure of purest beauty. Le Corbusier, however, the Picasso of
modern architecture, deals not with the structural problem of building,
but with the esthetic problem of an architectural style. And he uses
modern construction mainly for its emotional power of expression.

But when the idea of style prevails, form always precedes function.
It characterizes Le Corbusier's attitude towards the problem of structure
that in his *Trois Rappels à MM les Architectes* he deals, first of all, with
the plastic form, and then he next speaks of the surface, recommending
for its arrangement the "regulating line," the old and approved expedient
of academic composition. And only in the third place, he comes to the
plan, although he always calls it "the generator." Corbusier, the theorist,
declares the plan proceeds from within to without; Corbusier, the architect, however, is always ready to make in his ground plans far-going con-
cessions, at the cost of function, in favor of the exterior. And while Cor-

busier accused academicism of having made the ground plan into a work of graphic art, exhibiting an ornament of radiant stars, his own ground plans with their elaborate interplay of straight and oblique lines, of curves and spirals, almost recalling the abstract paintings of Picasso, are certainly no less ornamental. Thus, for all his radicalism, Corbusier in his conception is not so far from those adversaries whom he antagonizes most: from the academicians.

As a matter of fact, with his radicalism Le Corbusier has thoroughly overthrown the traditional doctrine of academicism, but only with the result of replacing it with another, no less abstract principle, with the doctrine of cubism. In architecture, however, cubism means rather a return to elementary geometry than a turn towards organic order. Nothing, indeed, could be more dangerous for the new spirit of building, so long as its ideas are not yet fully ripened, than a premature lapse into doctrine. The lesson of History gives warning: even in earlier times, French radicalism, "a mixture of emotion and logic, one-sidedly tending towards program, system and doctrine," has stifled by its urge toward systematization the hopeful beginnings of an organic style. . . .

And once again it is French radicalism that has reduced the ideas of modern building to the common denominator of the classical rule. In the command of these rules Le Corbusier proves his esthetic mastery. His work, infused with the spirit of Geometry as the source of its order, certainly affords us "the sublime satisfactions of Mathematics which gives us such a grateful perception of order." And demonstrating in his achievements this spirit of order, he may convince us as artist, but he cannot convert us to the belief that it is just the spirit of Geometry which determines the modern mode of thinking and affords the universal law under which our time is striving for a new order. And eyes which do see realize that the creations of modern technique which excite Le Corbusier's highest admiration have not originated from mathematical calculation alone; the machine, the automobile, the airplane, are typical creations of organic structure, and what they look like they really are—products based on the evolutionary laws of organic nature. . . .

THE MATHEMATICS
OF THE IDEAL VILLA:
PALLADIO AND LE CORBUSIER
COMPARED (1947)

Colin Rowe

There are two causes of beauty—natural and customary. Natural is from geometry consisting in uniformity, that is equality, and proportion. Customary
beauty is begotten by the use, as familiarity breeds a love to things not in themselves lovely. Here lies the great occasion of errors, but always the true test is
natural or geometrical beauty. Geometrical figures are naturally more beautiful
than irregular ones: the square, the circle are the most beautiful, next the
parallelogram and the oval. There are only two beautiful positions of straight
lines, perpendicular and horizontal; this is from Nature and consequently necessity, no other than upright being firm.

SIR CHRISTOPHER WREN

Palladio's Villa Capra, called the Rotonda, has perhaps more than any
other house, imposed itself on the imagination of subsequent generations,
and as the ideal type of central building, it has become part of the general
European experience. Mathematical, abstract, four square, without apparent function, its dry aristocratic derivatives have enjoyed universal diffusion; when he writes of it Palladio is lyrical.

The site is as pleasant and delightful as can be found, because it is upon
a small hill of very easy access, and is watered on one side by the Bac-
chiglione, a navigable river; and on the other it is encompassed about
with most pleasant risings, which look like a very great theatre and are
all cultivated about with most excellent fruits and most exquisite vines;
and, therefore, as it enjoys from every part most beautiful views, some
of which are limited, some more extended, and others which terminate
with the horizon; there are loggias made in all four fronts.

When the mind is prepared for the one by the other, a passage from Le Corbusier's *Précisions* is unavoidably reminiscent of this. No less lyrical, but rather more explosive, he is describing the site of his Maison Savoye at Poissy [Fig. 15].

> The site: a spreading grassy meadow in the shape of a flattened dome. . . . The house is a box hovering in the air . . . in the midst of fields overlooking the orchard. . . . It fits well into the rustic countryside of Poissy. . . . The occupants who had come here because they found this rural setting beautiful . . . will contemplate it in its preserved state from the top of their roof garden or through their long windows facing in all directions. Their home life will be enfolded in a Virgilian dream.

The Savoye House has been given a fair number of interpretations: it may be a machine for living in, an arrangement of interpenetrating volume and external space, another emanation of space, time and architecture. It is probably all these things; but the suggestive reference to the dreams of Virgil, and a certain similarity of site, solution and feeling put one in mind of the passage in which Palladio describes the Rotonda. The landscape there is more agrarian and bucolic, there is less of the untamed pastoral, the scale is larger, but the effect is somehow the same.

Palladio, writing elsewhere, amplifies the ideal life of the villa. Its owner, from within the fragment of created order, will watch the maturing of his possessions, and savour the piquancy of contrast between his fields and his gardens; reflecting on mutability, he will contemplate through the years the antique virtues of a simpler race, the harmonious ordering of his life and estate will be an analogy of paradise.

> The ancient sages commonly used to retire to such places, where being oftentimes visited by their virtuous friends and relations, having houses, gardens, fountains and such like pleasant places, and above all their virtue, they could easily attain to as much happiness as can be attained here below.

Perhaps these were the dreams of Virgil. Freely interpreted, they have gathered round themselves, in the course of time, all those ideals of Roman virtue, excellence, Imperial splendour and decay, which make up the imaginative reconstruction of the ancient world. It would have been, perhaps, the landscape of Poussin that Palladio would have longed to penetrate, to roam among the portentous apparitions of the antique: it is possibly the fundamentals of this landscape, the poignancy of contrast between the disengaged cube and its setting in the rustic countryside, between geometrical volume and landscape which has the look of unimpaired nature, which lie behind Corbusier's Roman allusion. If architecture at the Rotonda forms the setting for the good life, at Poissy it is certainly the background for the lyrically efficient one; and if the contemporary pastoral is not yet sanctified by conventional usage, apparently the Virgilian nostalgia is still present. From the hygienically equipped boudoirs, pausing while ascending the ramps, the memory of the Georgics no doubt interposes itself, and, perhaps, the historical reference adds relish as the car pulls out for Paris.

A more specific comparison that presents itself is that between Palladio's Villa Foscari [Fig. 14], the Malcontenta, and the house which in 1927 Corbusier built for M. de Monzie at Garches [Fig. 13]. A diagrammatic comparison will reveal the fundamental relationships.

In general idea, as can be seen, the system of the two houses is closely similar. They are both conceived as single blocks, with one projecting element and parallel principle and subsidiary façades. Allowing for variations in roof treatment they are blocks of corresponding volume, eight units in length, by five and a half in breadth, by five in height. In both cases six "transverse" lines of support, rhythmically alternating double and single bays, are established; but the rhythm of the parallel lines of support, as a result of Corbusier's use of the cantilever, differs slightly. At the villa at Garches it is ½ : 1½ : 1½ : 1½ : ½, and at the Malcontenta 1½ : 2 : 2 : 1½. In plan, Corbusier thus obtains a sort of compression for his central bay, and interest seems transferred to his outer bays, which are augmented by the extra half unit of the cantilever; while Palladio secures a dominance for his central division, and a progression towards his portico, which focuses interest there. In both cases the projecting element, terrace or portico, occupies 1½ units in depth.

Structures, of course, are entirely different, and both architects look to structure to some extent as a justification for their dispositions. Palladio employs a solid bearing wall, and of this system he writes:

> . . . it is to be observed, that those (rooms) on the right correspond with those on the left, so that the fabric may be the same in one place as in the other, and that the walls may equally bear the burden of the roof; because if the walls are made large in one part and small in the other, the latter will be the more fit to resist the weight, by reason of the nearness of the walls, and the former more weak, which will produce in time very great inconveniences and ruin the whole work.

Palladio is concerned with the logical disposition of motifs dogmatically accepted; but he attempts to discover a structural reason for his planning symmetries. Corbusier, who is proving a case for structure as a basis of the formal elements of design, contrasts the new system with the old. He is a little more inclusive.

> I want to remind you of the "frozen plan" of stone
> houses and what we have attained with the house made
> of steel or reinforced concrete:
>   free plan
>   free façade
>   free skeletal structure
>   long windows or sealed windows

stilts [*pilotis*]
roof garden
and the interior equipped with built-in cabinets
and freed from the encumbrance of furniture.

Palladio's structural system makes it almost necessary to repeat the same plan on every level of the building; and point support allows Corbusier a fairly flexible arrangement; but both architects make a claim, which is somewhat in excess of the reasons they advance. Solid wall structures, Palladio declares, demand absolute symmetry; a frame building, Corbusier announces, requires a free arrangement: these must be, at least partly, the personal exigencies of high style, for asymmetrical buildings in the traditional manner in fact remain standing, and frame buildings of conventional plan continue to give aesthetic satisfaction.

In both houses the principal rooms are on the first floor, linked to the garden by an external feature and flight of steps. The main floor of the Malcontenta shows a cruciform hall, and symmetrically disposed about it are two suites of three rooms each, two staircases and a portico. At Garches the central hall remains; one of the two staircases occupies a similar position, but the other has been turned through an angle of ninety degrees; the entrance hall has been revealed from this level by an asymmetrical well, and the external feature corresponding to the portico becomes partly a re-entrant volume, obliterating a line of support and placed in a less perceptible relationship to the main room. The cruciform shape has disappeared, and a Z-shaped balance is achieved by throwing the small library into the main apartment. There is a subsidiary cross axis at Malcontenta, which is suggested at Garches by the central voids of the end walls. These convey a certain careful character to the plan, but there is no through vista. . . .

In the Villa at Garches the exploitation of the structural system has led to the conception of the wall as a series of horizontal strips, alternating void and solid, a system which places equal interest in both centre and extremity of the façade, and is maintained by Corbusier's almost complete suppression in elevation of the wider spans of the double bays, which are arranged to read as two separate bays. Any system of central vertical accent, and inflection of the wall leading up to it, is profoundly modified. The immediate result in the garden elevation at Garches shows itself in the displacing of portico and roof pavilion from the central position which they occupy in the Malcontenta. They are separated, the one occupying the three bays to the left of the façade, and the other a central position in the solid, but an asymmetrical one in the whole elevation. The diagonal of the staircase forms the balance.

The entrance elevation retains the central feature in the upper storey, but it is noticeable that the further development of this feature within itself is asymmetrical. The downward indication of weights in this sort of façade is impossible; and to see the central feature, interrupted by the horizontal voids, centrally repeated in the base, would be grotesque.

Displacement and breaking up of the feature are again compensated by diagonal relationships; and in the ground floor entrance marquise and service door fulfil these purposes.

The other chief point of difference lies in the idea of the roof. In the Malcontenta it forms a pyramidal superstructure dominated by the temple fronts of the upper pediments, which occur above, and augment the central features of the main wall. Interest and silhouette are provided by the highly romantic chimneys, which possess a mediaevalizing quality, recalling the complicated machicolations of the now disappeared courtyard walls. Garches has a flat roof on two levels, treated partly as enclosure cut out of the block, and scattered with the irregular incident of gazebo, perforation and pavilion. The main plastic elements, the framed terrace of the entrance elevation and the pavilion of the garden front, are placed respectively in symmetrical and asymmetrical relation to the façades below. As at the Malcontenta, they are dominant features in the composition, but in neither case are they placed in direct vertical relationship with the principal features of the lower wall.

Corbusier's treatment of the base is not continuous. In the cantilevered façades it is affirmed by set-backs or horizontal voids, elsewhere it is not expressed.

Mathematics and musical concord as the basis of ideal proportion was a common belief in Palladio's North Italian circle, where there was felt to be a correspondence between the perfect numbers, the proportions of the human figure and the elements of musical harmony. Sir Henry Wotton, as Ambassador at Venice, reflects some part of this attitude when he writes:—

> The two principal Consonances that most ravish the Ear are, by the consent of all Nature, the Fifth and the Octave, whereof the first riseth radically from the Proportion between two and three, the other from the double Interval between one and two, or between two and four, etc. Now if we shall transport these Proportions, from audible to visual Objects, and apply them as shall fall fittest . . . , there will indubitably result from either, a graceful and harmonious Contentment to the Eye.

It was not in fact suggested that architectural proportions derived from musical harmonies, but rather that the laws of proportion were established mathematically and universally diffused. The Platonic and Pythagorean universe was compounded of the simpler relationships of numbers, and such a world was formed within the triangle made by the square and cube of the numbers 1, 2, 3. Its qualities, rhythms and relationships were established within this framework of numbers up to 27; and if such numbers governed the works of God, it was fitting that the works of man should be similarly constructed, and that a building should be a representative in microcosm, of the same process exhibited to a larger scale in the workings of the world. In Alberti's words "Nature is sure to act consistently and with a constant analogy in all her operations," what is patent in music must also be so in architecture, proportions are a reflection of the harmony of the universe, their basis, scientific and religious, was quite unassailable. Palladio had the satisfaction of an entirely objective aesthetic.

Corbusier has expressed similar convictions about proportion. Mathematics bring "comforting truths," and "one only stops his work with the certainty of having reached the precise result." It is, indeed, exactness, precision, neatness that he seeks, the overall controlling shape; and within, not the unchallengeable clearness of Palladio's volumes, but a sort of planned obscurity. Consequently, while in the Malcontenta geometry is diffused through the internal volumes of the building, at Garches it resides only in the total block and the disposition of its supports.

The theoretical basis on which Palladio rested broke down in the eighteenth century, when proportion became a matter of individual sensibility and inspiration; and Corbusier, in spite of the comforts which mathematics afford him, occupies no such unassailable position. The functionalist theory was, perhaps, an attempt to re-assert a scientific aesthetic with the objective value of the old. Its interpretation was crude. Results can be measured in terms of the solution of a particular process; proportions are apparently accidental and gratuitous. It is in contradiction of this theory that Corbusier imposes mathematical patterns upon his buildings: these are the universal "comforting truths."

Thus, either because, or in spite of theory, both architects share a common standard, a mathematical one, defined by Wren as "natural beauty"; and within the limitations of a particular programme, it is not surprising that the blocks should be of corresponding volume—8 : 5½ : 5. Corbusier has carefully indicated his relationships by regulating lines, dimensions and figures, and over all he places the ratio of the golden section, $A : B = B : (A + B)$. Thus he indicates the ideal with which he would wish his façade to correspond, although in actual fact the figures $3 : 5 = 5 : 8$ thus represented are only approximate.

Palladio also provides his plan with cryptically explanatory dimensions, and thus the rooms comprising the suites of three can be read as a progression from a $3 : 4$ to $2 : 3$ relationship. They are numbered $12 : 16$, $16 : 16$, and $16 : 24$.

The façade is divided vertically into four main units, the two central ones being really a single division by their common expression as portico. The horizontal divisions are complicated by the introduction of the order, which presupposes alongside the "natural" proportions, a series of purely "customary" relationships. In fact these horizontal divisions are uneven although, as the figures show, they roughly approximate to a division into fifths—a fifth part to the attic and approximately three-fifths of the remaining wall surface to order and entablature.

Corbusier also divides his façade into four units; but in his case horizontally. The two central units are partly unified by their placing alongside the garden terrace, and could be considered as corresponding to Palladio's piano nobile. The vertical divisions are in the relationship indicated by the equation $(3 : 5)$, which Palladio uses horizontally. In both cases there are elaborations in detail of dominant, complicated by imposition upon subsidiary system. It is by vertical extension into arch and vault, diagonal of roof line and parapet, that Palladio modifies the geometrical asperities of his cube; and the use of the circular and pyramidal elements with the square seems both to conceal and amplify the real nature of the volumes. Some of these resources are the prerogatives of solid wall construction, freedoms of the "frozen plan," and the introduction of arched forms and pitched roofs is a liberty which Corbusier at Garches is unable to allow himself. In the frame building it is not, as in the solid wall structure, the enclosing walls that are a dominant, but the horizontal planes of floor and roof. The quality of partial paralysis, which Corbusier has noticed in the plan of the solid wall structure, in the frame building is transferred to the section. Perforation of floors giving a certain vertical movement of space is possible; but the sculptural quality of the building as carving has disappeared, and there can be none of Palladio's firm sectional transmutation and modelling of volume. Extension must be horizontal, following the established horizontal planes; free section is replaced by free plan, paralysed plan by paralysed section; and the limitations in both cases are equally severe; as though the solid wall structure had been turned on its side, the former complexities of section and subtleties of elevation are now transferred to plan.

The shapefulness and spatial audacities of the Garches plan continue to thrill; but it is an interior which seems to be regulated by the intellect only, operating, as it were, inside a stage vacuum. There is a permanent tension between the organised and the apparently fortuitous. To the intellect it is clear, to the senses deeply perplexing; and it seems not to be possible to stand anywhere in it, at any one point and receive the palpable impression of the whole. Both buildings can be absorbed from without; but from within, in the cruciform hall of the Malcontenta, there is a clue to the whole building, which is crystallised and focused there. At Garches, the theoretical equidistance between floor and ceiling conveys an equal importance to all parts of the volume in between. Allowed a sufficient height, it might be treated as a single volume, but otherwise the development of focus becomes a somewhat arbitrary proceeding. Corbusier accepts this limitation, and accepts the principle of horizontal extension; at Garches the central focus has been consistently broken up, concentration at one point is disintegrated, and replaced by a peripheral dispersion of incident. The dismembered fragments of the central focus become, in fact, a sort of serial installation of interest round the extremities of the plan.

The system of horizontal extension comes up against the rigid bounding lines of the rectangular block, which is fundamental to the programme. Elaborate external development is, therefore, impossible, and Corbusier logically employs the opposite resource, inversion in the place of extension, gouging out large volumes of the block as the terrace and the roof garden, and exposing them to the outer space. Thus the peripheral incident, which replaces the focus, sometimes becomes one and the same with the inversions, which represent an essentially similar feature to Palladio's vertical extension.

This system of regular diffusion of interest and irregular develop-ment of points of concentration throws into intense relief the geometrical substructure of the building. A comparable process to that in the plan takes place in the elevations, where the horizontal window treatment con-veys equal interest to the centre and verge of the façades, and produces similar disintegration of vertical emphasis and displacement of the cen-tral feature. Elimination of focus immediately transfers interest to ex-tremities of the block, which acquire a clarity and tautness, as though they were trying to restrain the peripheral incident from flying out of the block altogether.

A specific comparison is less easy to make between the Villa Ro-tonda and the Savoye House of 1930, the houses which seemed to pro-voke it. The problem, although at first it appears to be more severe, in actual fact offers a wider range. The emotional impression, concentrated in two fronts at Garches and the Malcontenta, is diffused here through all four, resulting in a more complex internal disposition and a greater genial-ity of external effect. The structural system of the Poissy house is less clear, and its central character is somewhat discounted by the canti-levered prolongations of what are presumably the east and west façades; and by the "directed" expression of the ground floor, with its porte-cochère and utility entrances. There is a noticeable easiness and lack of tension in these façades; but there are analogous developments from the earlier houses in both cases. Such is Palladio's development of central emphasis in both plan and elevations; and Corbusier's extended interest throughout his façades and dispersing of focus. The complicated vol-umes of the roof gardens replace the Palladian pitched roof and cupola; Palladio's four projecting loggias are replaced within the block as the first floor roof garden, which could also be considered, as the dominant ele-ment of this floor, to correspond to the domed salon of the Rotonda.

Symbolically, and in what might be called the sphere of "customary" beauty, these two groups of buildings are in different worlds. Palladio sought complete clarity of plan, the most lucid organisation of conven-tional elements based on symmetry, as the most memorable form of order, and mathematics as the supreme sanction in the world of external forms. In his own mind his work was essentially that of adaptation, the adapta-tion of the ancient house; and at the back of his mind were always the great halls of the Imperial thermae, and such buildings as Hadrian's villa at Tivoli. He has several schemes of archaeological reconstruction of Greek and Roman domestic buildings, based on Vitruvius and Pliny, and incorporating elements, which in Greek and Roman practice would have been found only in public buildings, but which he regarded as general. Rome for him was still alive, and if the ancients had adapted the temple from the house, their large scale planning was no doubt similarly reflec-tive. Development was, therefore, less a matter of innovation, than an extension of ideas already implicit.

Corbusier has an equal reverence for mathematics, and would ap-pear to be sometimes tinged with a comparable historicism. He seems to find a source in those ideals of suitability and comfort displayed in the ingenious planning of the rococo hotel, the background of a social life at once more amplified and intimate. The French have an unbroken tradition of this sort of planning; and one discovers, in a beaux arts utilisation of an irregular site, elements which, if they had not preceded Corbusier, would have been curiously reminiscent of those suave boudoirs and vestibules. Corbusier admires the Byzantine architecture of the Mediterranean world, and there is also present a purely French delight in the more comprehensible aspects of mechanics . . . the little pavilion on the roof at Garches is at the same time a temple of love and the bridge of a ship, the detail is precise, the most complex architectural volumes are fitted with running water.

Geometrically, both architects may be said to have approached something of the Platonic archetype of the villa, which the Virgilian dream could be held to represent. The idealisation of the cube house must lend itself very readily to the purposes of Virgilian dreaming. Here is set up the conflict between the contingent and the absolute, the natural and the abstract; the gap between the ideal world and the too human exigencies of realisation receives its most pathetic presentation. The bridging must be as competent and compelling as a well-executed fugue, charged as in these cases with almost religious seriousness, or sophisticated, witty allusion; it is an intellectual feat which reconciles the mind to the fundamental discrepancy of the programme.

Palladio is the convinced classicist with the sixteenth century repertoire of well-humanised forms. He translates this "customary" material with a passion and a high seriousness fitting to the continued validity that he finds it to possess: the reference to the Pantheon in the superimposed porticoes; to the thermae in the cruciform salon; the ambiguity, profound, in both idea and form, in the equivocal conjunction of temple front and domestic block. These are charged with meaning, both for what they are and for what they signify; and their impression is poignant. The ancient house is not re-created, but there is in its place a concrete apparition of antique virtue, excellence, Imperial splendour and stoicism: Rome is there by allusion, the ideal world by geometry.

By contrast, Corbusier is in some ways the most ingenious of eclectics. The orders, the Roman allusion, are the apparatus of authority, customary, and in a sense universal forms. It is hard for the modern architect to be quite so emphatic about any particular civilisation; and with Corbusier there is always present an element of wit, suggesting that the historical reference has remained a quotation between inverted commas, possessing always the double value of the quotation, the associations of both old and new context. The world of classical Mediterranean culture, on which Palladio drew so expressively, is closed for Corbusier. The emblematic representations of the moral virtues, the loves of the Gods and the lives of the Saints, the ornamental adjuncts of humanism, have lost their former historical monopoly. Allusion is dissipated at Garches, concentrated at the Malcontenta; with the one cube the performance is mixed, within the other, Roman. Corbusier selects the irrelevant and the particular, the fortuitously picturesque and the incidentally significant forms of mechanics, as the objects of his virtuosity. They retain their original implications of classical landscape, mechanical precision, rococo intimacy; one is able to seize hold of them as known objects, and sometimes as basic shapes; but they become only transiently provocative. Unlike Palladio's forms there is nothing final about their relationship: their rapprochement would seem to be affected by the artificial emptying of the cube, when the senses are confounded by the apparent arbitrariness, and the intellect more than convinced by the intuitive knowledge that here, in spite of all to the contrary, there is order and there are rules.

Corbusier has become the source of fervent pastiches, and witty exhibition techniques: the neo-Palladian villa became the picturesque object in the English park. Content is different in both cases, and a bad portico is usually more convincing than an ill-executed incident. It is the magnificently realisable quality of the originals which one fails to find in the works of neo-Palladians and exponents of "le style Corbu." The difference is that between the universal and the decorative or merely competent; perhaps in both cases it is the adherence to rules which has lapsed.

CONCLUSION: FUNCTIONALISM AND TECHNOLOGY (1960)

Reyner Banham

. . . [In] Le Corbusier's house, *Les Heures Claires,* built for the Savoye family at Poissy-sur-Seine and completed in 1930 [Fig. 15] the vertical penetrations are of crucial importance in the whole design. They are not large in plan but, since they are effected by a pedestrian ramp, whose balustrades make bold diagonals across many internal views, they are very conspicuous to a person using the house. Furthermore, this ramp was designed as the preferred route of what the architect calls the *promenade architecturale* through the various spaces of the building—a concept which appears to lie close to that almost mystical meaning of the word "axis" that he had employed in *Vers une Architecture.* The floors connected by this ramp are strongly characterised functionally—*on vit par étage*—the ground floor being taken up with services and servants, transport and entrance facilities, and a guest room; the first floor given over to the main living accommodation, virtually a week-end bungalow complete with patio; and the highest floor a roof garden with sun-bathing deck and viewing platform, surrounded by a windscreen wall.

This, of course, is only the functional breakdown; what makes the building architecture by Le Corbusier's standards and enables it to touch the heart, is the way these three floors have been handled visually. The house as a whole is white—*le couleur-type*—and square—one of *les plus belles formes*—set down in a sea of uninterrupted grass—*le terrain idéal* —which the architect has called a Virgilian Landscape. Upon this traditional ground he erected one of the least traditional buildings of his career, rich in the imagery of the Twenties. The ground floor is set back a considerable distance on three sides from the perimeter of the block, and the consequent shadow into which it is plunged was deepened by dark paint and light-absorbent areas of fenestration. When the house is viewed from the grounds, this floor hardly registers visually, and the whole upper part of the house appears to be delicately poised in space, supported only by the row of slender pilotis under the edge of the first floor—precisely that species of material-immaterial illusionism that Oud had prophesied, but that Le Corbusier more often practised.

However, the setting back of the ground floor has further meaning. It leaves room for a motor-car to pass between the wall and the pilotis supporting the floor above; the curve of this wall on the side away from the road was, Le Corbusier claims, dictated by the minimum turning circle of a car. A car, having set down its passengers at the main entrance on the apex of this curve, could pass down the other side of the building, still under the cover of the floor above, and return to the main road along a drive parallel to that on which it had approached the house. This appears to be nothing less than a typically Corbusian "inversion" of the test-track on roof of the Matté-Trucco's Fiat factory, tucked under the building instead of laid on top of it, creating a suitably emotive approach to the home of a fully motorised post-Futurist family. Inside this floor, the entrance hall has an irregular plan, but is given a business-like and ship-shape appearance by narrow-paned industrial glazing, by the plain balustrades of the ramp and the spiral staircase leading to the floor above, and by the washbasin, light fittings, etc., which, as in the *Pavillon de l'Esprit Nouveau*, appear to be of industrial or nautical extraction. On the main living floor above, the planning shows less of that *Beaux-Arts* formality that had appeared in the slightly earlier house at Garches, but is composed much as an Abstract painting might have been composed, by jig-sawing together a number of rectangles to fit into a given square plan. The feeling of the arrangement of parts within a pre-determined frame is heightened by the continuous and unvaried window-strip—the ultimate *fenêtre en longueur*—that runs right round this floor, irrespective of the needs of the rooms or open spaces behind it. However, where this strip runs across the wall of the open patio it is unglazed, as is the viewing window in the screen wall of the roof-garden, a fulfilment, however late and unconscious, of Marinetti's demand for villas sited for view and breeze. The screen wall, again, raises painterly echoes: in contrast to the square plan of the main floor, it is composed of irregular curves and short straights, mostly standing well back from the perimeter of the block. Not only are these curves, on plan, like the shapes to be found in his *Peintures Puristes*, but their modelling, seen in raking sunlight, has the same delicate and insubstantial air as that of the bottles and glasses in his paintings and the effect of these curved forms, standing on a square slab raised on legs, is like nothing so much as a still-life arranged on a table. And set down in this landscape it has the same kind of Dadaist quality as the statue in the Barcelona Pavilion. . . .

. . . The course of a lifetime of work . . . was born from a seed which has germinated since the beginning . . . proposing and imposing a course of conduct.

LE CORBUSIER*

GARCHES TO JAOUL:
LE CORBUSIER AS DOMESTIC
ARCHITECT IN 1927 AND 1953 (1955)

James Stirling

Villa Garches [Fig. 12], recently reoccupied, and the two houses for Mr. Jaoul [Fig. 21] and his son, now nearing completion, are possibly the most significant buildings by Le Corbusier to be seen in Paris today, for they represent the extremes of his vocabulary: the former, rational, urbane, programmatic, the latter, personal and anti-mechanistic. If style is the crystallization of an attitude, then these buildings, so different even at the most superficial level of comparison, may, on examination, reveal something of a philosophical change of attitude on the part of their author.

Garches, built at the culmination of Cubism and canonizing the theories in "Towards a New Architecture," has since its inception been a standard by which Le Corbusier's genius is measured against that of the other great architects of this century. Inhabited, again by Americans, after fifteen years' splendid isolation, it has been painted in a manner more "de Stijl" than the original: walls white inside and out, all structural members black and single planes of primary colour on areas of lesser consequence. It is never possible to see more than one coloured plane from any single viewpoint. On the principal façade, the underside of the

* Le Corbusier, *Oeuvre complète 1952–1957* (Zurich: Editions Girsberger, 1958), p. 9.

entrance canopy is painted sky-blue as the underside of the slab over the terrace. Inside, one wall of the living area is painted yellow, etc.

As with the still deserted Poissy, the deterioration at Garches was only skin-deep; paint decay, broken glass and slight cracks in the rendering; there has been no deterioration to the structure nor any waterproofing failures. Though the landscape has thickened considerably to the rear of the house, trees have not yet grown close against the main façades; where this has happened, at La Roche, Cook and Planeix, the balanced asymmetry of the elevations, as total compositions, has been grossly disfigured. The one instance among the Paris buildings where trees are sympathetic is the Pavillon Suisse where they have grown the full height of the south elevation, significantly one of the most repetitive façades that Le Corbusier has produced. In more extreme examples of additive elevations, as in many American buildings, the presence of trees, naturalistic incidents, might almost be considered essential. The disembowelled machine parts of the Armée du Salut outbuildings have a similar juxtaposition to the neutral backdrop of the slab [Fig. 18].

If Garches appears urban, sophisticated and essentially in keeping with "l'esprit parisien," then the Jaoul houses seem primitive in character, recalling the Provençal farmhouse community; they seem out of tune with their Parisian environment. Their pyramidal massing is reminiscent of traditional Indian architecture and they were in fact designed after Le Corbusier's first visits to that country. Frequently accused of being "internationalist," Le Corbusier is actually the most regional of architects. The difference between the cities of Paris and Marseilles is precisely the difference between the Pavillon Suisse and the Unité, and at Chandigarh the centre buildings are indebted to the history and traditions of a native Indian culture; even a project for the Palace of the Soviets makes considerable reference to Russian constructivism. Therefore, it is perhaps disturbing to encounter the Jaoul houses within half a mile of the Champs Elysées.

Assuming that the observer has become familiar with the architecture of Le Corbusier through the medium of the glossy books, then the first impression registered on arriving at the Jaoul houses is unique for they are of the scale and size expected, possibly because of the expressed floor beams. Usually, the scale is either greater or smaller than anticipated, that of Garches being unexpectedly heroic.

Differing from the point structure and therefore free plan of Garches, the structure of Jaoul is of load-bearing, brick cross-walls, cellular in planning by implication. It would, however, be a mistake to think of these buildings as models for cross-wall architecture as this aspect is visually subordinated to the massive, concrete, Catalan vaults occurring at each floor level. These vaults are to be covered with soil and grass to resist thermal expansion and the timber shutter-boards have been set to leave a carefully contrived pattern. Internally one-inch solid steel tiles are positioned at approximately fifteen-foot centres to resist diagonal thrust into the brick walls. At the external centre point of these vaults, bird-nesting boxes are formed, and occasionally concrete rainwater heads are projected from the side-beams, though the pipes drop internally. Rising from the underground garage through to the top of each house are dog-leg stairs, cast in situ; they are a development from the Marseilles fire-escape stair, with the treads cantilevered either side of the vertical concrete slab. By English standards, the brickwork is poor, but then the wall is considered as a surface and not a pattern. Masonry, rubble, or, perhaps more rationally in view of the vault construction, mass concrete walls could be substituted without difference to the principle of design.

Perhaps the only factor that Garches and Jaoul have in common is the considerable influence of the site on both. All Le Corbusier's buildings tend to fall into one of two categories: those in which the peculiarities of the site are a paramount factor in conception—most notably the Armée du Salut—and those where the site is of little consequence, being subordinated to a preconception or archetype, e.g., the Unité [Fig. 22]. To some extent this may account for the lack of inevitability, sometimes felt with buildings of this latter category, most particularly the Pavillon Suisse where, except as an archetype per se, there seems little justification for raising the building above ground, there being no circulation or view through. If the entrance hall, approachable from any direction, had been under and not to the rear of the slab, the raising of the block would not appear so arbitrary. None the less, the town-planning ideas which generated this form retain their urgent validity.

The exact relationship and planning of the two Jaoul houses have been motivated by the nature of the site. The circulation is on two levels and of two kinds. Cars drive straight off the road into the garage, a large underground cavern from which separate stairs rise through to each house. Walking circulation is above this garage on what appears to be natural ground level but which is actually a made-up terrace on which the houses stand. This level is linked to the road by a ramp. The differentiation of circulation on superimposed levels and the free movement around the houses are reminiscent in another medium of the suspended routes into the Armée du Salut.

At Maison Jaoul the only entire elevation that can be seen from a single viewpoint is to the rear and has to be observed over the garden wall of the adjoining private property. Owing to the narrowness of the plot, all other façades have to be viewed either episodically through the trees or close up at an oblique angle. The solid-void relationship of the exterior does not appear to follow any easily apparent scheme. This is a development from Le Corbusier's earlier work where at La Roche the drawing board elevation also cannot be seen at right angles and the studied balance of window to wall is destroyed. This is due not only to the trees which have grown since but especially to the necessity of viewing the elevation at a sharp angle.

The hierarchic presentation of external elements occurs also in the work of Frank Lloyd Wright, where the most important feature is the corner, and this may account for much of the undergrowth against the façades proper. It may be argued that the only exterior which can maintain interest, as the eye moves at an equal distance around the corner, is the cage or box. The most notable example of this is the Lake Shore Apartments where it would be inappropriate to suggest a "principal façade." Poissy [Fig. 15] almost comes into the category of the box but only on three sides; the fourth, receiving no undercut, becomes a vertical plane differing from the dynamic horizontality of the others. At Garches there is no point in moving around the corner for there is a very definite axis and the side elevations are of little consequence, their window openings positioned functionally make no attempt to arrive at a formal composition. The site boundary lines, defined by tall, closely planted trees, are about six feet from each of these side elevations, making it almost impossible to see them. The long façades, on the contrary, may be seen head on from a considerable distance by the approaching visitor and their balanced asymmetry is masterfully exploited.

Internally, space departs radically from the structure; an explosion in terms of Cubist space is contained within the four peripheral walls which externally give little evidence of this phenomenon, contained except where it escapes and rushes out along the direction of the terrace, to be finally dissipated in the heavy landscape. However, space is not contrived for the sake of effect only, it invariably has a psychological as well as a functional context. For instance, on passing through the front door, the immediate double height and the presence of a stair indicate that the main floor is above. Similarly, the diagonal spatial stress across the first floor suggests the route through the house.

The main living areas are flooded with an even intensity of light, but, where accommodation and circulation are of lesser consequence, natural lighting becomes more restricted and as one moves through the house a continuous contrast in definition is attained. "The elements of architecture are light and shade, walls and space." The natural light which penetrates to the interior of the Jaoul houses is consistently subdued and not dissimilar to that found inside many Frank Lloyd Wright buildings.

Eventually somebody will have to consider the numerous similarities between Le Corbusier and Wright, and their common differences from the work of Mies van der Rohe. For instance, the pattern of circulation, repetitive on all floors as in the Pavillon Suisse and many of Le Corbusier's larger buildings, becomes in some of his and Wright's domestic works a route so complex and involved, as at Planeix, that it is with the greatest difficulty that the stranger finds his way out. To a lesser extent, this applies at Jaoul and again, similar to Wright, the spatial effects, though exciting, are unexpected, encountered suddenly on turning a corner or glimpsed on passing a slit in the wall. Where double height does occur in one of the living rooms it appears as a dead area, having no secondary use such as the vertical height of the Unité flats which lights and ventilates the bedroom. If the space inside Garches can be considered dynamic, then here it is static; there is certainly no question of being able to stand inside and comprehend at a glance the limits of the house, as at Garches.

Implicit in the structural system, rooms tend to be small boxes with the living areas more generous. The internal finishes have a greater variety and richness of surface than at Garches, where, with the exception of the floor, the materials, though not the form, of the walls and ceilings are neutralized. Inside Jaoul, concrete is left shutter-marked, walls are plastered or brick fair-faced, floors are tiled and there is a considerable variety and quantity of timber and, most significantly, the ceiling or underside of the vaults is frequently finished in a dark clay tile which cannot be expected to amplify "the magnificent play of light on form." The "fourth wall"—the incorporation of shelving and opaque materials into the window opening—is symptomatic of Le Corbusier's recent attitude to surface depth. Windows are no longer to be looked through but looked at. The eye finding interest in every part of the surface impasto, does not, as at Garches, seek relief from the hard textureless finish by examining the contours and form of the plane.

Maison Jaoul is no doubt dimensioned according to "Le Modulor" [Fig. 27], a development from the application of the golden section by regulating lines as at Garches, where it is possible to read off the interrelations of squares and sections as the eye traverses the façade and where, internally, every element is positioned according to an exact geometrical hierarchy. In fact, Garches must be considered the masterpiece of Neo-Palladianism in modern architecture, conceived in plan, section, elevation from two proportions which, owing to their particular interrelationship, achieve an organic or harmonic whole as distinct from an additive total. The variety of dimensions available from "Le Modulor" are considerable and as Bodiansky[1] has said, "there is always a figure near at hand to adjust to." This considerable flexibility may create a visually non-apparent geometry, as at Jaoul, but here the restrictions of the site already mentioned must be remembered when considering whether this is a valid criticism.

Garches is an excellent example of Le Corbusier's particular interpretation of the machine aesthetic. The body of the house, built by quite conventional methods for its time, has skin-walls of concrete block rendered to a monolithic, poured or sprayed effect; an aesthetic for a structural system not yet in being. Yet while Garches is not the product of any high-powered mechanization, the whole spirit of the building expresses the essence of machine power. To be on the first floor is to witness the Mumfordian end product of twentieth-century technology, "the silent, staffless power-house." The incorporation of railroad and steamship fabrication is decidedly technocrat and the integration of architecture to specialist requirements extremely considered as the boiler-house disposed like an industrial engine-room or the timber-strip flooring obviously laid by ship's carpenters. The type of detailing in synthetic materials here and at the Armée du Salut is almost the last of the steam-age period; crude maybe, it is nevertheless powerful. After this date, the number of synthetic materials per building increases, and, as at the Pavillon Suisse,

[1] The structural engineer for the Marseilles Unité.

the detailing becomes more refined but somehow less memorable. There is no reference to any aspect of the machine at Jaoul either in construction or aesthetic. These houses, total cost £30,000, are being built by Algerian labourers equipped with ladders, hammers and nails, and with the exception of glass no synthetic materials are being used; technologically, they make no advance on medieval building. The timber window-wall units may be prefabricated but as with technology one suspects that prefabrication must begin with the structure.

To imply that these houses will be anything less than magnificent art would be incorrect. Their sheer plastic virtuosity is beyond emulation. Nevertheless, on analysis, it is disturbing to find little reference to the rational principles which are the basis of the modern movement, and it is difficult to avoid assessing these buildings except in terms of "art for art's sake." More so than any other architect of this century, Le Corbusier's buildings present a continuous architectural development which, however, has not recently been supplemented by programmatic theory.

As homes the Jaoul houses are almost cosy and could be inhabited by any civilized family, urban or rural. They are built by and intended for the status quo. Conversely, it is difficult to imagine Garches being lived in spontaneously except by such as the Sitwells, with never less than half a dozen brilliant, and permanent, guests. Utopian, it anticipates, and participates in, the progress of twentieth-century emancipation. A monument, not to an age which is dead, but to a way of life which has not generally arrived, and a continuous reminder of the quality to which all architects must aspire if modern architecture is to retain its vitality.

RONCHAMP: LE CORBUSIER'S CHAPEL AND THE CRISIS OF RATIONALISM (1956)

James Stirling

With the simultaneous appearance of Lever House in New York and the Unité in Marseilles [Fig. 22], it had become obvious that the stylistic schism between Europe and the New World had entered on a decisive phase. The issue of art or technology had divided the ideological basis of the modern movement, and the diverging styles apparent since Constructivism probably have their origin in the attempt to fuse Art Nouveau and late 19th century engineering. In the U.S.A., functionalism now means the adaptation to building of industrial processes and products, but in Europe it remains the essentially humanist method of designing to a specific use. The post-war architecture of America may appear brittle to Europeans and, by obviating the hierarchical disposition of elements, anonymous; however, this academic method of criticism may no longer be adequate in considering technological products of the 20th century. Yet this method would still appear valid in criticizing recent European architecture where the elaboration of space and form has continued without abatement; and the chapel by Le Corbusier may possibly be the most plastic building ever erected in the name of modern architecture [Fig. 25].

The south tower of the chapel, emerging as a white thumb above the landscape, can be seen for many miles as one approaches the Swiss border. The rolling hills and green woodlands of the Haute-Saône are reminiscent of many parts of England and Wales, and the village of Ronchamp spreads along either side of the Dijon-Basle road. After climbing a steep and winding dirt-track, leading from the village through dense woodland, one reaches the bald crown of the hill on which the chapel is situated. The sweep of the roof, inverting the curve of the ground, and a single dynamic gesture give the composition an expression of dramatic inevitability. The immediate impression is of a sudden encounter with an

---

unnatural configuration of natural elements such as the granite rings at Stonehenge or the dolmens in Brittany.

Far from being monumental, the building has a considerable ethereal quality, principally as a result of the equivocal nature of the walls. The rendering, which is whitewashed over, has been hand thrown and has an impasto of about two inches. This veneer suggests a quality of weightlessness and gives the walls something of the appearance of papier-mâché.

Notwithstanding that both roof and walls curve and splay in several directions, the material difference of rendered walls and natural concrete roof maintains the conventional distinction between them. They are further distinguished on the south and east sides by a continuous 9-inch glazed strip, and though the roof is not visible on the north and west sides its contours are suggested by the outline of the parapet. There is a similarity between the chapel and the Einstein tower[1] which is even less conventional, but only inasmuch as the walls and roof are fused into one expression.

The whitewashed rendering is applied to the interior as well as to the exterior and the openings scattered apparently at random over the south and north walls splay either inwards or outwards, similar to the reveals of gun-openings in coastal fortifications. On the inside of the west wall these openings splay inwards to such a degree that from the interior the surface takes on the appearance of a grille. It is through this grille that most of the daylight percolates to the interior, yet the overall effect is one of diffuse light so that, from a place in the congregation, no particular feature is spotlighted as in the manner of a Baroque church.

Where the roof dips to its lowest point, a double-barrelled gargoyle projects outwards to shoot rainwater into a shutter-patterned concrete tub. This element is surprisingly reminiscent of South Bank festivalia and something of the same spirit is conveyed by Le Corbusier in his stove-enamelled murals covering both sides of the processional entrance door. The same applies to the inscriptions on the coloured glass insets to the window openings. These linear applications suggest a final flourish and appear superfluous and even amateur in comparison with the overpowering virtuosity in moulding the contours of the solid masses.

The usual procedure in examining buildings—an inspection of the exterior followed by a tour of the interior—is reversed, and sightseers emerging on to the crown of the hill proceed to walk around the building clockwise, completing one and one-half circles before entering the chapel where they tend to become static, turning on their own axis to examine the interior.

Echoing the sag of the roof, the concrete floor dips down to the altar-rail which appears to be a length of folded lead. The various altars are built up of blocks of polished pre-cast concrete (probably with a marble aggregate) which are cast to a marvellous precision. The roof,

---

[1] [By Erich Mendelsohn, Neubabelsberg, near Berlin: 1919–1921.—ED.]

together with the concrete alms-boxes and swivel-door, represents an incredible French ingenuity in using this material.

The wall adjacent to the choir gallery stairs is painted a liturgical purple and the whitewash on the splayed reveals of the openings returns on to the purple wall to a width of three inches, thus resembling the painted window surrounds on houses around the Mediterranean coast. Small areas of green and yellow are painted over the rendering on either side of the main entrance and also on the reveals to the opening which contains the pivoting statue of the Madonna. The only large area of colour is confined to the northeast chapel and tower; this has been painted red for its entire height so that light pouring down from the top gives this surface the luminosity of "Dayglow." The three towers which catch the sun at different times of the day and pour light down on to the altars are in fact vertical extensions of each of the side chapels.

Even with a small congregation, the superb acoustics give a resonance suggesting a cathedral space and the people using the chapel do so naturally and without any sign of embarrassment. As a religious building, it functions extremely well and appears to be completely accepted. It is a fact that Le Corbusier's post-war architecture has considerable popular appeal. The local population, both at Marseilles and at Ronchamp, appears to be intensely proud of their buildings. Remembering the pre-war conflicts, it is difficult to ascertain whether the change is a social one, or whether it lies in the public or Le Corbusier. Garches [Fig. 12] is still regarded with suspicion by the public, either on account of its style or the manner of living of its inhabitants.

It may be considered that the Ronchamp chapel being a "pure expression of poetry" and the symbol of an ancient ritual, should not therefore be criticised by the rationale of the modern movement. Remembering, however, that this is a product of Europe's greatest architect, it is important to consider whether this building should influence the course of modern architecture. The sensational impact of the chapel on the visitor is significantly not sustained for any great length of time and when the emotions subside there is little to appeal to the intellect, and nothing to analyse or stimulate curiosity. This entirely visual appeal and the lack of intellectual participation demanded from the public may partly account for its easy acceptance by the local population.

Basically it is not a concrete building, although it has all the appearance of a solidifying object; the walls, however, are constructed in weight-bearing masonry. The initial structural idea of outlining the form by a tubular metal frame wrapped over with wire-meshing onto which concrete was to be sprayed for some reason was not carried out. With no change in the conception, this outline was filled in with masonry, rendered over and whitewashed to the appearance of the initial idea. The interior of the west wall became so interrupted with openings that it was found necessary to imbed in the masonry a concrete frame to form around the window openings. This freedom from the precept of the correct use and expression of materials, apparent in other post-war European architecture, has little parallel in the New World where the exploitation of materials and the development of new techniques continues to expand the architectural vocabulary.

With the loss of direction in modern painting, European architects have been looking to popular art and folk architecture, mainly of an indigenous character, from which to extend their vocabulary. An appreciation of regional building, particularly of the Mediterranean, has frequently appeared in Le Corbusier's books, principally as examples of integrated social units expressing themselves through form, but only recently has regional building become a primary source of plastic incident. There seems to be no doubt that Le Corbusier's incredible powers of observation are lessening the necessity for invention, and his travels round the world have stockpiled his vocabulary with plastic elements and *objets trouvés* of considerable picturesqueness. If folk architecture is to re-vitalise the movement, it will first be necessary to determine what it is that is modern in modern architecture. The scattered openings on the chapel walls may recall de Stijl but a similar expression is also commonplace in the farm buildings of Provence. The influence of popular art is also apparent in the priest's house and the hostel buildings. The external woodwork is painted sky blue and areas of smooth rendering painted over in patterns are decoratively applied to the outside walls; their situation and appearance do not express any formal, structural or aesthetic principle. All the walls of these outbuildings are in concrete, and large stones have been placed in the mix close against the shuttering, so that when the boarding is removed the surface of these stones is exposed. . . .

If the application of technology is of little consequence, nevertheless the appearance of industrial products still has some importance for Le Corbusier, as shown by the handrails to the stairs on the chapel. These handrails, which appear to be cut-offs from an extruded section of rolled steel joist, are in fact specially cast and the top flange is set at an acute angle to the web. The movable louvre is a logical development in resisting intense sunlight and it is surprising to find them above two of the entrances to the chapel; however, a closer inspection reveals that they are 4-inch static concrete fins set at arbitrary angles, suggesting movability.

The desire to deride the schematic basis of modern architecture and the ability to turn a design upside down and make it architecture are symptomatic of a state when the vocabulary is not being extended, and a parallel can be drawn with the Mannerist period of the Renaissance. Certainly, the forms which have developed from the rationale and the initial ideology of the modern movement are being mannerized and changed into a conscious imperfectionism.

Le Corbusier, proceeding from the general to the particular, has produced a masterpiece of a unique but most personal order.

LE CORBUSIER'S CHANGING ATTITUDE TOWARD FORM (1965)

Peter Serenyi

No discussion of Le Corbusier's architecture of this decade can begin without considering, however briefly, his earlier development. Between 1919 and 1922 Le Corbusier embarked on a new path which he has never entirely abandoned since. In the realm of domestic architecture the Maison Monol of 1919 [Fig. 5] and the Maison Citrohan of 1920–1922 [Fig. 6] mark the beginning of a new style. In these two projects lie the roots of all his later houses, culminating in the Maison Jaoul of 1954 [Fig. 21] and the Villa Shodan of 1956 [Fig. 23]. Moreover, all his *unités* owe their origin to the Immeubles Villas of 1922 [Fig. 8], while the Ville Contemporaine of 1922 [Fig. 7] is the ancestor of Chandigarh [Fig. 28].

The historical events that preceded Le Corbusier's "Period of Invention" provide us with the best clues to a better understanding of the origins of his style; for the chaos and disorder resulting from World War I made him painfully aware of the need to create a new order based on a more stable world. It is not surprising, therefore, that both the Maisons Monol and Citrohan as well as the Ville Contemporaine revert to a distant past. While the former find their sources in the architecture of the tribal societies of the Eastern Mediterranean world, the latter recalls a Platonic order based on numbers. . . .

More than once Le Corbusier has referred to the immediate postwar years as the starting point for modern architecture. "If we pose the question," he proclaimed in 1928, " 'has the architectural moment of our epoch arrived?' the answer is 'it has; because since the end of the war period we possess a modern conception of architecture.' This fact is certain and can be verified in every country." [1] Let me add that Gropius,

---

---

[1] Le Corbusier, "The Town and the House," *Architectural Review*, LXIV (1928), 224.

who has always been more articulate in verbal than in visual images, summed up the effect of World War I on modern architecture even more precisely. He declared that "the full consciousness of my responsibility in advancing ideas based on my own reflections only came home to me as the result of the war, in which these theoretical premises first took definite shape. After the violent interruption . . . every thinking man felt the necessity for an intellectual change of front. Each in his own particular sphere of activity aspired to help in bridging the disastrous gulf between reality and idealism. It was then that the immensity of the mission of the architects of my own generation first dawned on me." [2]

As mentioned earlier, Le Corbusier invented two kinds of private houses shortly after the war: the Maisons Monol and Citrohan. The latter, angular and firm, stands erect on the ground, dominating the setting; while the former, undulating and soft, rests on the ground, absorbing the setting. To use Le Corbusier's own words: "In the one, strong objectivity of forms, under the intense light of a Mediterranean sun: *male* architecture. In the other, limitless subjectivity rising against a clouded sky: *female* architecture." [3] In his private houses, then, it is the individual human figure—isolated and lonely, to be sure—that is expressed symbolically. It is no coincidence, therefore, that most of his houses were built for single men or women, who were either artists or intellectuals.

Before turning to the period under discussion, let me preface my brief remarks by proposing a chronology for Le Corbusier's artistic development: I. Formative Years, 1887 to 1918; II. Period of Invention, 1919 to 1922; III. First Mature Phase, 1922 to 1928; IV. Period of Reassessment, 1928–1929 to 1945; V. Fulfillment, 1945 to the present.

Although the terminating date for this Symposium has no particular relevance to Le Corbusier's development, the years 1928–1929 do mark a turning point in his style. As is well known, it was during these years that he designed the finest, and indeed, the last house in the Purist style: the Villa Savoye [Fig. 15]. Yet it was also during these very same years that he conceived the Villa at Carthage—an entirely fresh interpretation of the well-known Citrohan type [Fig. 16]. This renewal of artistic imagination was made largely possible through his encounter with Rietveld's work, more specifically with the Schröder house. . . . On the façade of the Villa at Carthage, for example, two earlier elements —the studio and the ribbon window—are fused with the help of De Stijl vocabulary. As in Rietveld's house of 1924, there is a strong interplay between lines and planes, between solids and voids, and between verticals and horizontals. But unlike Rietveld's design, the various parts of the Villa at Carthage enjoy a lesser degree of independence, owing this quality, among others, to the tightness of the composition and to the

[2] Walter Gropius, *The New Architecture and the Bauhaus* (London: Faber and Faber Ltd., 1935), p. 48.
[3] Le Corbusier, *The Modulor* (Cambridge, Mass.: Harvard University Press, 1958), p. 224.

uninterrupted nature of the roof line. But in later versions of the Villa at Carthage the spaces and masses are gradually loosened up, culminating in the dynamic composition of the Villa Shodan [Fig. 23].

Another descendant of the Citrohan project—the Maison Errazuris of 1930 [Fig. 19]—marks the second change in his style during the period under discussion. In this case it is primarily Le Corbusier's attitude toward nature that leads him to a reassessment of form. For example, the exterior silhouette now becomes an active form, jutting upward from the ground itself. During the 1920s such visual activity was restricted to ramps or stairs, carefully concealed behind the external envelope. In fact, a comparison between this house and the Villa Savoye shows how the outline of the ramp is transformed into the space-enclosing mass, thus anchoring the entire interior volume to the site. There are, of course, a number of variations on the theme of the Maison Errazuris which were designed during this period, but with one exception, none of them was ever executed.[4] The exception is the house in Mathes of 1935. Here the functional independence of the wall—so characteristic of his houses of the 1920s—is entirely given up in favor of creating a masonry structure that serves both as a space-defining and as a load-bearing element, hence foreshadowing his houses of the past ten years.

Unlike its opposite, the Maison Monol had no successor during the 1920s. Some of its basic features, such as the vaulted roof and the long, continuous spaces, first appeared in Le Corbusier's own studio-apartment of 1930–1933. Yet the first Monol type house was built only in 1935. This well-known structure, located in the suburbs of Paris, occupies an important place in Le Corbusier's *oeuvre* [Fig. 20]. Unlike the Maison Citrohan and its later derivations, this week-end house does not stand upright on the ground, dominating the setting; instead, it rests on it, spreading its parts on the terrain itself. In this house—as in all Monol type structures—Le Corbusier expresses a more subservient attitude toward nature. This is most visible in the low, earth-hugging structure, built partially of natural materials, and covered with grass. Moreover, the area defined by the external walls of the house and the small pavilion is transformed into an outdoor room, whose space becomes at one with nature. As is well known, the later descendants of this house range from the project of La Sainte Baume of 1948 to the Maison Jaoul of 1954.

Before leaving the discussion of Le Corbusier's houses, let me turn, however briefly, to their interiors. During the 1920s his houses were built around staircases and ramps, creating an air of tension which was only resolved on the roof garden. As Le Corbusier has pointed out, the roof garden is a place "where the sky is always open; and far from the street, one can experience a feeling of security and well being." [5] This secluded area, high above the street and removed from the tensions of everyday

---

[4] For other examples of the Maison Citrohan with the butterfly roof see: Clarke Arundell of 1939; Lannamezan House of 1940; MAS prefabricated house of 1939–1940.

[5] Jean Badovici, ed., *Le Corbusier et Pierre Jeanneret* (Paris: Editions Albert Morancé, 1927), I, 13.

life, must be understood as an Arcadia—an earthly paradise, as it were—an area where the isolated and lonely man can become at one with nature in peace and tranquility. In this decade, however, Le Corbusier abandoned the roof garden in favor of creating a more restful interior space. Moreover, the importance of the ramps and stairs was taken over by the fireplace. In the 1920s his fireplaces were isolated and often fragile sculptural forms, whose primary function was to define or to divide space. This can best be seen in the living room of the Villa Church at Ville d'Avray and in the library of the double house at Stuttgart. In the 1930s, however, Le Corbusier's fireplaces acquire a more plastic quality, serving as a means to anchor the house more emphatically to the ground. Such fireplaces can be found in the house of Mme. de Mandrot, in the Errazuris project, and in the house at Mathes, not to mention his numerous unexecuted projects.

Turning to his public buildings, let me restrict my comments to some aspects of his apartment houses and office buildings, mentioning only two important changes that occurred during the decade under discussion. First, the flatness of the roof line, so characteristic of his projects for large buildings in the 1920s, is abandoned in favor of creating a more complicated superstructure on the roof tops. Moreover, while the roof garden is gradually given up in his private houses during this period, it acquires a significant role in his public buildings, foreshadowing the spacious roof gardens of the past twenty years. Also, the relationship between the public space on the roof and the natural surrounding is now firmly established. The project for the Rentenanstalt of Zurich, designed in 1933, serves as a good example to illustrate these points.

More important, however, is the realization of Le Corbusier's best known trade-mark: the *brise soleil*. One of the first projects in which this feature appears is the apartment house for Algiers of 1933. To enumerate the various sources for this motif lies outside the scope of this brief essay. Let me mention only one source whose origin goes back to Le Corbusier's peculiar use of window frames in the 1920s. In one of the windows of the living room of the Villa Church, for example, the glass pane is surrounded by a freestanding frame so as to give it the effect of a painting. In Algiers, on the other hand, the freestanding window frame of the previous decade is turned outside and is treated monumentally.

There is another kind of *brise-soleil*, which has, as it were, an independent life of its own. This type first appeared in the project for a Law Court for Algiers of 1938. Its composition has many visual sources. The one which I would like to emphasize particularly is van Doesburg's project for a house for an artist of 1923 [Fig. 24]. As in the van Doesburg project, large rectangular frames make up the façade of Le Corbusier's Law Court, creating a rich, plastic effect. Although the rigidity of Le Corbusier's *brise-soleil* has little to do with van Doesburg's looser and more fragmented composition, the original qualities of De Stijl spirit were later incorporated into the *brise-soleil* of Chandigarh [Figs. 29 and 30].

The year 1929 also marks an important change in Le Corbusier's attitude toward the city. His various projects for the rebuilding of Paris of the 1920s were essentially utopian diagrams, based on a neoclassical tradition best summed up in Laugier's dictum: "uniformity in detail and variety in general effect." The Mundaneum of 1929 [Fig. 17], intended for an actual site near Geneva, marks the first real effort on Le Corbusier's part to create a civic space based on the Acropolis. In this city plan the rigid symmetry of the earlier 1920s is given up in favor of a more open composition so that the various buildings acquire a greater sense of independence. Moreover, the axis of the city links the mountains with the lake. But it was only in the project for the University of Brazil of 1936 that most of his ideas first adumbrated in the Mundaneum were more fully developed. Here the dynamic asymmetry of the Acropolis is reinterpreted in a vigorous modern language. The buildings of the University are indeed "animated by a single thought, drawing around them the landscape and gathering it into the composition," to use Le Corbusier's own earlier words.[6]

Needless to say, the development of what one might best call Le Corbusier's "Acropolic style" of city planning was not the only significant event of this period of reassessment. There were also his "anti-city" city plans and the plan for a farm, which played an equally significant role in preparing the way toward fulfillment. Let me begin with the former.

Ever since 1920, when Le Corbusier made the first sketches for the Ville Contemporaine, his cities contained an element of fear—a fear of the big city, to be more exact. The most amusing illustration of this fear can be found in the various cartoons reproduced in *The City of Tomorrow*, accompanying the chapter "Newspaper Cuttings and Catchwords." The best of these, of course, is at the head of the chapter, with the caption: "Heartrending farewells of the father of a family about to cross the street in front of the Gare de l'Est." [7] On the more serious side, there is his long diatribe on the evils of the street, first published in 1929.[8] Here he condemns all conventional streets and boulevards, urging the immediate adoption of his elevated arteries of circulation, which would, as we know so well, not only separate pedestrian from vehicular traffic, but also trucks from cars and cars from bicycles. . . . There is also his Ville Contemporaine and the Plan Voisin for Paris in which, to paraphrase John Summerson, the park is not in the town but the town in the park.[9] Nothing done before or after, however, surpasses the plan for Hellocourt of 1935 in terms of being an "anti-city" city. With the pretentious title "urbanisation d'Hellocourt," Le Corbusier introduces a few scattered skyscrapers, separated by wide open spaces and large areas of greenery.

[6] Le Corbusier, *Towards a New Architecture* (London: John Rodker Publisher 1927), p. 188.

[7] Le Corbusier, *The City of Tomorrow and Its Planning* (London: The Architectural Press, 1947), p. 141.

[8] Le Corbusier, *Oeuvre complète 1910–1929* (Zurich: Les Editions Girsberger, 1937), pp. 118–19.

[9] John Summerson, "Architecture, Painting and Le Corbusier," in his *Heavenly Mansions* (New York: W. W. Norton & Co., 1963), p. 191.

Aristotle once said that "men come together in cities in order to live; they remain together in order to live the 'good life,'—a common life, for noble ends." [10] In Hellocourt, however, men stay apart; in fact, they escape from one another by isolating themselves in lonely towers, or "lookouts"—to use Le Corbusier's term—to live a private life freed from communal responsibility. . . .

While addressing himself to these two entirely different attitudes towards human order, during these very same years Le Corbusier also searched for a means to reconcile them, for if seen in the proper light, the Ferme Radieuse of 1934–1938 must be understood as a desperate effort on Le Corbusier's part to reconcile the one and the many, the country with the city, individuality and collectivity, indeed existentialism with classicism. In it, he combined the sense of freedom and openness of such plans as Hellocourt with the more formal organization of his "Acropolic style" of city planning. Unity between these two is achieved with the help of De Stijl vocabulary. As a comparison with van Doesburg's painting *Rhythm of a Russian Dance* of 1918 indicates, the fragmentation of form combined with the continuity of space—so characteristic of De Stijl compositions in general—reappears in Le Corbusier's plan for this civic space. The two buildings at each end serve as primary space definers, while the others mark the boundaries for the space that flows between the first two, creating a spatial and formal rhythm that is closely reminiscent of van Doesburg's painting. Though each building is treated as a separate unit, the whole composition is brought into unison by a flowing space. Unlike the plan for Nemours, for example, where only a series of diagrammatic roads links the buildings together, here the whole town revolves around and emanates from a space that is both living and active. Moreover, in order to achieve a greater sense of unity between man and nature, each building is covered with a Monol-type vaulted roof, which firmly anchors the interior spaces to the ground.

Although it is an ideal town, planted not on an actual site but simply on a blank sheet, the Ferme Radieuse is far removed from its ancestor, the Ville Contemporaine. The gradual reassessment of form and content which is first visible in the plan for the Mundaneum of 1929 comes to an end here. It is a process of transformation without which such mature plans as St. Dié and Chandigarh would remain incomprehensible.

To conclude, the numerous important changes that took place in Le Corbusier's style during the decade under discussion were realized: first, through his reassessment of nature; second, through his renewed encounter with De Stijl; and third, through his fresh attitude toward his own work of the 1920s. All these changes paved the way for his most mature style of the post-1945 period. One can, therefore, justly call these years a period of reflection and reassessment.

[10] Aristotle, *On Civics,* quoted by Frederick Hiorns in *Town Building in History* (London: George G. Harrap and Co., Ltd., 1956), p. 10.

FORMAL AND FUNCTIONAL INTERACTIONS: A STUDY OF TWO LATE PROJECTS BY LE CORBUSIER (1966)

Alan Colquhoun

The French Embassy building in Brasilia and the Hospital in Venice seem to represent two extremes in the work of Le Corbusier [Figs. 31, 32]. The Embassy refers directly to the concept of simple volumes intended to "release constant sensations" and to the related idea of the "surface" which form the basis of Le Corbusier's classicising tendencies.[1] The Hospital, on the other hand, seems to derive from opposing tendencies which are typified in his investigations into patterns of growth, his interest in the irregular and spontaneous forms of folk architecture and the direct transformation of a functional organism into its appropriate form.

Yet if we look more closely we can see that the polarity of these attitudes is present in both projects, and that each owes more to its complementary principle than at first seems the case. The most immediately striking fact in the Embassy project is its division into two buildings of simple but contrasting volumes. An architect wishing to express the functional interaction between the residence and the chancellery would have developed his scheme in a single complex. But in such a solution it would have been difficult to avoid the administration overpowering the residence. Le Corbusier has evidently wanted to make the Ambassador's house carry the traditional meanings associated with embassies, and to do this he has had to separate the two buildings completely.

[1] *Vers une Architecture* (Paris: Editions Vincent, Fréal & Cie., 1958); and *Oeuvre complète 1910–1929* (Zurich: Les Editions Girsberger, 1960).

The residence has the low cubic form of a villa, placed across the lower half of the site and looking towards the lake, dominating the site from the east and screening its upper half. The chancellery is situated near the western site boundary, where it has a more direct relation to the centre of the city—a cylindrical seven-storey tower, its height giving it views over the residence towards the lake, its cylindrical form enabling it to act as the complement of the smaller, rectangular mass of the residence.

A driveway links the two buildings and the opposite ends of the site, switching across the site between one building and the other, and underlining their complementarity by giving the site rotational symmetry—a frequent device of Le Corbusier. . . .

In this solution, a circular *brise-soleil* screen encloses an irregular orthogonal building, whose walls and floors only extend to the inner face of the circle at certain points. The impression of an object within an object which this gives is enhanced by the fact that the enclosing arc only extends for about three-fifths of a circle, allowing the corner of the enclosed building to emerge sharply from its sheath at the point of lift-shaft and staircase. The effect of this is to slice off the circle in response to the driveway, and to divide the building into an entrance and movement zone, and a quiet working zone. Balconies prolong the *brise soleil* on the driveway side, and their random spacing allows the lowest one to detach itself and to be read as a canopy over the entrance. A central hall on each floor, offset slightly from the centre of the circle, gives onto rows of offices facing north and east. These offices and their private balconies vary from floor to floor, giving constantly new relations with the inner surface of the *brise-soleil*. The cylinder is therefore hollowed out, and its interior surface is always felt as independent of the enclosed structure.

This concept of the simple solid differs radically from that of the renaissance. The platonic form of the circle acts as a field within which a functional arrangement is established. This arrangement, which has been freely chosen, resembles topologically the generants of the circle, but results in a "chaotic" plastic organization. It is necessary to express both the functional and the platonic systems, since to express only the first would result in *apparent* disorder, and to express only the second would deny the functional reality and assert a form that was empty of meaning. . . .

The same ambiguities exist in the Ambassador's house, working within a different set of functional and formal determinants. The problem has been reduced to three elements: a main body consisting of the reception rooms and their offices; an "attic" containing the Ambassador's private apartments; and a vast porch-vestibule linking the two and containing the main staircase. The entrance and reception rooms are on the first floor, and two broad ramps connect this level with the ground, one leading to the entrance porch from the west, the other leading from the reception rooms on the east to a *parterre* surrounding a pool. From the

south east corner of this site the entrance ramp seems like a podium supporting the chancellery, and by suppressing the intervening ground, ties
the two buildings together.

The motif of a porch at one end of a block is a recurrent one in
the work of Le Corbusier. It first appears at Garches [Fig. 12] (though
this itself is a derivative of the *Esprit Nouveau* pavilion) and reappears,
slightly modified, in the High Court at Chandigarh [Fig. 30]. In the
Ambassador's house it acts as a lens through which the chancellery is
related to the Ambassador's house and the lower end of the site (the two
buildings are sited so that the chancellery can be seen through the porch
from the east boundary, and so that the offices on the east face of the
chancellery look through it towards the lake). It is the eye of the building,
the aedicule through which one enters its mysterious inner spaces and by
means of which they enter into relationship with the public space of
site or city. Both at Garches and in the embassy, its deep penetration
at one end of the block activates the building diagonally, and creates a
counter movement to that implied by the strictly orthogonal shell.

The classical overtones of this porch are obviously intentional, and
its position implies an ironical rejection of symmetry and gives it a
curious, rhetorical independence. Equally subversive is the way in which
it breaks through the solid wall of the attic, and in doing so allows one
to attribute to this floor an importance equal to that of the reception
rooms—an importance which is reinforced by the "domestic" scale of
their *brise-soleil*.

The apartment floor is a derivative of the director's flat in the
Maison Suisse. Here, however, the walls are not penetrated as they are
in that building, partly because the linking action of the porch makes
this semantically unnecessary, and partly because at the Maison Suisse
the *pilotis* necessitate the visual hollowing out and lightening of the
top floor. Here the absolute privacy of the Ambassador's residence is
established and roof patios form private open spaces which repeat, on an
intimate scale, the public open spaces related to the reception rooms.

Both in this building and in the chancellery the *brise-soleil* belong
to the type first used in India, consisting of deep reveals supported
independently of the main structure. The earlier *brise-soleil* were conceived as projections from the glass wall. Their use as independent structures is one of the major developments in Le Corbusier's later style (although he continued to use them in their original form in certain late
buildings). When used in this way they become perforated walls, which
re-establish the transitional space between outside and inside lost when
the solid wall was destroyed and replaced by a "dimensionless" and im-
penetrable skin. The continuous penetrability of this element at ground
level made it possible to dispense with *pilotis* without implications of
weight and massiveness, and in this way also made it possible to put the
principal rooms on the first floor. In the Ambassador's house, the ground
floor can be read either as open or solid, thus permitting it to be partially
concealed by solid ramps, which give the impression of the ground floor
rising to meet the first floor. Where rooms occur on the ground floor, the

brise-soleil carry right down to the ground, but where the space is void, the spacing is doubled to suggest vestigial *pilotis*, without however, destroying the surface value of the *brise-soleil*.

While the organizational problems in the Brasilia buildings are relatively simple, those in the hospital at Venice are complex and specialized. It is possible (even within the height restrictions imposed by the site) to imagine a solution in which vertically organized blocks of different classes of accommodation would be related horizontally, but Le Corbusier has decided to separate the different classes vertically, so that each level serves a different purpose, and a cross section at any one point is, in principle, typical of the whole organization. This has obvious advantages both from the point of view of administration and that of extensibility. But it also repeats the pattern of the city, with its overall texture—a solid mass of building penetrated by canals and courts. In Venice, the city itself is the building, and the hospital is an extension of this building, spreading, tentacle-like, over the water. . . .

Despite the uniqueness of this building in the work of Le Corbusier —a uniqueness that can be explained by the complexities of the problem and by the peculiarities of the site—a number of prototypes exist in his earlier work. At Poissy [Fig. 15] the flat cube, projected into the air and open to the sky, was first established as a "type" solution. It seems clear that this sort of "type" solution cannot be equated with the *"Objet Type"* discussed by Reyner Banham in his *Theory and Design in the First Machine Age*, since Le Corbusier frequently uses the same type in different contexts. We must assume that his concept of "type" relates to a mythic form rather than to the means of solving particular problems, and that, as with physiognomic forms or musical modes, a number of different contents can be attached to the same form. A similar idea is apparent in the *Musée Illimitée*, also connected with the problem of extensibility as at Venice, though solving it in a different way. In the 1925 *Cité Universitaire* project a solid single-storey block of studios was proposed, where the rooms were lit entirely from the roof.

There are also a number of projects where a building on *pilotis* extends over water, possibly stemming from Le Corbusier's early interest in reconstructions of prehistoric lake dwellings in central Europe. La Tourette [Fig. 26] resembles such schemes through the way in which the building is projected over rough sloping ground which, like water, offers no foothold for the inhabitants of the constructed world suspended above it.

But in the hospital scheme the potential symbolism of these forms has been harnessed to a new and unique problem. The *pilotis* space forms a shaded region in which the reflections of sunlight on water would create continual movement. Over this space, which is articulated by innumerable columns whose grouping would alter with the movement of the observer, floats a vast roof, punctured in places to let in the sunlight and give a view of the sky. This roof is in fact an inhabited top storey, whose deep fascia conceals the wards behind. It is the realm of the sky, in whose calm regions the process of physical renewal can take place, remote from the world of water, trees and men which it overshadows. But apart from its suggestions of sunlight and healing, it has more sombre overtones. The cave-like section of the wards, the representation in the drawings of the sick almost as heroic corpses laid out on cool slabs, the paraphernalia of ablution, suggest more personal obsessions and give the impression of a place of masonic solemnity, a necropolis in the manner of Ledoux or Soane. Typical of Le Corbusier is the way in which the logic of a total conception has been relentlessly applied to the organization of the wards, and has resulted in a solution which stands the accepted idea of "convenience" on its head. There is a civic *gravitas,* a ritualistic seriousness, about this scheme, wholly at variance with a society whose values are based on the likely opinions of the average man multiplied by n, and it is possible that such a *"machine à guérir"* may not commend itself to the committee in whose hands the fate of the building lies. In spite of its different purposes, and the different organizational patterns which these produce, the Venice hospital resembles the Brasilia scheme in the way in which it evokes complex and overlapping responses. The analytical way in which the constituent functions are separated allows them to develop pragmatically around and within fixed patterns. The form is not conceived of as developing in a one-to-one relation with the functions, but is based on ideal schemata with which the freely deployed functions, with their possibilities of unexpected sensuous incident, engage in a dialogue. The building is both an agglomeration of basic cells, capable of growth and development, *and* a solid which has been cut into and carved out to reveal a constant interaction of inside and outside space.

The impression of complexity, here as at Brasilia, is the result of a number of sub-systems impinging on schemata which, in themselves, are extremely simple.

Fig. 1
LE CORBUSIER:
Villa Fallet (1905–7)
La Chaux-de-Fonds, Switzerland
(Photo Fernand Perret, La Chaux-de-Fonds)

Fig. 2
LE CORBUSIER:
House for His Parents (1912)
La Chaux-de-Fonds, Switzerland
(Photo Fernand Perret, La Chaux-de-Fonds)

Fig. 3
LE CORBUSIER:
Villa Schwob (1916–17)
La Chaux-de-Fonds, Switzerland
(Photo Fernand Perret,
La Chaux-de-Fonds)

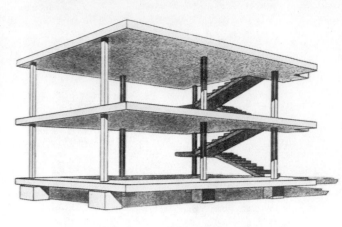

Fig. 4
LE CORBUSIER:
Project for *Domino Houses*
(1914–15)
(Le Corbusier, *Oeuvre complète 1910–1929*)

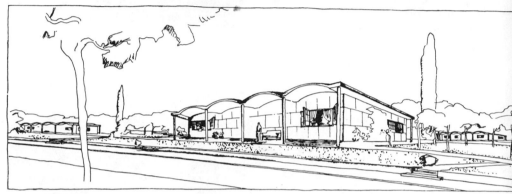

Fig. 5
LE CORBUSIER:
Project for *Monol Houses* (1919)
(Le Corbusier, *Oeuvre complète 1910–1929*)

Fig. 6
LE CORBUSIER:
Project for *Citrohan House,* second version (1922)
(Le Corbusier, *Oeuvre complète 1910–1929*)

Fig. 7
LE CORBUSIER:
Project for *A Contemporary City* (1922)
(Le Corbusier, *Oeuvre complète 1910–1929*)

Fig. 8
LE CORBUSIER:
Project for *Villa-Apartment Blocks* (1922)
(Le Corbusier, *Oeuvre complète 1910–1929*)

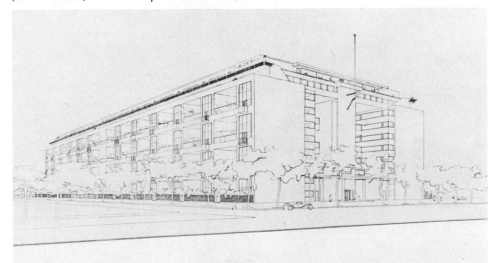

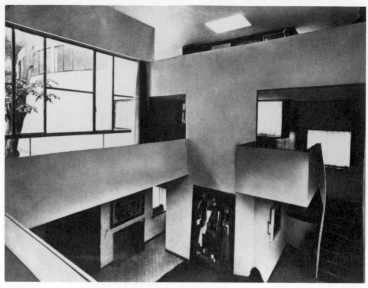

Fig. 9
Entrance hall of *La Roche House* (1923)
Paris
(Le Corbusier, *Oeuvre complète 1910–1929*)

Fig. 10
LE CORBUSIER:
Housing Settlement (1924–26)
Pessac, near Bordeaux
(S. Giedion, *Space, Time and Architecture,* 5th edition, 1967. Harvard University Press.)

Fig. 11
LE CORBUSIER:
Housing Settlement in Pessac, as seen today
(Photo Philippe Boudon)

Fig. 12
LE CORBUSIER:
Villa Stein (1927)
Garches, near Paris
(Le Corbusier, *Oeuvre complète 1910–1929*)

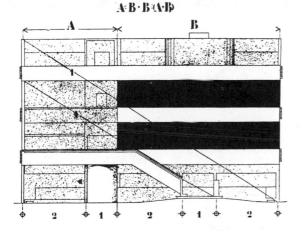

A·B·B(A·B)

A   B

2   1   2   1   2

Fig. 13
LE CORBUSIER:
Villa Stein (1927) Garden façade
(Le Corbusier, *Oeuvre complète
1910–1929*)

Fig. 14
PALLADIO:
Villa Foscari, "Malcontenta"
(1560)
Near Venice
(Andrea Palladio,
The Four Books of Architecture.
Dover Publications, Inc.)

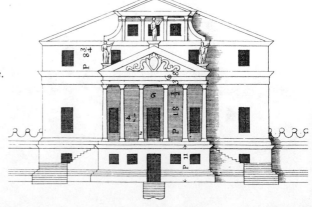

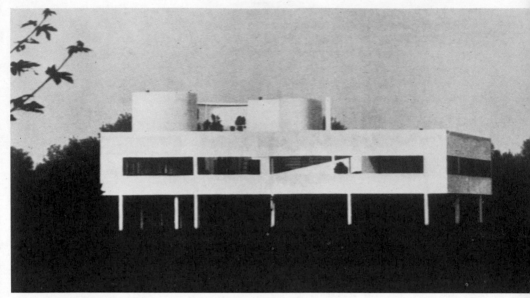

Fig. 15
LE CORBUSIER:
Villa Savoye (1928–31)
Poissy, near Paris
(Le Corbusier, *Oeuvre complète 1929–1934*)

Fig. 16
LE CORBUSIER:
First scheme for *Villa* (1928)
Carthage, Tunisia
(Le Corbusier, *Oeuvre complète 1910–1929*)

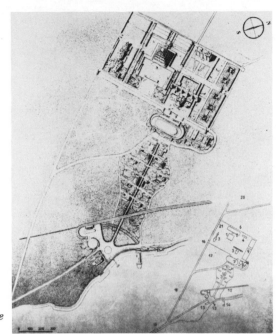

Fig. 17
LE CORBUSIER:
Project for the *Mundaneum*
(1929)
(Le Corbusier, *Oeuvre complète
1910–1929*)

Fig. 18
LE CORBUSIER:
Salvation Army Hostel (1929–33)
Paris
(Le Corbusier, *Oeuvre complète 1929–1934*)

Fig. 19
LE CORBUSIER:
Project for *Errazuris House*
(1930)
(Le Corbusier, *Oeuvre complète
1929–1934*)

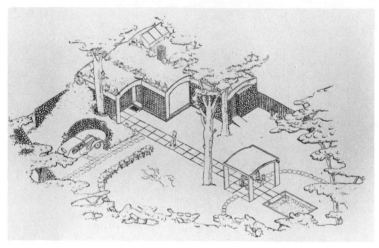

Fig. 20
LE CORBUSIER:
Weekend House (1935)
Celle-St. Cloud, near Paris
(Le Corbusier, *Oeuvre complète 1934–1938*)

Fig. 21
LE CORBUSIER:
Jaoul House (1952–56)
Neuilly, near Paris
(Photo Lucien Hervé, Paris)

Fig. 22
LE CORBUSIER:
Apartment House Block (top half)
(1945–52)
Marseilles
(Photo Wayne Andrews)

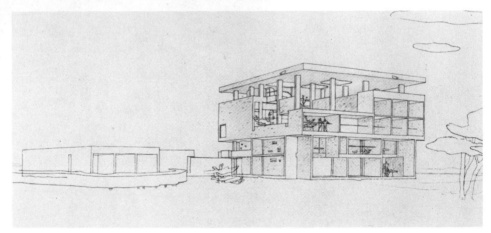

Fig. 23
LE CORBUSIER:
Villa Shodan (1952–56)
Ahmedabad, India
(Le Corbusier, *Oeuvre complète 1952–1957*)

Fig. 24
THEO VAN DOESBURG:
Project for an *Artist's House* (1923)
(With permission of Florian
Kupferberg Verlag, Mainz,
from Theo van Doesburg,
*Grundbegriffe der neuen
gestaltenden Kunst* (*Principles of
Neo-Plastic Art*)

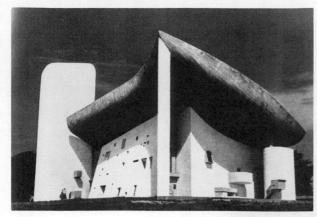

Fig. 25
LE CORBUSIER:
Chapel at Ronchamp (1950–1955)
Near Belfort
(Photo P. and E. Merkle, Bâle)

Fig. 26
LE CORBUSIER:
Monastery of La Tourette
(1957–60)
Eveaux-sur-Arbresle, near Lyons
(Photo Bernhard Moosbrugger,
Zurich)

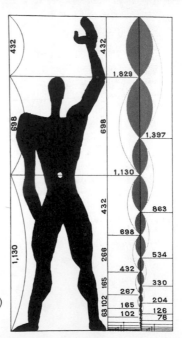

Fig. 27
LE CORBUSIER:
The Modulor (1942–51)
(Le Corbusier, *Oeuvre complète 1938–1946*)

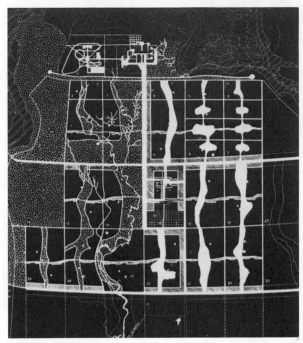

Fig. 28
LE CORBUSIER:
Plan of Chandigarh (1951)
India
(Le Corbusier, *My Work*)

Fig. 29
LE CORBUSIER:
The Secretariat (1951–58), *The Assembly Building* (1951–62)
Chandigarh, India
(Photo Willy Boesiger, Zurich)

Fig. 30
LE CORBUSIER:
The High Court (top half) (1951–56)
Chandigarh
(Photo Jacqueline Vautier-Jeanneret, Geneva)

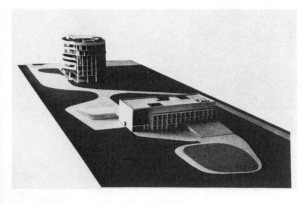

Fig. 31
LE CORBUSIER:
Project for *French Embassy* (1964)
Brasilia, Brazil
(Photo Willy Boesiger, Zurich)

Fig. 32
LE CORBUSIER:
Project for *Venice Hospital* (1965)
(Photo Guillermo Jullian de la Fuente, Paris)

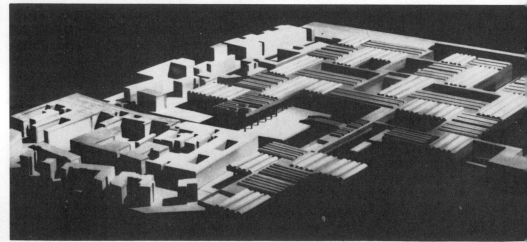

. . . The "Modulor" is a working tool, a precision instrument . . . a *tuned*
piano. The piano has been tuned: it is up to you to play it well.

LE CORBUSIER*

MODULOR (1954)

Peter Collins

The ideas which Le Corbusier has publicized in his long career usually
have two characteristics in common; firstly, an element of paradox in the
way they are expressed, and, secondly, a grandness of conception as regards their application and their ultimate benefit to humanity. The paradoxical nature of his theories has been neatly described by Mr. John
Summerson in one of his essays in *Heavenly Mansions;* the grandness of
his conceptions is apparent to the most superficial observer, and relates
Le Corbusier more closely to the revolutionary architects of the eighteenth century than do the novel shapes of his buildings, or the intensity
of his humanitarian ideals.

The *Modulor,* as an idea, is as breathtakingly ambitious as the *Unité
d'Habitation* [Fig. 22] in its aim to provide an objective ideal solution to
a general human problem; it is also the most paradoxical theory of design
which could be enunciated by a violent opponent of academicism. Le
Corbusier envisages every architect and engineer having on his drawing
board not only a foot or decimetre scale for measuring, but also a *Modulor* scale for proportioning, so that every object designed for human use
shall correspond to a single all-pervading harmony [Fig. 27].

There is no need to describe here the *Modulor* in detail. The years of
research during which it was formulated have been described by Le Corbusier carefully and at times grandiloquently, and every architect should
study his book, which has just been skilfully translated by Peter de

"Modulor" by Peter Collins. From *The Architectural Review,* 116 (July 1954), pp.
5–8. Copyright The Architectural Review. Reprinted by permission of the editor.

* Le Corbusier, *The Modulor* (Cambridge, Mass.: Harvard University Press, 1958),
pp. 130–31.

Francia and Anna Bostock.[1] Briefly, the problem was to find a series of proportions all related directly to the human stature, and the solution adopted was to evaluate dimensions in the Fibonacci series based on the length 6 ft.

The Fibonacci series is a simple series of numbers in which each additional figure is formed by adding the two previous numbers, thus 1, 2, 3, 5, 8, 13, 21, etc. This can be expressed algebraically as a, b, $a + b$, $a + 2b$, $2a + 3b$, $3a + 5b$, $5a + 8b$, etc. The principal virtue of this series is that the larger the numbers become the more does $\dfrac{a}{b}$ tend to equal $\dfrac{b}{a + b}$ etc. Now the formula $a : b :: b : a + b$, or $\dfrac{a}{b} = \dfrac{b}{a + b}$ is the expression of the "golden section," and can be expressed numerically to four figures as $\dfrac{.618}{1} = \dfrac{1}{1.618}$. It will be seen, however, that these figures are not quite accurate, as by multiplying across we get $1 = .999924$.

So much, then, for the general arithmetic of the theory, which was explained in detail by Matila Ghyka in the February, 1948, issue of THE ARCHITECTURAL REVIEW. Before the reader of *The Modulor* accepts all its implications, he will have to decide, firstly, to what extent any modular system of design can be justified, and, secondly, whether any such system can have objective and universal validity.

To discuss the first question, we must begin by distinguishing between the various meanings of the word "module." Firstly, it can mean a standard measurement of which all elements of a design are multiples. In practice this type of module is inevitably used by every craftsman, since it can be taken as the maximum amount of tolerance. If a joiner works to the nearest $\frac{1}{16}''$, then $\frac{1}{16}''$ is his module. The aim of the Modulor Society is to design not to the dimension of tolerance, but to a module of four inches, which will, by ensuring that everything is in multiples of this dimension, increase the standardization of manufactured articles, and enable a great number of diverse elements to be fitted together perfectly.

Another type of module is the basic measurement used to regularize the rhythm of elements in a building. At Le Havre, for example, Perret established a module of 1 ft. 9 ins. for his facades, but this dimension is used only for the general disposition of the parts, and is seldom actually found in the buildings except in the *inter-axial* spacing of various elements.

Thirdly, we have the modular system of the classical orders which was set out by Vitruvius, although modified by every major architect of the Renaissance, since its precise values are not supported by the great monuments of Greece and Rome. The Vitruvian system is not concerned with measurements as such but with proportion, and is an algebraic system for standardizing the relationship of parts, whatever the scale.

[1] *The Modulor: A harmonious measure to the human scale universally applicable to architecture and mechanics.* By Le Corbusier. Faber & Faber. 25s.

Two other systems of proportioning independently of scale may be mentioned. One is the method of relating all proportions to those of musical intervals. This method, which has been dealt with exhaustively by Professor Wittkower in *Architectural Principles in the Age of Humanism,* is similar to the method proposed by Le Corbusier, except that the relationship of units is based not on the "golden section," but on harmonic proportions. Aware of the "divine proportion" which links all musical sounds by simple arithmetic relationships, the Renaissance theorists concluded that such proportions might be objectively valid throughout the entire universe, and sought to apply them to obtain harmony in architectural design. Palladio was the only architect we know of who made a serious attempt to incorporate these proportions fully into his buildings, basing them on the Vicentine foot of approximately 13¾ English inches. Yet even within the wide limitations of Renaissance planning and structural requirements he found difficulty in putting the system into practice, hence the frequent disparity between the dimensions of his original drawings and those of his finished buildings.

The other system is the control of design by simple geometric forms such as triangles, squares, circles, golden sections, etc. This method, advocated by Le Corbusier in *Towards a New Architecture,* has behind it a long tradition in Gothic as well as Classical design, and it was the basis of the early French academic system. François Blondel, the first Academy professor in Paris, claimed it as the basis of his design for the Porte S. Denis, and although his successor in office, Jacques-François Blondel, has demonstrated in *L'Architecture Françoise* that the true measurements of the Porte S. Denis do not in fact coincide with the proportions published in François Blondel's *Cours d'Architecture,* this edifice has always been regarded as one of the classic proofs of the method, and was accepted as such by Le Corbusier. François Blondel's teaching was attacked by Claude Perrault, who claimed in his *Ordonnance des Cinq Espèces de Colonnes* that if certain proportions in buildings seem more beautiful than others, it is only because we have grown accustomed to them. The controversy between those who believe in objective systems of proportioning and those who do not has continued almost uninterrupted from the seventeenth century until the present day.

The novelty of the *Modulor* is that it combines two modules in one, a module of measurement and a module of scale. As a module of measurement it is to some extent limited by the fact that it is not capable of equal subdivision. A more serious limitation is that although the dimensions at the base of the scale are reasonably small (if less accurate expressions of the "golden section") they rapidly assume astronomic values as the logarithmic spiral progresses. Le Corbusier tried to overcome this difficulty by introducing a second spiral, or "blue" series, running half way between the "red" series, but in fact only the latter is based strictly on the height of a man. Nevertheless, even this subdivision is inadequate, and the *Modulor* tape sub-divides both series again by processes of interpolation to which Le Corbusier refers vaguely as "secondary operations" (*p. 160*). As an example of this defect in the system, let us examine his illustration of the interior of a room in the *Unité d'Habitation*. The height of the room is 226 cms. (7 ft. 5 ins.) but the only *Modulor* dimension below this is 183 cms., i.e., the height of a man, so that to obtain a height for the door Le Corbusier is in a dilemma, as the door is a flush door unbroken by small panels. He overcomes this difficulty adroitly by employing narrow push-plates 86 cms. high (*Modulor* dimension) and screwing them 53.4 cms. (*Modulor* dimension) from the ground. This leaves a distance (undimensioned in the drawing) for which the only possible *Modulor* dimension is 53.4 cms., thus giving a door of total height 192.8 cms., or 6 ft. 4 ins. Judging from other dimensions on the drawing, however, the door almost certainly measures 200 cms., and indeed Le Corbusier remarks elsewhere in his book that his doors are not kept strictly to *Modulor* dimensions. This departure is justified as "a personal interpretation of the *Modulor*, the limitations which it imposes and the liberties which it allows" (*p. 100*).

Even the smaller dimensions suffer from this kind of inflexibility. The floor thicknesses of the *Unité d'Habitation* are of two dimensions, 33 cms. for the intermediate "balcony" floors, and 53.4 cms. for the fire-resisting floors between each flat. On consulting the *Modulor* scale, it will be seen that the structural engineer must have been asked to accommodate his calculations to values among the following *Modulor* dimensions: 26.7 cms., 33 cms., 43.2 cms., 53.4 cms., and 69.8 cms. In other words, thickness of the fire-resisting floor had to be either 1 ft. 5 ins., 1 ft. 10 ins., or 2 ft. 4 ins., differences not implying great economy of design in reinforced concrete.

The norm on which all the *Modulor* values are calculated is the height of a man. Originally Le Corbusier selected 175 cms., the conventional height of a man in the metric scale, which is equivalent to approximately 5 ft. 9½ ins. (This compares with 5 ft. 7½ ins. under the *ancien regime*, for the pre-revolution French foot was 15/16 of an English foot.) He found, however, that dimensions calculated on 175 cms. were very difficult to translate into inch measurements, and so in 1946 he changed the norm to 183 cms., or 72 ins. Seventy-two inches falls simply within the Fibonacci series: ½″, 1″, 1½″, 2½″, 4″, 6½″, 10½″, 17″, 27½″, 44½″, 72″, etc., and was therefore a much more convenient norm for a system intended for the standardization of dimensions in countries using both metric and English scales. It will be seen that the norm is a purely conventional dimension, adopted because of its practical arithmetic value, like the value of middle C in the musical scale.

The difficulty of selecting the correct value from "a hundred or a thousand" possibilities is recognized by Le Corbusier, who adds: "I still reserve the right at any time to doubt the solutions furnished by the *Modulor*, keeping intact my freedom which must depend solely on my feelings rather than on my reason" (*p. 63*). Yet only on the previous page he laments that American industrialists have not already seized upon the *Modulor* to apply it "on a mass scale in the dimensioning of manufactured articles." One can imagine the chaos which would result if the norm were to be changed once mass production had started!

But however perfect the figure accepted, the *Modulor* is still just another of those rigid *academic* systems which the great architects of the past ignored when it suited them, and the inferior architects used to justify their mediocrity. No amount of scorn poured on "Beaux-Arts" star-shaped plans (*pp. 61, 72, 223*) will clear Le Corbusier's theory of a classification which he, more than any other writer of this century, has done his best to render opprobrious. The other systems do, however, have the advantage of being able to call on the evidence of a number of celebrated buildings the beauty of which is uncontested, even if the precise means whereby that beauty was obtained is not. As a demonstration of the value of the *Modulor*, Le Corbusier explains how its dimensions have been exclusively applied to the *Unité d'Habitation*, but he does not show how his theories relate to acknowledged masterpieces of the past, as he did when he put forward his earlier doctrine in *Towards a New Architecture*. He has not given us those major dimensions of Notre Dame, the Capitol, or the Petit Trianon which correspond to the *Modulor*, and it would be interesting to know whether the experiment was tried when Le Corbusier was formulating his system. It seems more than likely that it was tried and failed, for a whole chapter in his book is devoted to demonstrating how the dimensions of a small Gothic doorway at Chaalis, or the height of a balustrade in Sancta Sophia, correspond to the *Modulor* scale based on 183 cms. The very sparseness of his evidence undermines rather than supports his theory, and the fact that he was able to find such scraps of corroborative evidence earlier when using the 175 cm. *Modulor* (*p. 49*) suggests that some door somewhere is bound to fit any system.

We are given reasons, which some may consider plausible, why the Parthenon cannot be expected to conform (*p. 209*), but unless Le Corbusier is claiming that the *Unité d'Habitation* is the first and only complete building ever to be erected to a harmonious and human scale, the onus is on him to show us that other buildings of perfect harmony and scale must have been *instinctively* designed to the proportions he proposes.

For this is the stumbling block of all novel systems of proportioning. Renaissance architects adopted Vitruvian canons *because they believed that the Greeks had actually used such canons to obtain the perfect beauty of their temples*. With new systems there is no such justification, for, if buildings were designed intuitively in the past without such systems, they can be so designed in the future. Le Corbusier exercises this intuition when he claims the right to disregard the *Modulor* if it produces results which are obviously unsatisfactory to the eye (*p. 130*). This he considers an example of his freedom from academic servitude, but it is also the most devastating refutation which the *Modulor* can suffer.

"I will fight against any formula and any set of instruments which take away the least particle of my freedom. I want to keep that freedom so intact that at the very moment when the golden figures and the diagrams point to a perfectly orthodox solution I may reply: 'That may be so, but it is not beautiful.'" (*p. 183*).

LE CORBUSIER'S MODULOR (1963)

Rudolf Wittkower

At a recent meeting at the Royal Institute of British Architects in London to which I was a party (June 18, 1957), the motion was before the house "that Systems of Proportion make good design easier and bad design more difficult." The motion was defeated. But in the debate Le Corbusier's Modulor was constantly referred to, and the distinguished architect, Misha Black, even said apologetically that "it must inevitably be in our minds as we discuss the motion." Indeed, after the Modulor we must be for it or against it; it would mean deluding ourselves if we tried to be escapist or neutral.

In 1948 Le Corbusier surprised the architectural world with his *Modulor*. The book was quickly sold out. Le Corbusier himself, whom I may (perhaps not too charitably) describe as a cross between a prophet and a salesman of rare ability, brought the story up to date in 1954, with the publication of his *Modulor 2*.

What was the reason for the world-wide response to the Modulor? Was it due to Le Corbusier's prophesy or his salesmanship? Each may have played a part, but many a prophet has cried in the wilderness, unheard. In all fairness, we must admit that the time was ripe for the Modulor.

The Beaux Arts tradition, according to which proportion is something vague, indefinable, irrational—a "something" that must be left to the individual architect's sensibility—that tradition is as dead as a doornail. If it is not, it should be.

Be that as it may, I find it difficult or even impossible to give paternal advice to practitioners regarding the suitability of the Modulor for the design of, say, skyscrapers. As an historian I am concerned with the past rather than with the future, and I can only discuss the Modulor in its historical context. Such an investigation may at least help to assess the validity of Le Corbusier's basic assumptions.

So far as I can see, the belief in an order, divine and human, derived from numbers and relations of numbers was always tied to higher civilizations. All systems of proportion are implicitly intellectual, for they are based on mathematical logic. Without a grasp of geometry and the theory of numbers, no system of proportion is imaginable.

It must be regarded as one of the most extraordinary events in the early history of mankind when a bridge was created between abstract mathematical thought and the phenomenal world that surrounds us; when geometry and numbers were found to govern the skies as well as all creation on earth. The Bible reflects this remarkable alliance between life and mathematics, between endless variety and numerical limitation. In the *Wisdom of Solomon* (XI, 20), we read, "By measure and number and weight thou didst order all things."

The intellectualism of this daring hypothesis must not lead us astray, for in reality we are here faced with a biologically conditioned sublimation. The quest for symmetry, balance, and proportional relationships is deeply embedded in human nature. Modern antagonists always claim that systems of proportion interfere with, and even impede, the release of creative energies. In actual fact, however, such systems are no more, and no less, than intellectual directives given to an instinctive urge which regulates not only human behaviour but even the behaviour of higher species of animals.

Man's predisposition for ordering complex sensory stimuli can easily be tested. For instance, we interpret automatically irregular configurations as regular figures (see Arnheim, *Art and Visual Perception,* fig. 44). Such incontestable observations permit us to conclude that we seek ordered patterns; systems of proportion are the principal vehicles to satisfy this urge.

All systems of proportion in Western art and architecture, the only civilization we are concerned with, are ultimately derived from Greek thought. Pythagoras, living in the sixth century B.C., is credited with the discovery that the Greek musical scale depends on the division of a string of the lyre in the ratios 1:2 (octave), 2:3 (fifth), 3:4 (fourth), and 1:4 (double octave). In other words, the ratios of the first four integers 1:2:3:4 express all the consonances of the Greek musical scale. This discovery of the close interrelationship of sound, space, and numbers had immense consequences, for it seemed to hold the key to the unexplored regions of universal harmony. Moreover, if the invariable of all octaves is the ratio 1:2, it must be this ratio, the Greeks argued, that is the cause of the musical consonance. Perfection and beauty were therefore ascribed to the ratio itself.

Plato, in his *Timaeus,* expounded a geometrical theory which was no less influential. He postulated that certain simple figures of plane geometry were the basic stuff of which the universe was composed. I have no doubt that it was mainly owing to Plato's never-forgotten cosmological theory that such figures as the equilateral triangle, the right-angled isosceles triangle, and the square were charged with a deep significance and played such an important part in the Western approach to proportion.

We have overwhelming evidence that many medieval churches were built *ad quadratum* or *ad triangulum,* reflecting a platonic pedigree. Milan Cathedral is a well-known example: discussions on whether the church should be erected according to triangulation or quadrature dragged on for years.

From the fifteenth century on, attention was focused on musical proportion. Although never entirely excluded from consideration, the Renaissance and post-Renaissance periods preferred an arithmetical theory of proportion derived from the harmonic intervals of the Greek musical scale, in contrast to the Middle Ages, which favoured platonic geometry. The Renaissance, in addition, fully embraced ancient anthropometry. Following Vitruvius (whose treatise reflects Greek ideas), Renaissance theory and practice pronounced axiomatically that the proportions of architecture must echo those of the human body. This ancient theory lent itself to being incorporated into a Christian conception of the world. The Bible tells us that Man was created in the image of God. It logically follows that Man's proportions are perfect. The next axiom appears unavoidable: man-made objects, such as architectural structures, can only be attuned to universal harmony if they follow man's proportions. You may approve or disapprove of these deductions; you may find Renaissance architects' demonstrations of the connection between man and architecture naive and even funny, but some of you may detect that we are moving close to the Modulor. Moreover, because of—or in spite of—such convictions, the world was enriched by most beautiful buildings.

To postulate such a relationship between human and architectural proportions is, perhaps, not so far-fetched. The human body lends itself to an investigation of metrical relationships between parts and between the parts and the whole. You can express the parts in terms of submultiples of the whole; or you can operate with a small unit of measurement such as the face or the hand as a module, the multiples and submultiples of which guarantee metrical coordination.

Precisely the same principles may be applied to architectural structures: all the parts may be metrically interrelated by making them submultiples of a grand unit or multiples of a small unit. For the Renaissance, the *tertium comparationis* between man and buildings consisted in this: just as the beauty of the human body appears to be regulated by and derived from the correct metrical relation between all its members, so the beauty of a building depends on the correct metrical interrelation of all its parts.

In the eighteenth century the old approach to proportion broke down. Enlightenment and empiricism militated against the notion that mathematical ratios as such can be beautiful. Romantic artists had no use for intellectual number theories which would seem to endanger their individuality and freedom. In the nineteenth century it was mainly scholars who kept the interest in problems of proportion alive.

The mid-nineteenth century, however, saw two events which had a direct bearing on the modern approach to proportion—and on Le Corbusier's Modulor. First, Joseph Paxton built the Crystal Palace in London, the first structure of colossal size erected of standardized units over a grid. The logic inherent in the industrial revolution enforced a dimensional order. Secondly, the German, Adolf Zeising, published a book, *Neue Lehre von den Proportionen des menschlichen Körpers,* 1854, in which he persuasively argued that the Golden Section was the proportion pervading macrocosm and microcosm alike.

The wonderful properties of the Golden Section, of course, had been known to the Greeks. The Golden Section is the only true proportion consisting of two magnitudes (instead of 3 or 4), and in it as you know, the ratio of the whole to the larger part always equals that of the larger to the smaller part:

$$\frac{a}{b} = \frac{b}{a + b} = \frac{.618}{1} = \frac{1}{1.618}$$

In the early thirteenth century Leonardo da Pisa, called Fibonacci, discovered that on a ladder of numbers with each number on the right being the sum of the pair on the preceding rung, the arithmetical ratio between the two numbers on the same rung rapidly approaches the Golden Section. Thus, for practical purposes, the Golden Section may be approximated to such ratios as 5:8, 8:13, 13:21. (Expressed algebraically, the Fibonacci series runs: a, b, a + b, a + 2b, 2a + 3b, 5a + 8b. . . .)

Although the Golden Section remained a treasured heirloom of Western thought, it played no significant part in art and architecture. But after Zeising, the Golden Section found enthusiastic partisans, and a straight line leads from him to Hambidge's *Dynamic Symmetry* (1917) and to Matila Ghyka's books in the nineteen-twenties and thirties—from Ghyka to Le Corbusier.

Here briefly are the constituent elements of the Modulor one after another:

First, the Modulor [Fig. 27] is a measuring tool based on the human body. Anthropometry is its essence. Le Corbusier is thus in line of descent from Vitruvius and the Renaissance. When you look at his design of the "Stele of the Measure," built at the Unité d'Habitation at Marseille, you are right back at the anthropometric Renaissance exercises which seemed so strange before.

Secondly, basic geometrical units, the square and the double square, form Le Corbusier's point of departure. Quadrature, we saw, played an overwhelming part in the Middle Ages, and the square and the double square with their ratio of 1:2 has Pythagorean connotations. Le Corbusier saw these units in their relation to man: the solar plexus lies at the centre of a man with arm raised. Needless to say, this was well known to Renaissance artists.

Thirdly, two Golden Section means are introduced, one added to the square, the other subtracted from the double square. The Golden Section added to the square determines the relationship between the two parts of the body, up to the solar plexus and from there to the head. The Golden

Section subtracted from the double square determines the relationship from the foot to the fork and from the fork to the tips of the fingers of the upraised arm.

The proportions of the human body defined in terms of the Golden Section were derived by Le Corbusier from his erroneous belief that "it has been proved, particularly during the Renaissance, that the human body follows the Golden Rule." In actual fact, Renaissance artists found in the human body only commensurate musical proportions. Le Corbusier's implicit acceptance of the Golden Section stems from the mystique of Matila Ghyka.

Fourthly, the Modulor is no module in the ordinary sense. It consists of a scale of dimensions derived from the six-foot man. As we have seen, the irrational divisions of the Golden Section can be approximated by numbers of the Fibonacci series (Le Corbusier used centimeters, but he may as well have used inches.) In his Modulor, the figures 43, 70, 113 belong to a Fibonacci series which originated from the square (the red series, in Le Corbusier's terminology), and 86, 140, 226 belong to another Fibonacci series, which originated from the double square (the blue series). In other words, the ratio of 1:2 is always present.

By combining the two series, one arrives at a series the terms of which have a special bearing on man in space, as Le Corbusier attempts to demonstrate. These Fibonacci series, single or in combination, may be prolonged in both directions. An illustration published by Le Corbusier shows that each series can be drawn as a grid which engenders a great variety of spatial shapes.

Another figure gives the points of intersection of the superimposed red and blue series, and here the interweaving of the original unit, the double unit and the Golden Section may be noticed.

For the Modulor, Le Corbusier makes some special claims: First, the spatial combinations obtained by the Modulor are infinite. Secondly, the Modulor is a perfect means of unification in the mass production of manufactured articles. In contrast to an arbitrary module, it offers the possibility of harmonious integration of standardized products. Such considerations show Le Corbusier in line of descent from Paxton and competing with the propagators of standardization through modular coordination. Thirdly, in contrast to the technologists among architects, who consider a module esthetically neutral, for Le Corbusier esthetic satisfaction overrides all other considerations. Harmony, regulating everything around us, is his ultimate quest. His aesthetic judgment is buttressed, thus, by a metaphysical belief in a divine order of things. Fourthly, the Modulor is a precision instrument, comparable to the keyboard of a piano; like the keyboard, the Modulor does not interfere with the individual freedom of the performer. Nor does it help to make bad designs good.

Meanwhile, modular coordination is on the march. An almost unbelievable amount of research has been devoted to it in recent years. The main purpose of these enterprises is to economize on all levels: in the architect's and the contractor's office as well as in the factory. Designs consist of multiples of the basic module, and since F. Bemis's *Evolving*

House, published in 1936, the four-inch grid has been given preference in this country [U.S.A.]. The difference between the static—sterile, one is tempted to say—quality of the normal modular grid and the dynamic quality of Le Corbusier's grid is most striking.

What is the balance sheet? As I see it, Le Corbusier's Modulor, the creation of one man, has to assert itself against the combined efforts of hundreds or even thousands working on modular coordination. The odds favour the advocates of modular coordination: their work is scientific, sober, and objective. It is to the point, easily intelligible, and eminently practical. Le Corbusier's is the opposite in every respect: it is amateurish, dynamic, personal, paradoxical, and often obscure. When you think you have it all sorted out, you wonder how practical the Modulor really is. Le Corbusier's own buildings at Marseille, St. Dié, Algiers, Chandigarh, supply the answer.

Nevertheless, all his claims have been challenged. Against his faith in the immense variability of design offered by the Modulor, it is said that its range enforces an unsatisfactory limitation. Against his canon derived from the six-foot man, it is claimed that in order to be universal, other human heights should be taken into account. His assertion of freedom of design guaranteed by the Modulor is dismissed as "just another rigid academic system." His play with the Golden Section and the Fibonacci series is criticized as schoolboy mathematics wrapped in a cloak of mystification.

I do not want to continue this list of censure, for when all is said and done, it is only Le Corbusier whose instinct guided him to the sources of our cultural heritage; who transformed it imaginatively to suit modern requirements; who attempted a new synthesis, and once again, intellectualized man's intuitive urge with which I began. It is only Le Corbusier who brings to bear on the old problem of proportion a prophetic, unceasingly searching, and, above all, poetic mind . . . the poetic and illogical mind of a great artist.

Since the breakdown of the old systems of proportion, no architect has been so deeply engaged and none has believed so fervently that "architecture is proportion."

Architectonic arrangements vary according to the nature and form of the society whose image they are. In every age they translate the fundamentals that constitute the social state, they are the faithful reflection of them and characterize them beautifully.

VICTOR CONSIDÉRANT AS QUOTED BY LE CORBUSIER[*]

LE CORBUSIER: THE ARCHITECTURE OF TOMORROW? (1926)

Steen Eiler Rasmussen

. . . Le Corbusier's architecture has, in my opinion, never been more clearly expressed than in his last work: the Pessac housing settlement near Bordeaux [Fig. 10]. The black and white illustrations give only a faint impression of this elegant world. The foundations of the houses are black, the walls alternately sienna brown, bright blue, bright aquamarine, white, bright yellow or grey. The various sides of the houses are not of the same color; one side for example is dark brown, the other bright green, and these colors meet directly at the corner; this is perhaps the strongest way of making the walls appear immaterial. The impression is strange and fantastic, but not chaotic. All these brightly colored surfaces with green plantings spaced in an architectonic order are placed in rows and arranged along axes. All the windows are standardized and made of the same materials. Imagine the whole settlement inhabited, the roof gardens overgrown with live vegetation, gaily colored wash flapping in the wind in the shaded service yards, while children run about playing. Is this then the architecture of tomorrow? . . .

Yet the value of Le Corbusier's architecture for the future will be entirely dependent on his conception of the task of this architecture. If the program is wrongly conceived, then no matter how ingenious the solutions, they still cannot truly express our times. . . .

---

[*] Le Corbusier, *Looking at City Planning* (New York: Grossman Publishers, 1971), p. 71.

If we examine the individual houses, whether those in Pessac or in Le Corbusier's *Vers une Architecture* . . . we eventually discover that on the whole they are based on rather few practical ideas. His books are so full of witty and apt comments on traditional architecture that one may get the impression that he in particular is a champion of functionalism, and may even be a constructivist. But that is quite wrong. The impression one gets from his own works is that they are artistically determined creations, and this impression is borne out by his own statements. In a conversation between Le Corbusier and Dr. Hegemann . . . the artist declared that his aim was "to create something poetical." And these houses are indeed poetic and beautiful with their bright rooms, clear surfaces and imaginative exteriors. Yet I doubt whether they represent the housing of the future. They are mass-produced, to be sure, and are built in a fairly industrialized manner, but they are nevertheless hardly economical, even though they may be cheap in Bordeaux because of special labor conditions. The cost of the roof garden alone and of the whole bizarre interior arrangement presumably outweighs all the savings gained by omitting the customary ornamentation. Even if it is not so cold in Bordeaux in the winter, the reinforced concrete walls are poor insulation against the summer heat. Finally, it is doubtful whether the housing is at all serviceable for the worker population for whom it was intended, since actually it ought to be inhabited by extremely cultivated people. In fact, the people for whom a public-spirited man, M. Frugès, built these houses are reluctant to move in. That may be stupidity, just as it was doubtless out of stupid prejudice that the workers refused to use sprayed cement in the beginning and insisted upon more expensive concrete block construction, even for the curved walls. Yet it would seem that a project like Pessac should be based upon a careful study of the needs and wishes of its future residents. The result would perhaps be less poetic but it would make a more important contribution toward solving the urgent question of modern worker housing.

Hence many doubts arise. But we should probably consider these buildings as preliminary results, as links in a chain of experiments which, perhaps, point toward the future. Once the houses are lived in, their architect will be able to gather new information which he can later utilize for further construction. Thus a process of selection will perhaps produce the appropriate housing for the times, and it will then become the accepted solution, as were the houses of former times. . . .

LIVED-IN ARCHITECTURE (1969)

Philippe Boudon

CONCLUSION

Apart from providing a monograph of the Pessac project this study has enabled me to shed some light on the problems of standardization, functionalism and architectural semiotics, with which architects and town planners are now having to contend on a wide scale. It has also drawn attention to certain new problems, which might best be described as "toposociological" and which clearly call for further investigation. Because of its place in the history of architecture, because of the personality of its creator and the goal which he had set himself, the Pessac project lent itself particularly well to the analysis of such problems. By now some forty years have passed since Le Corbusier built his workers' settlement. But the questions which he asked himself then are still being asked today, and in much the same form.

Certain aspects of the Pessac development have now been clarified. In the first place we have seen that the Q.M.F.[1] [Fig. 10] were not an "architectural failure": the modifications carried out by the occupants constitute a positive and not a negative consequence of Le Corbusier's original conception [Fig. 11]. Pessac could only be regarded as a failure if it had failed to satisfy the needs of the occupants. In point of fact, however, it not only allowed the occupants sufficient latitude to satisfy their needs, by doing so it also helped them to realize what those needs were. Because of the individuality of certain houses in the district—and it was in these that the most extensive conversions were carried out—the district itself acquired a highly individual character. It is, in fact, a small world in itself, closed and open at one and the same time and imbued with an individuality that I was privileged to study. On the other hand, there

"Conclusion." From Philippe Boudon, *Lived-in Architecture* (Cambridge, Mass.: The MIT Press, 1972), pp. 161–64. Copyright 1969 by Dunod, Paris. Reprinted by permission of the author and Dunod, the original publisher.

[1] ["Quartiers Modernes Frugès"—ED.]

were certain zones in the settlement where the houses were far more impersonal with the result that they were converted to a much lesser extent; this merely goes to show that, in certain circumstances, a settlement is more likely to inhibit individuality than encourage it. The dwellings in Maine-Montparnasse are doubtless less susceptible to conversion than the Pessac houses, and it is improbable that they will ever be embellished with frontons or baskets of flowers. But this only means that the architectural failure of Maine-Montparnasse is likely to pass unnoticed. . . .

But, of course, Le Corbusier built other things besides the Q.M.F. In his *unités d'habitation* the balance between the individual and the collective—in so far as it exists—will have been struck in a different way. And in this connexion we might well ask ourselves whether the "failure of Pessac"—which is how Le Corbusier regarded this project—influenced his later designs.

Of course, what Le Corbusier *said* and what he *did* were often two different things. For the architect, as for the artist, it is not enough to do a thing, he also has to see what he has done. That is what really matters. The duality of these two actions was clearly expressed by Le Corbusier: "You must always say what you see and, what is more, you must see what you see."

The importance which he attached to seeing things is understandable for, where the architect is concerned, looking at things, seeing things, is in itself an action. . . .

We have seen on numerous occasions that there was often a marked discrepancy between the statements made by the occupants and their actions. In fact, in a number of cases, these were diametrically opposed to one another. Moreover, we have also seen that there was a discrepancy between Le Corbusier's intentions and his finished works. But although both the occupants and Le Corbusier were less than consistent, in the final analysis they complemented one another extremely well for, by designing open-plan interiors, Le Corbusier provided the occupants with a perfect basis for their conversions.

This consistency of action between architect and occupants seems to have derived in the first instance from the "construction game" utilized by Le Corbusier in Pessac, which led on quite naturally to the "conversion game" subsequently played by the occupants. Thus, the rules of the game framed by Le Corbusier proved extremely fertile.

Of course, the whole basis of these games was standardization, for this determined the form and size of the component elements. But both the architect and, subsequently, the occupants were able to play about with these components until they discovered suitable arrangements. This was done by the occupants in terms of their own individual houses and by the architect in terms of the whole district. The geometrical permutations were considerable, which meant that differentiation was assured. In the final analysis my own enquiry has also been concerned with topographical considerations for, after first investigating the ecology of the Q.M.F., I have been able to proceed to a topographical analysis. Gradually, the *situational* factor has emerged more and more clearly and has been defined in terms of open and closed, of external and internal, characteristics. Such antitheses appear primarily within a situational framework; and so, before playing black or white, it is necessary to know how to play on the antithesis between black and white. Consequently, instead of trying to decide whether, in the final analysis, Le Corbusier's architecture is open or closed, I have preferred to concentrate on its antithetical character, which derives from the polarity between external and internal or—and this comes to the same thing in the end—open and closed conditions. This polarity is, of course, one of the fundamental characteristics of urban space and—in so far as it is possible to conceptualize space or, conversely, to spatialize mental concepts—it helps us to effect the transition from urban space—or architecture—to thought. Meanwhile, the question as to whether Le Corbusier's architecture is open or closed must remain unanswered. . . .

LE CORBUSIER AT PESSAC (1972)

Brian Brace Taylor

PART I: INTRODUCTION

Jeanneret embarked upon his first investigations of minimal-standard, house-type suitable to contemporary needs by consulting the encyclopedic works on the subject by French social researchers. The methods of analysis and classification employed by certain of these late 19th century political economists were incorporated by Jeanneret into his own approach to housing the masses. Those analyses which he studied in the *Bibliothèque Nationale* in Paris in 1914–1915 aided Jeanneret in defining a system for designing house-types that responded to specific social and economic conditions in France. Although he was already familiar with a great many kinds of habitations in other European countries, and especially with pre–World War I housing experiments in Germany, he sought out studies of the French dwelling which discussed the essential biological, social and cultural aspects of shelter.

The Enquête sur les conditions de l'Habitation en France, Les Maisons-Types (1894) is a two-volume compilation of data obtained from contributors throughout France. The factual information about rural habitation-types and their conditions, but particularly the introduction by Alfred de Foville explaining the method and purpose of the survey, provided the framework for Jeanneret's first designs of modern working-class dwellings. The goals of the *Enquête* stated by Foville were to clarify existing conditions in order to promote reforms and to develop a taste for methodical observation among his readers. In pursuit of these aims the *Section des sciences économiques et sociales du Comité des travaux historiques et scientifiques* circulated a questionnaire to professional people in all regions of France. The assumption upon which this questionnaire was based is described as follows:

From Brian Brace Taylor, *Le Corbusier at Pessac* (Cambridge, Mass.: Carpenter Center for the Visual Arts, Harvard University, 1972), pp. 1–2, 4–5, 7–10. Copyright Brian Brace Taylor. Reprinted by permission of the author.

In nearly all regions there exist for the use of peasants, landowners or not, hundreds, even thousands of dwellings which are rather similar, and it is this house-type, this characteristic unit, whose elements should be clarified and defined.

Foville, who was a statistician by profession and founder of the French Institute of Statistics, addressed the committee's questionnaire to private individuals as well as to public officials who might possess knowledge and interest in the realm of housing reform. The philosophy and motivation behind Foville's inquiry was substantially different from other studies of the period, for example, Charles Garnier's l'Habitation humaine (1892). In contrast to a purely academic interest in the architectonics and decoration of ancient dwellings, Foville's direct concerns were biological and social, economic and technical, and ultimately even political.

> . . . A man constructs his house and, in doing so, puts a part of himself into it. But with time, the house shapes the man also. . . . it is, therefore, more than a mirror; it is almost a mould.

This concept of the house as an active, formative, physical entity rather than simply a passive, indicative one, betrays a deterministic philosophy of reform which subsequently appears in Le Corbusier's concept of planning: re-form the conditions of habitation and you can eventually improve man's moral behavior.

Jeanneret extracted factual data from Foville's Enquête which he copied into his notebooks. Information concerning housing in four particular regions appears in these notes: the Loire, the Meuse, Avesnes, and Montbeliard; for these areas he noted the physical characteristics of houses—for example, that the dimensions of winegrowers' houses of the Loire are eight meters by five meters, the number of inhabitants, their distribution for sleeping, the moral conditions which this reflects, and the use of dwellings for purposes other than habitation, such as shops or ateliers. Most of this information pertained to northern and eastern regions, especially the Montbeliard, which is close to the architect's native city. The houses of this region, which were well-organized, well-ventilated and well-lighted, were offered by Foville as a model to other communities; the social and economic organization which the groupings of these houses reflected was also recommended by the author. These "industrial villages," where members of families engaged in both agriculture and watchmaking, exercised an influence on Jeanneret's earliest studies for his DOM-INO houses, as will be seen in a moment. The issue of physical and moral "hygiene" associated with typical houses described by Foville received special attention from Jeanneret. He transcribed from the Enquête that,

> The grossness of moral behavior is directly proportional to the degree of intimacy which prevails between men and beasts in our diverse sorts of rural dwellings. Proximity should not degenerate into cohabitation.

In his notes the architect recorded typical arrangements of sleeping accommodations for different members of a family: parents; children grouped according to their sex; grandparents; and domestics. There exists a very clear tendency of Jeanneret to search for the *norms* in human needs, behavior, and use of space in the family domicile.

This social survey, providing a large sample of standardized, traditional responses to questions of shelter, was of immediate and long-term significance in Jeanneret's formulation of minimal family dwellings for the masses. However, the attitudes which lay behind this particular survey were founded upon the desire to explain, and subsequently to control, the links between uses of physical space and social, economic, and moral behavior. These same intentions eventually emerge in Jeanneret's own stated views on workers' housing. The fundamental motivation in pursuing "methodical" and "scientific" inquiries into housing conditions was that of "social engineers" who wished to direct the progress of social life according to their own ideals.

The activists in this 19th century reform movement were not, however, the architects of the period but were either political economists, statisticians, and engineers, or, philanthropic industrialists. The former group contributed the technique of making surveys to establish norms, yet a moral purpose is everywhere apparent in their analyses. Jeanneret's early conceptions of an ideal worker's dwelling, based upon rural, traditional precedents, were strongly affected by these engineers, hygienists, and economists. . . .

GARDEN CITY HOUSING
FOR INDUSTRY

The garden city concept was an English innovation rooted in co-operative ideas of 19th century reformers. Essentially, the proposal was to create self-sufficient satellite communities of 30,000–50,000 residents around existing cities. Land was to be purchased and held in common in order to avoid speculation; social evils found in urban centers, stemming from unsanitary, high-density dwelling accommodations mingled with large industrial concentrations, might be eliminated by rational suburban planning.

The connotation of garden city in France, where the problems of urban concentration associated with industrialization were in general less acute than in England, was from the outset synonymous with residential suburb. They were rarely created as joint stockholding enterprises, let alone cooperative lines. The phenomenon of garden city soon after its introduction became identified with, then replaced, the term workers' city in the vocabulary of contemporary reformers. Part of the reason for this resides in the fact that France already had a strong reformist tradition, for the most part carried on by philanthropists, which sought to displace the worker from the center city. A large garden was considered an

indispensable element for the workers' family dwelling; a vegetable garden (*potager*) was viewed as an influential element in improving the
economic self-sufficiency, physical well-being, and moral behavior of
the working classes. Reformers such as Foville, Charles Lucas, Emile
Cheysson and others, saw a kitchen-garden annexed to an individual
dwelling as a means for stabilizing the working-class population near
factories; a certain agrarian idealism (perhaps sentimentalism) is perceptible in the French image of family "home," an image shared by
workers and bourgeoisie alike. The aim of upperclass reformers of peace-
fully controlling working-class society by keeping it in pleasant surroundings outside the urban center was an important dimension to the French
interpretation of garden city. It was ultimately influential upon Le Corbusier's view of the function of garden cities within a framework of contemporary cities.

Jeanneret had already produced a preliminary project for a residential garden suburb in La Chaux-de-Fonds in May 1914. During the preceding decade, the idea of garden suburbs had gained a considerable
number of adherents on the Continent as well as in England. The planning
and design of several such suburbs by the English architects Barry
Parker and Raymond Unwin received much attention in architectural
reviews, and Jeanneret had made tracings of some of the designs reproduced. A first-hand encounter with similar experiments in Germany,
particularly at Hellerau, near Dresden, where his brother Albert was
teaching music, excited Jeanneret's imagination enormously. His desire
to imitate prototypes of unified housing ensembles, situated around
cul-de-sacs with park-like landscaping, is most apparent in the architectural detailing of the La Chaux-de-Fonds project. A vision of a refined
cultural and residential life in a quiet, picturesque, and healthful natural
environment became the basis of his many suburban schemes which followed. The site planning for La Chaux-de-Fonds, for DOM-INO units,
and a scheme for St. Nicholas d'Aliermont reflect this newly-formalized
ideal which seemed an improvement over the older model of *corons* laid
out along a strict orthogonal. . . .

JEANNERET AND TAYLORIZED
INDUSTRIALIZATION

While engaged in the engineering and construction studies discussed
above, Jeanneret was confronted by the controversial analyses and systems of the American mechanical engineer Frederick Winslow Taylor
which were aimed at increasing the efficiency of industrial production.
His *Principles of Scientific Organization of Factories*, published in French
in 1912, must surely have been one of the many publications which
Jeanneret consulted. For many years he spoke of taylorism as one of the
fundamental bases of his proposals for mass-produced housing.

It was Taylor's contention that one should study the traditional
working methods of workers in all epochs, classify them, compare them,

and deduce the rules, laws, and formulae which should guide us. This empirical method of research practiced by Taylor was precisely the kind in which Jeanneret had engaged when consulting Foville on housing or when analyzing regional house-types at St. Nicholas.

The research of F. W. Taylor aimed at the precise determination of the time and human movements required in executing certain clearly defined tasks. The fundamental goal of such studies was economic in nature, an augmentation of the productive power of the worker without increasing his fatigue. Taylor's "science" was clearly applied science more than it was purely speculative, or theoretical. In industries where men were operating machines, the machine provided a kind of constant against which man's behaviour could be measured and regulated; or, as Le Corbusier remarked, the Machine commands the Man. (Compare Charlie Chaplin's portrayal of this in the film *Modern Times.*) The assumption was, that if the characteristics and standards of performance of the machine were ascertainable and controllable, then so too was man's performance in relation to it able to be determined and programmed for the greatest efficiency, and quality of output.

The connection which Taylor made between his mechanical model of individual actions and social behavior is one which Jeanneret was inclined to accept. The behavioral determinism evident in Foville's statement that the house can shape the man is analogous to that found in Taylor's belief that a well informed, well directed and disciplined worker will be happy and prosperous in his job, resulting in greater wealth and *harmony* among all classes of a society. Jeanneret would claim subsequently that social equilibrium could be attained when the family and communal life of the industrial worker was organized in garden cities, and his productive capacities "scientifically" managed in the factory. The difficulties and compromises which Jeanneret eventually encountered in trying to achieve the *Quartier Moderne Frugès* at Pessac can be explained, in part, by something that Taylor himself warned against— namely, a premature attempt to apply his procedures to a given situation, and on too broad a scale.

Although Jeanneret's experiences as a designer and administrator of industrial enterprises produced the conviction that a "systems approach" was what was necessary, he was in no position at the time of Pessac to control the taylorization of any production of building materials or of a building site as he would have liked. The procedural model that he would have liked to follow is contained in a brochure published in 1925 by Michelin and Company concerning their successful efforts to "taylorize" the construction of their own company housing at Clermont-Ferrand. What they were able to attain in industrialized building at the time was known to Jeanneret through a copy of this brochure, and in fact, he visited Clermont-Ferrand with Pierre Jeanneret, we are told, to see the work for himself. As we shall see ultimately, Michelin dealt with projects as well as technical and organizational expertise on a much larger scale than Jeanneret found available in his personal efforts along similar lines.

PART II: INTRODUCTION

The opportunity to design a model residential community at Pessac, near Bordeaux, for a private developer was the first occasion for Le Corbusier to actualize those proposals for low-cost mass-produced housing which had slowly taken shape during the preceding years of research and experimentation [Fig. 10]. It became, primarily, an attempt to establish by example the validity of principles set forward in the earliest DOM-INO studies [Fig. 4]. The project for a modern residential neighborhood for workers (along garden city lines) must also be understood within the framework of Le Corbusier's 1922 diagram for a potential urban agglomeration of three million [Fig. 7]; that is, the *Quartier Moderne Frugès* (QMF) amounts *not* to the nucleus of such a city but to the elaboration of one sector. Yet, in order for us to comprehend fully Le Corbusier's capacity to make an architectural statement that addressed itself to the realities of his situation, we should note the general social context of house construction in France at the time, and the fact that in design problems he was now in collaboration with his cousin Pierre Jeanneret.

PUBLIC POLICY CONCERNING HOUSING

Public policy concerning low-income, workers' housing on a national level in France first took shape in the 1890s with the passage of the Siegfried Law (1894), followed in 1908 by the Ribot Law, which served as the major existing piece of legislation during the post-World War I reconstruction. The Ribot Law defined a policy by which government funds were made available to corporations (*sociétés*) rather than to individuals for constructing inexpensive, private dwellings. French legislators continued for many years to encourage private, limited-profit initiatives rather than public building programs in order to solve housing needs.

The Ribot Law made possible credit of 60% to 80% of the cost of house and property combined. The prospective homeowner was free to choose his own architect or to choose from a series of standard house-types furnished by a building company; the law stipulated only that these plans conform to specified codes. For example, the minimum surface for habitable rooms was 9 square meters; storerooms, dressing rooms, etc., could not have dimensions greater than 1.25 meters by 1.80 meters or the house would not receive a certificate as a sanitary dwelling, since larger spaces would inevitably be converted into additional bedrooms. All toilets had to be lighted and ventilated directly. And finally, the maximum surface area allowed for a garden was one thousand square meters. The stipulations of this law were expanded and modified slightly after World

War I, but no new, far-reaching attempt at low-cost housing legislation was actually passed until the Loucheur Law (1928). . . .

PESSAC: THE INITIATORS AND THEIR GOALS

. . . M. Henri Frugès . . . was himself a man of extra-creative energy and versatility. Author, composer, musician, painter, designer, he possessed an artistic sensibility that permitted him to be especially susceptible at the time to Le Corbusier's architectural achievements and goals. That Le Corbusier held the talents of M. Frugès in high esteem was frequently apparent. Requests by him to M. Frugès to design "oriental" carpets for the *Esprit Nouveau* Pavilion and for the inauguration of Pessac itself, or invitations to his Parisian friends to attend concerts given by M. Frugès are but isolated examples of Le Corbusier's appreciation of his artist-client. The remarkable collaboration between Le Corbusier and M. Frugès was possible and fruitful, because of a mutual respect for the practical experience and artistic judgment which each brought to the task.

It was in keeping with events of the period in France, and of Le Corbusier's prior experiments in workers' housing, that an industrialist from Bordeaux, one of the wealthiest in southwestern France, should arrive at the architect's door with a commission for company housing. As the first letters of M. Frugès clearly state, his principal reasons for interest in Le Corbusier's ideas on mass housing were *rapidity* and *economy* of construction. His program entailed half a dozen dwellings for his workers, on a rural site near one of his factories. His motivation[1] was to stabilize his working population and assure their continual availability at the factory, suggesting that M. Frugès was a classic example of the French social and political tradition concerning workers' communities.[2] A meeting between M. Frugès and the architect resulted in an important reorientation of this originally modest program.

Two decisions taken at the outset by architect and client were certainly inextricably linked. One related to the technical system of construction which Le Corbusier proposed, namely the cement-gun technique of the Ingersoll-Rand Company; the cost of purchasing this equipment was not justified by the scale of M. Frugès' initial proposal. Thus the other decision taken at the time that the gunite system was adopted, enlarged the scope of the building program. It was enlarged to include *several* model residential *quarters* in the Southwest of France. Le Corbusier, it would seem, had little trouble in persuading his client that he could regain the initial investment in equipment by constructing and selling a high volume of very inexpensive houses which he would design. As the architect later recalled to M. Frugès, their goal was "to build in

[1] Boudon, Philippe, *Pessac de Le Corbusier* (Paris: Dunod, 1969).
[2] M. G. Raymond, *La Politique pavillonnaire* (Paris: Institut de sociologie urbaine, Centre de recherche d'urbanisme, 1966).

the southwest," which enabled him, as the designer/planner, to experiment with a technical system that intrigued him as well as to achieve some of his urbanistic schemes in reality.

The grandeur of their joint endeavor had a special, rather ancient, precedent in the region that both men were well aware of. This was the rich tradition of thirteenth-century *villes neuves* in southwestern France. Le Corbusier was familiar with these medieval towns from an article which had appeared in January, 1925, which had been translated from English for his use. The English and French conquerors alike had settled large tracts of land by founding such planned new towns as Creon, Sauveterre, Monpazier, and Libourne. Streets set out in a carefully rectilinear grid, with a main plaza at the center, characterize the urban pattern of many of these colonial settlements; a noteworthy architectural element, namely, a covered arcade around the four sides of these plazas and termed "*cornières*," was a feature which M. Frugès specifically requested the architects to include in the *Quartier Moderne Frugès* at Pessac. M. Frugès' stature as industrialist, community leader, and artist suggests that he wished to see himself as a *grand seigneur* of the 20th century, developing the region by means of model communities.

Le Corbusier, on his side, believed in garden cities as the principal means in his period for urbanizing the rural countryside. In 1923 he articulated the following distribution of population for cities:

> Those of power, the leaders, are located at the center of the city. Then their auxiliaries, down to the most humble, whose presence is required in the center of the city at a fixed hour, but whose limited destiny tends simply towards familial organization. . . . We classify three sorts of population: citizens; workers whose life unfolds half of the time in the center and half in the garden cities; the laboring masses divide their time between suburban factories and the garden cities.

The decongestion and "deproletarianization" of existing city centers through the creation of "cities of repose" in the country for workers were the ideal social aims of Le Corbusier's urbanism. The ways in which this coincided with the social and economic goals of M. Frugès the industrialist should be clear. . . .

LE CORBUSIER, FOURIER, AND THE
MONASTERY OF EMA (1967)

Peter Serenyi

The climactic point of an architectural system is not when it seems to fulfill itself but when it makes the utmost effort to reconcile the irreconcilable.[1]

No better words than these written by Emil Kaufmann can summarize Le Corbusier's aim during his "Period of Invention," stretching from 1918 to 1922. To reconcile the irreconcilable, that is, to reconcile such polarities as private and public, individuality and collectivity, personal and impersonal, unity and diversity—just to name a few examples—was one of Le Corbusier's most urgent tasks during this period of search and invention.

The world he encountered, and soon shared, in Paris in 1917 was the world of the painter, the sculptor, the poet and the musician. In short, it was the world of the Bohemian, the outsider, the rebel, the uprooted wanderer—a world which had nothing to do with propriety, conventionality, and established order, qualities which one usually associates with the world of architecture. In fact, in trying to explain the drastic change that occurred in his architecture after the war he tells us, at one point, that "it was only in 1919—at the age of 32—that I was really able to see the 'architectural phenomenon' . . .."[2] And at another place he adds that "the secret of my quest must be sought in painting."[3] It is not surprising, therefore, that one of his first major architectural inventions of the immediate post-war period was the Maison Citrohan [Fig. 6], a studio house, primarily designed for the single artist. This was followed by the invention of a communal dwelling—the Immeubles Villas of 1922—in which Le Corbusier attempted to tackle the larger human question: how to relate man to man within an existing framework of society. The means

"Le Corbusier, Fourier, and the Monastery of Ema" by Peter Serenyi. From *The Art Bulletin*, XLIX (1967), pp. 277–86. Reprinted by permission of the editor-in-chief.

[1] Emil Kaufmann, *Architecture in the Age of Reason* (Cambridge, Mass.: Harvard University Press, 1955), p. 123.
[2] Le Corbusier, *Modulor 2* (Cambridge, Mass.: Harvard University Press, 1958), p. 297.
[3] *Ibid.*, p. 296.

he chose to solve this problem will provide us with the best clues to an understanding of his concept of society.

The Immeubles Villas [Fig. 8] is a project for an apartment super-block consisting of many individual Maisons Citrohan, put next to or on top of one another, and linked together by corridors and open terraces. The entire building revolves around an open courtyard, which provides recreational facilities for the inhabitants. Moreover, communal facilities, such as restaurants, common rooms, and the like are placed on the top floor so as to make domestic life free of dirt and drudgery. Through the creative act of joining and linking together individual "cells"—to use Le Corbusier's own term—he created a communal order whose nature and meaning can only be understood if we consider its sources.

In the text describing the Immeubles Villas, Le Corbusier informs us that the whole concept of this project was born after he evoked the memory of a monastery he had visited in Italy.[4] From his other writings we know that this was the Monastery of Ema, near Florence, which he had visited in 1907.[5] And it was this monastery which made him "conscious of the harmony which results from the interplay of individual and collective life when each reacts favorably upon the other. Individuality and collectivity comprehended as fundamental dualism."[6] Moreover, referring to this early period of search and invention, he tells us in his book *The Modulor*: "His studies were complex and far-reaching: basic measures of urbanism . . . determination of the cellular unit . . . the mesh of communications . . . in reality, a process of fundamental architectural organization which he had already experienced once, fifteen years earlier, at the Charterhouse of Ema in Tuscany (individual freedom and collective organization)."[7]

For Le Corbusier, then, the image of the ideal communal life is embodied in monasticism, in which individual will and general will are in complete accord with one another. He even urged a group of architectural students that "devoting yourself to architecture is like entering a religious order. You must consecrate yourself, have faith and give. As a just reward, architecture will bring a special happiness to those who have given her their whole being. This happiness is a sort of trance that comes with radiant birth after the agonies of labor. It is a power of invention, of creation which allows man to give the best that is in him to bring joy to others, the everyday joy found only in the home."[8]

It is revealing that his sermon on architecture begins with a reference to monastic life and ends with a note on the home. It must be remembered that Le Corbusier likes to consider the home as a monastic cell, created,

[4] Le Corbusier, *Oeuvre complète 1910–1929* (Zurich: Les Editions Girsberger, 1960), p. 40.

[5] See especially Le Corbusier, *Précisions sur un état présent de l'architecture et de l'urbanisme* (Paris: Les Editions Crès et Cie., 1930), pp. 91f.

[6] Le Corbusier, *The Marseilles Block* (London: Harvill Press, 1953), p. 45.

[7] Le Corbusier, *The Modulor* (Cambridge, Mass.: Harvard University Press, 1954), pp. 27f.

[8] Le Corbusier, *Talks with Students* (New York: The Orion Press, 1961), p. 34.

ideally at least, for the single individual; for the family, as a small, intricate social group, has no place in Le Corbusier's art or mind. He never thinks of the family as a complex unit made up of various, different, and unique members, precariously held together by loyalty and love. And with this thought in mind, we are led directly back to the Immeubles Villas of 1922, which is nothing but a collection of single figures put on top or next to one another by the architect. For each unit, as said earlier, is really a Maison Citrohan, or a studio apartment, symbolizing the single artist, uprooted and lonely. It is a secular monastery made of concrete, steel and glass in which the solitary confinement of the individual cells is counteracted by the openness of the communal areas on the top floor and in the courtyard; hence individual freedom and collective organization are united in harmony.

The Carthusian Monastery of Ema is located on a pleasant hill about ten miles outside of Florence. The oldest section of the monastery was built in the fourteenth century, but the larger part of the building dates from the sixteenth century. One of the most conspicuous features of the monastery consists of innumerable cells which project from the main body of the building, providing private apartments for each monk. It was to this aspect of the complex Le Corbusier addressed himself when he said that there is a "harmony which results from the interplay of individual and collective life." There is indeed an interplay between these cells, symbolizing privacy and individuality, and the building as a whole, symbolizing collective order. In fact, these cells remind one of so many Maisons Citrohan crowning the hill. It is not surprising that Le Corbusier was deeply impressed by the monastery complex, which left a lasting effect on his conception of communal buildings.

It must be remembered, however, that the Monastery of Ema in particular and monasticism in general were not the only sources which inspired Le Corbusier in formulating his concept of the ideal communal life. The nineteenth century French social philosopher Charles Fourier played an equally important role in this process. Le Corbusier makes references to Fourier in his various books: for example in *Manière de penser l'urbanisme* of 1945 and *L'Unité d'Habitation de Marseille* of 1950.

François-Marie-Charles Fourier was born in Besançon on April 7, 1772, and died in Paris on October 9, 1837.[9] . . . During his early life one major historical event left a permanent imprint on his mind: the French Revolution. After 1793, for example, his property was taken away by the Republicans, only to be followed by a forcible conscription by their army, in which he fought, understandably enough, with considerable unwillingness. While in Lyons, he was even imprisoned a number of times by the revolutionary forces, and almost guillotined on one occasion.

As John Wahlke has pointed out, it was the horrors of 1793 which clearly revealed to Fourier the need for discovering a new world order.[10]

[9] For the best biography of Fourier see Charles Pellarin, *The Life of Fourier* (New York: W. H. Graham, 1848).

[10] John C. Wahlke, "Charles Fourier and Henri Saint-Simon: Two Theorists of the Reaction" (unpublished doctoral dissertation, Harvard University, 1952).

"Such was the first consideration," said Fourier in his first book, "which made me suspect of the existence of a Social Science as yet unknown, and which excites me to attempt the discovery of it." [11] Therefore, his primary aim—like that of Le Corbusier—was to reestablish a unity and order among mankind which had been lost through the disruptive historical events he himself had experienced at first hand. Both Fourier and Le Corbusier were deeply disturbed by the disorder of their own time, and both, in their own way, wanted to stabilize the course of events which surrounded them. To achieve order, Fourier—as did Le Corbusier a century later—invited the world to unite in action. "Unity of action," he said, "is the end of nature and it is the aim of God in the material and in the social world." [12]

To what extent Le Corbusier understood the nature of Fourier's world order is best revealed by his first reference to this nineteenth century social philosopher. After having enumerated the great architects of the nineteenth and twentieth centuries, such as Sullivan, Berlage, and Wagner, he tells us that "a part of their ideas, although coming from far away horizons, is to be found in certain prophetic propositions of Fourier, formulated around 1830, at the time when the machine itself was born." [13] It is revealing, although not surprising, that Le Corbusier equates the birth of the machine with Fourier's visionary, if not necessarily prophetic, ideas. For Fourier himself was deeply interested in the newly emerging machines of his own time, and tried to create a world order patterned on them.

As he looked around himself, Fourier could see nothing but strife, chaos, and disorder among his fellow human beings. The only order he could find was in the Newtonian concept of the cosmos and in the frictionless and smooth-running modern machine. No wonder, therefore, that with his flair for precision and meticulousness, he tried to create a social order based on the "Newtonian world machine"—to use J. H. Randall's term—and on the effortlessly running mechanical instruments of his own time. Yet before envisaging this new world order, he attempted to define the very nature of man.

As a self-proclaimed heir to Newton, Fourier argued in his first book that "there must exist a unitary social code, founded by God and revealed by attraction." [14] He then adds that while it was Newton who discovered material attraction, it was he who found the key to human nature: passional attraction. Whereupon he proceeds to describe the nature of man by suggesting that there are twelve passions that he possesses. There are five "sensitive passions," corresponding to the five senses of man; followed by the four "affective passions," which he identifies as love, ambition, friendship, and family sense. Finally, he concludes

[11] Charles Fourier, *Théorie des quatre mouvements et des destinées générales* (Leipzig: 1808), p. 80. (Publisher unknown.)

[12] Charles Fourier, *Oeuvres complètes* (Paris: Librarie Sociétaire, 1841–48), VI, 85.

[13] Le Corbusier, *Manière de penser l'urbanisme* (Paris: Editions de l'Architecture d'Aujourd'hui, 1946), p. 44.

[14] Fourier, *Théorie*, p. 141.

his list by the three "distributive passions," identifying them as the "butterfly passion," the "cabalist" or "intriguing" passion, and the "composite passion." [15] . . .

A more general, yet a more profound, echo of Fourier's theory of attraction can be found in Le Corbusier's best known book, *Towards a New Architecture*. Fourier had argued that "there is a unity of man with himself, a unity of man with God and a unity of man with the universe." [16] And at another place he added that "unity of action is the end of nature, it is the aim of God in the material and in the social world." [17] Moreover, he had claimed that the key to this unity can be found in his theory of attraction, based on the interaction of the passions. Le Corbusier, on the other hand, introduced what one might best call a theory of "resonance," based not on the interaction of the passions but rather on the belief that there exists in the world an all-embracing "axis." A significant passage from his book illustrates the point:

> We say that a face is handsome when the precision of the modelling and the disposition of the features reveal proportions which we *feel to be harmonious* because they arouse, deep within us and beyond our senses, a resonance, a sort of sounding-board which begins to vibrate. An indefinable trace of the Absolute which lies in the depths of our being. This sounding-board which vibrates in us is our criterion of harmony. This is indeed the axis on which man is organized in perfect accord with nature and probably with the universe, this axis of organization which must indeed be that on which all phenomena and all objects of nature are based; this axis leads us to assume a unity of conduct in the universe and to admit a single will behind it. The laws of physics are thus a corollary to this axis, and if we recognize (and love) science and its works, it is because both one and the other force us to admit that they are prescribed by this primal will. If the results of mathematical calculation appear satisfying and harmonious to us, it is because they proceed from the axis. If, through calculation, the airplane takes on the aspect of a fish or some object in nature, it is because it has recovered the axis. If the canoe, the musical instrument, the turbine, all results of experiment and calculation, appear to us to be "organized" phenomena, that is to say as having in themselves a certain life, it is because they are based upon that axis. From this we get a possible definition of harmony, that is to say a moment of accord with the axis which lies in man, and so with the laws of the universe—a return to universal law. [18]

In their desperate effort to regain the lost unity between man and man, and between man and the universe, both Fourier and Le Corbusier devised a theory based on intuition, whose primary purpose was to create order in face of disorder. While Fourier's passional theory is that of a

---

[15] *Ibid.*, p. 81.
[16] Fourier, *Oeuvres complètes*, II, 26.
[17] *Ibid.*, VI, 85.
[18] Le Corbusier, *Towards a New Architecture* (London: John Rodker Publisher, 1927), pp. 187–96.

social philosopher, Le Corbusier's theory of "resonance" is in keeping with his own audio-visual upbringing. Yet despite the differences that exist between these two theories, they have this essential presupposition in common: the basic link between all men and things can be regained by empathy. In fact, to "touch the axis," or to keep the passions in equilibrium in all men at all times, both Fourier and Le Corbusier believed that they must create an entirely new environment in which the theory of "resonance" or "attraction" can be made to work. And it is no accident that it was in the lack of the right kind of housing in which they both found the roots of all evil. Fourier declared that "if the civilized world after 3000 years of study and practice in architecture, has not yet learned how to construct comfortable and healthy residences, it is not very surprising that it has not learned how to direct and harmonize the passions." [19]

Le Corbusier echoes Fourier's warning in his oft-quoted passage: "The problem of the house is the problem of the epoch. The equilibrium of society depends upon it. Architecture has for its first duty, in this period of renewal, that of bringing about a revision of values, a revision of the constituent elements of the house." [20]

Both Fourier and Le Corbusier were deeply affected by the major war of their own times, and by the calamities that followed. While both wanted primarily to create unity and order in their own uneasy world, their means were different. Yet in their quest for harmony and equilibrium they both turned to a Newtonian concept of the universe and to the smoothly running machines of their own time. "The law of gravity," says Le Corbusier, "keeps the universe in equilibrium." [21] And elsewhere he adds that the "machine will lead to a new order both of work and leisure." [22] Both Fourier and Le Corbusier believed that only by remaking the whole world could humanity be saved from total despair and destruction. To put it in different terms, if only humanity would make it possible for them to realize their vision of a new world, it could regain the axis or the passional equilibrium it had lost over the centuries. To leave a deeper imprint on the mind of the reader, both Fourier and Le Corbusier charged their writings with a dual theme: life or death; hope or despair; salvation or abjection; cosmos or chaos; in short, architecture or revolution. The eschatological spirit is always counteracted by a spirit of hope and anticipation made available to those who were willing to follow their lead. So it is in the light of a deeply felt human struggle for life and order that we must judge the content of their message, and not from the point of view of practicality or attainability.

The question that still remains to be answered is in what specific terms did Fourier conceive of his utopian world. So far its general aims and its models have been mentioned, not its concrete form. Here again a

[19] Albert Brisbane, *Concise Exposition of the Doctrine of Association* (New York: J. S. Redfield, 1844), p. 28.
[20] Le Corbusier, *Towards a New Architecture*, p. 210.
[21] Le Corbusier, *The City of Tomorrow* (London: John Rodker Publisher, 1929), p. 20.
[22] Le Corbusier, *Towards a New Architecture*, p. 95.

passage from Le Corbusier's writing provides us with the best introduction: "Look back. Think of Charles Fourier, and his 'wild ideas' of houses supplied with communal services. 'Perhaps one day,' he wrote, 'water itself will be conducted through iron pipes into every house.' That was about 1830, and Fourier was dismissed as a madman. So don't let's be afraid of ideas." [23] Needless to say, here Le Corbusier refers to one of the best known aspects of Fourier's writings, the *Phalanstère*. Fourier gave us a long and detailed description of the physical form his utopia should take.[24] It should, first of all, consist of a large building which would provide living quarters for eighteen hundred inhabitants, ranging from large and spacious apartments for the wealthy to modest ones for the poor. It should also provide space for communal areas, such as dining halls, play rooms, and workshops. Finally, as partly indicated by Le Corbusier's passage, Fourier envisaged such novelties as running water, central heating, gas light, and covered walk-ways so as to make life as pleasant as possible.

As Le Corbusier a century later, Fourier by no means advocated the abolition of private property, or the equalization of wealth. He believed, instead, that the members of the *Phalanstère* should retain their socio-economic distinction, while at the same time sharing their intellectual qualities with one another. The difference in the size and the rent of the apartments would help to retain the former, while the communal areas would insure the latter.

The physical makeup of the building understandably reflects Fourier's theory of passions, which is based on his own personality. The first five "sensitive passions," emphasizing the primacy of the individual, are embodied in the apartments. Fourier attached great importance to the apartments as a means to enable the inhabitants to retain their privacy and desired solitude. He even envisaged special separating walls between the apartments—later to be realized by Le Corbusier in the Marseilles Block—to insure a sense of isolation in each of them. . . . Fourier wanted every member of the *Phalanstère* to remain at one place only for a short time, changing work and habitat at frequent intervals. With the preconception that extended stay creates friction, Fourier envisaged a world in which each member of a *Phalanstère* would move to another so as to maintain peace and equilibrium. In short, the edifices Fourier had envisaged for mankind would bring about a world in which every human being would be turned into a vagabond, rootless and lonely —just like Fourier himself. . . .

To understand the link between Fourier and Le Corbusier, we must consider, however briefly, the social and architectural tradition that led to the invention of the *unité* concept in 1922. A vision though it was, Fourier's *Phalanstère* was actually realized, if only for a short time, and

23 Le Corbusier, *The Marseilles Block*, p. 22.
24 For a detailed description of Fourier's *Phalanstère* see Victor Considérant, *Description du Phalanstère et considerations sociales sur l'architectonique* (Paris: Librarie Sociétaire, 1848), and Brisbane, *Concise Exposition of the Doctrine of Association.*

if only at an isolated place, by Jean-Baptiste Godin in his *Familistère* at Guise. After having rejected Saint-Simon, Owen, Cabot, and Communism in general, Godin discovered Fourier's theory of universal unity in 1842.[25] It immediately attracted his imagination. He shared Fourier's view that before a productive association can be achieved, people must be placed in an environment conducive to collective living. With an iron-foundry providing the economic resources, Godin built his *Familistère* between 1859 and 1883. Similar to Fourier's *Phalanstère*, Godin's main building consisted of three parts, each built around an enclosed courtyard, and housing a total of twelve hundred people. Aside from the individual apartments, varying in size, the building contained numerous communal facilities, ranging from recreational areas in the covered courtyards to grocery, clothing, and furniture stores inside the structure. Additional buildings were built for the school, the kindergarten, the restaurant, and the theater. He also provided the members of the *Familistère* with such conveniences as running water, garbage disposal, and water closets, not to mention the clean-up crew that kept the building neat in appearance. All these, and more, were later incorporated into Le Corbusier's Immeubles Villas and later in his Unité d'Habitation in Marseilles.

While Godin was building his *Familistère*, Jules Borie published a book in 1865, under the title *Essai sur un nouveau mode de maisons d'habitation.*[26] In this book he describes a building which he claims to have invented himself, calling it *aérodomes*. Judging from the description, the building seems to be another link between Fourier and Le Corbusier, echoing certain elements of the *Phalanstère* and foreshadowing the Immeubles Villas of 1922. Borie envisaged his *aérodomes* as vast eleven-story buildings, 135 feet high, with schools, gymnasia, and children's recreational rooms on the flat roof. *Chambres mobiles*, or steam-elevators, would provide vertical access to each floor, while road bridges would link the various buildings, making it possible for the inhabitants to go from one to another "without ever descending into the street."[27]

Who introduced Le Corbusier to the social and architectural ideas of Fourier and the tradition that followed him? It seems to me that it was none other than Tony Garnier. Le Corbusier had met Garnier in Lyons during his first visit to France in 1908. He once referred to him as the man who "felt the imminence of the new architecture based on our new social condition."[28] The social condition to which Le Corbusier refers may not be so new, for, as Dora Wiebenson has pointed out, Garnier's ideas, most eloquently embodied in his Cité Industrielle of 1901–1904, go back to Fourier's utopia as transmitted to him by Zola's

[25] See especially Jean-Baptiste Godin, *Solutions sociales* (Paris: A. Le Chevalier, 1871), and E. Dallet, *Twenty-eight years of Co-partnership at Guise* (London: Labour Co-Partnership association, 1908).

[26] For a more accessible description of Borie's *aérodomes* see Peter Collins, *Concrete —The Vision of a New Architecture* (London: Faber and Faber, Ltd., 1959), pp. 272f.

[27] *Ibid.*, p. 273.

[28] Le Corbusier, *Oeuvre complète, 1910–1929*, p. 12.

book *Travail,* written shortly before the planning of the city.[29] Indeed, Garnier paid frequent tribute to Zola's book in the various lengthy inscriptions which adorn the public buildings in his *Cité.* Zola's work was itself inspired by Fourier's *Phalanstère,* as he himself admitted many times in the book.[30]

After having been exposed to the ideas of Fourier by the architect of Lyons, Le Corbusier had undoubtedly studied the writings of the social philosopher first-hand even before returning to La Chaux-de-Fonds at the end of 1909 . . . although it was perhaps not until the end of the war that he had envisaged a world order largely based on Fourier's *Phalanstère.* He tells us that after the war "I immersed myself in industrial and economic problems." [31] Fourier's writings were, no doubt, high on the list of books on economics and industry which were consulted by Le Corbusier during the immediate post-war years. We have only to examine the project for the Immeubles Villas of 1922 to confirm this assumption. Although the sources of the Immeubles Villas are varied, ranging from the Monastery of Ema to the Parisian studio-type house of the turn of the century, its essential features echo the ideas of Fourier, as expanded by men such as Godin and Borie. First and foremost, the very plan of Le Corbusier's building recalls that of the *Phalanstère* or the *Familistère.* The living quarters, for example, are built around a rectangular courtyard, which can be used for recreational purposes. Moreover, communal facilities such as dining halls, stores, and common rooms, already projected by Fourier and realized by Godin, reappear here. Finally, Borie's recreational rooms and gymnasia, intended for the top of his *aérodomes,* are incorporated into Le Corbusier's design in an identical way.

In the Immeubles Villas Le Corbusier fused two traditions of communal living: monasticism and Fourierism. Although they are different in nature and purpose, they have a great deal in common. They are both voluntary associations in which the will of the individual members is reconciled with the will of the community through the binding power of the respective institutions. Moreover . . . in both monasticism and Fourierism the idea of uprootedness is considered to be an essential part of life. While monks are sent to different places from time to time, members of the *Phalanstère* were to rotate their homes and jobs so as to remain unattached to a single place. Still living under the impact of World War I in a city hostile to his art, Le Corbusier—an uprooted, single, lonely man himself—wanted to combine these two traditions in his attempt to create a new collective world order based on harmony and equilibrium. It was a vain and desperate effort, to be sure, but it emanated from the same human need that has inspired thinkers from Plato to our own day to arrest change in an all too rapidly changing world.

[29] Dora Wiebenson, "Utopian Aspects of Tony Garnier's Cité Industrielle," *JSAH,* 19 (1960), 16–24.
[30] Emile Zola, *Labor* (New York: Harper and Brothers, 1901), pp. 208, 587f., 589.
[31] Le Corbusier, *Oeuvre complète 1910–1929,* p. 12.

In 1926 Le Corbusier built his first communal building—the Palais du Peuple—for the Salvation Army in Paris. It is a delicate, narrow structure, situated on an awkward lot. With its *pilotis*, ribbon windows, roof garden, and frontal orientation, it is related to the general type of the Maison Citrohan. Its function, on the other hand, is perfectly in keeping with Le Corbusier's notion of communal living. In one of his books he even paid tribute to the Salvation Army for its ability to "teach its inhabitants how to live." [32] The communal living taught by the Salvation Army was in complete accord with Le Corbusier's own idea that "to *savoir vivre* we must add *savoir habiter,* a know-how of dwelling," based on "normalization . . . standardization . . . measure and proportion" so as to achieve an "alliance between human values and numbers." [33] Neither Plato nor Fourier would have disagreed with this statement.

To see how much client and architect had in common, let us turn to two other designs commissioned by the Salvation Army. The first of these is the Asile Flottant—or floating asylum—built in 1929. The function of this boat was to provide lodging for freezing bums and streetwalkers during the winter and a place of recreation for the poor children of Paris during the summer. But above all, it provided Le Corbusier an opportunity to design something which he himself had always held in high esteem, namely, a ship. He was not the first architect to admire the ship as a symbol of modernity. Lethaby, for example, used the analogy of the ship with modern architecture; and it was a favorite theme of Viollet-le-Duc and his followers.[34] But to my knowledge, Le Corbusier was the first theoretician to use the ship not only as a model of good design but also as a symbol of a way of life. In the chapter entitled "Eyes which do not see" of his book *Towards a New Architecture,* Le Corbusier proclaims that the "steamship is the first stage in the realization of a world organized according to the new spirit," and adds that "if we forget for a moment that a steamship is a machine for transport and look at it with a fresh eye, we shall feel that we are facing an important manifestation of temerity, of discipline, of harmony, of a beauty that is calm, vital and strong." [35] Equally revealing is Le Corbusier's description of life on a ship in his book *Précisions,* which is immediately followed by an account of his first encounter with the Monastery of Ema.[36]

Judging from these descriptions and from the photographs in his *Towards a New Architecture,* Le Corbusier's ships are not the "storm-tossed boats" of the romantics—to use Lorenz Eitner's picturesque phrase —but they are, instead, ordered, disciplined, yet carefree entities, recalling monastic life itself. No wonder, therefore, that he considers life on a ship an ideal one, for it allows the passengers a great deal of privacy while at the same time it provides them with communal facilities. As in the monastery, then, the conflict between private and public—theoreti-

[32] Le Corbusier, *The Four Routes* (London: Dennis Dobson, Ltd., 1947), p. 183.
[33] Le Corbusier, *The Marseilles Block,* pp. 27–31.
[34] Collins, *Concrete,* p. 136.
[35] Le Corbusier, *Towards a New Architecture,* pp. 96f.
[36] Le Corbusier, *Précisions,* pp. 87–92.

cally at least—is brought into harmony. Furthermore, like the monastery, the ship is governed by a smoothly running non-political institution made up of the captain and his crew, who, in this context, are secular equivalents to the prior and his advisers. Finally, like the members of a monastic order, the passengers of a ship are temporary—uprooted—inhabitants of their freely chosen community. While the monk considers his monastery a transient station between earth and heaven, the passenger looks upon his ship as a bridge between two shores. While the habitat of the former is physically static but spiritually active, that of the latter is physically active but spiritually static. To have viewed these two together, as Le Corbusier did in his *Précisions*, is undoubtedly no coincidence. They must have appeared to him as two sides of the same coin—a coin that symbolizes his own desire to be free as a first class passenger, yet bound to the world as in a stable monastery; to be the center of spiritual activity, yet to have a blind following such as sea captains have in time of crisis. But above all, both images must have seemed to Le Corbusier as way stations for the earthly passenger in transit, uprooted and lonely.

The same year that the Asile Flottant was being built, Le Corbusier received another commission from the Salvation Army. This time he was asked to build a large eight story asylum—called the Cité de Refuge—to house not only dormitories for men and women as in the Maison du Peuple of 1926 but also to provide ample space for communal rooms, such as dining halls, recreation areas, and a library. Although it was commissioned in 1929, the actual construction did not start until 1932, and it was completed only a year later. Looking at the model of the building [Fig. 18], one is immediately reminded of the profile of a huge ocean liner. This impression is strongly substantiated by even a superficial glance at the plan of the building. With its streamlining and pointed nose, the plan again recalls a ship. In fact, a comparison between the entrance passageway of the asylum and the corridor of the liner "Empress of France," illustrated in *Towards a New Architecture*, shows to what extent certain specific features of a ship are incorporated into this building. Indeed, there is no other building by Le Corbusier which captures as faithfully the spirit of an ocean liner as the Asylum of the Salvation Army. In addition to the plan, profile, and interior, the whole operation of the building recalls life on a great ship—though steerage to be sure. For example, single men and women are placed in large dormitories, while mothers with children live in small cabin-like cells. There are nursery rooms for children and play rooms for adults. There is even an open "deck," or roof garden, for those who wish to catch some fresh air without leaving the building.

The Asylum of the Salvation Army is a transient habitat for the homeless, rootless, and lonely. As a ship, it carries men from one point of their life to another, while providing them with a life that is both collective and carefree. It is a life in which individual will and collective will are reconciled with the binding force of a non-political institution, whose power is based not so much on the collective will of the inhabitants as on their collective needs, that is, on the safest social cement in existence.

There are two buildings which represent the culmination of Le Corbusier's patient and weary search in the area of communal living: The Unité d'Habitation in Marseilles and the Monastery of La Tourette. The main sources of the Marseilles Block are the writings of Fourier, while those of La Tourette are in the Monastery of Ema.

The Unité d'Habitation [Fig. 22] was commissioned by Raoul Dautry, Minister of Reconstruction, during the concluding months of World War II. Le Corbusier's first design, comprising three separate buildings, was intended for a site called La Madraque, near the port of Marseilles. In 1946, however, Le Corbusier was asked to make a second plan for a site chosen by himself in the well-to-do neighborhood of the city on the Boulevard Michelet. Another year elapsed before the cornerstone was laid on October 14, 1947, and it was not until January, 1948, that construction was actually started on the building. Between its inception in the spring of 1945 and its official opening on October 14, 1952, Le Corbusier's client—the French Government—changed ten times, with seven different ministers of reconstruction. But fortunately for the architect, they all supported his expensive dream of an ideal community, whose cost amounted to about two billion French francs.

Looming high above the ground, this seventeen-story structure provides space for 1600 inhabitants (only 200 less than Fourier's *Phalanstère*); it contains 360 apartments of 23 types, and is equipped with 26 different kinds of communal facilities, ranging from shops on the seventh floor to a gymnasium on the roof garden. The Marseilles Block is built of rough concrete (*béton brut*) whose texture is enlivened by imprints of the wooden molds left on its surface. This visual activity is further heightened by the strong colors (although faded to some extent by now) such as red, yellow, blue, brown, and green. Finally, the liveliness of the texture and the colors of the walls are brought into focus by the overall plasticity of the building. The massive *pilotis*, thirty feet in height, the bold cantilevering, the *brise-soleil*, the jagged outline of the roof garden, all create a striking visual effect.

The interior, on the other hand, if judged on the basis of a self-sufficient "vertical garden-city"—to use Le Corbusier's own term—providing living, shopping, and recreational facilities for human beings of all ages and for families of varying sizes, that is, if judged on the basis of the multiple functions the building should fulfill, can be considered, to a large measure a failure.[37] Except for the studio-living room of the Maison Citrohan type, all other rooms in the apartments are far too narrow, offering little privacy to their occupants. Moreover, the master bedroom, overlooking the living room, collects all the noise and bad odors emanating from below. Finally, the shopping center on the seventh floor is a ghost town, and the children prefer to play in the neighboring park rather than on the roof garden.

---

[37] For a devastating criticism of the building, see Lewis Mumford, "The Marseilles Folly," in his *Highway and the City* (New York: Harcourt, Brace & World, Inc., 1963), pp. 53–66.

Why, then, did Le Corbusier design the building in such a way; could he not have foreseen at least some of these more obvious defects? The fact that he failed to avoid these mistakes and that he continued to build *unités* in practically the same manner long after the completion of the Marseilles Block reveals something about the nature of the collective order he had envisaged there. It seems to me that, ideally at least, each apartment of the Marseilles Block is designed for a single human being, living completely alone, while sharing the advantages of a larger collective order. Each apartment, then, must be understood as a bachelor's quarter and the whole building as a bachelor's hostel, with communal facilities available to the inhabitants at all times. Used by families of various sizes, the building is, at least to a large measure, a failure, but if it were used only by single men and women it would be a success. Le Corbusier even advises the inhabitant of the Unité to "go in by a single door; take one of the four lifts (twenty people to each) which serve the eight, superimposed internal streets." But here comes the sudden shift from a collective world to a completely private world. "You will then be alone," he continues, "you will meet no one, you will be in peace, sunlight and space, and the green world outside will stream in through your windows." [38] To express this sense of isolation structurally, Le Corbusier treated each apartment as an independent unit, or, to be more precise, as a single house. Each apartment, for example, is imbedded in a reinforced concrete frame—a rack, as it were—so that none touches its neighbor. Moreover, lead padding is placed between each apartment to insure complete soundproofing. Finally, most apartments have two open views, one facing the mountains, the other the sea.

Exactly fifty years after Le Corbusier visited the Carthusian Monastery of Ema in 1907, work was begun on his most perfect communal building: The Dominican Monastery of Sainte-Marie de La Tourette at Eveaux-sur-Arbresle, near Lyons. Through the intercession of the famous friend of modern art, Father Coutourier, the Dominicans of Lyons entrusted Le Corbusier in 1953 to build them a new monastery. It took more than three years for the architect to prepare all the plans for this ideal community. But with its completion in 1960 a building that is not only perfect visually but also functionally was brought into existence [Fig. 26].

Little can be added to the superb photographs of Bernhard Moosbrugger and the sound description of the visual and structural qualities of the monastery by Colin Rowe, except that within the walls of this ideal community individuality and collectivity are perfectly reconciled. [39] It is a community comprised of single men, whose voluntary vow binds them to adhere to the beliefs, laws, and traditions of the Order. It is a community

[38] Le Corbusier, *Oeuvre complète 1946–1952* (Zurich: Les Editions Girsberger, 1960), p. 95.

[39] Anton Henze and Bernhard Moosbrugger, *La Tourette: Le Corbusier's erster Klosterbau* (Starnberg: Josef Keller Verlag, 1963); Colin Rowe, "Dominican Monastery of La Tourette," *Architectural Review*, 129 (1961), 400–410.

whose aim is individual salvation through collective means. It is a way station, to be sure, but one in which a positive affirmation is made in favor of the rich possibilities and choices a transient existence can offer to man. To what extent the spirit of active existence permeates the entire structure is best revealed in its relationship to the setting, in the treatment and use of its materials, and finally in the powerful contrasts of its composition. In short, it is an eloquent visual and spiritual symbol that has taken the architect half a century to create. What was only a dream in 1907 has now become a reality.

From the long road which leads from the Immeubles Villas to the Unité d'Habitation of Marseilles two seemingly contradictory themes emerge: consistency and change. If there is change in the visual appearance of the buildings there is also consistency in their architectural content. While the early project is characterized by brittleness, thinness, and lack of permanence, the latter work is exemplified by forcefulness, plasticity, and permanence. Yet both the Immeubles Villas and the Unité of Marseilles express a communal order consisting, ideally at least, of single individuals, each symbolized by a Maison Citrohan, whose multiplication makes up both buildings. They are both based on Fourier's *Phalanstère*, stressing the need for reconciling such polarities as private and public and unity and diversity. In La Tourette, on the other hand, the ideals realized in the Monastery of Ema—"individuality and collectivity comprehended as a fundamental dualism," to use Le Corbusier's own words—are given a fresh meaning.

PART SEVEN / The City

A TOWN is a tool.
Towns no longer fulfil this function. They are ineffectual; they use up our bodies,
they thwart our souls. . . .
A town is a mighty image which stirs our minds. Why should not the town be,
even to-day, a source of poetry?

LE CORBUSIER°

A PLAN FOR
A CONTEMPORARY CITY (1922)

Waldemar George

Le Corbusier exhibited a diorama of his Contemporary City at the Salon d'Automne [Fig. 7]. The young architect's project was keenly discussed in the newspapers. Most of the critics reproached him for devising fanciful schemes which are out of touch with reality, and for building cities of the future on paper as if existing ones could be erased with a stroke. One cannot deny the validity of these objections. But Le Corbusier starts by sketching the general outlines of a project and then considers its eventual application to existing conditions. He has not only conceived the plan for a large city of three million inhabitants, but has also worked it out. He has confronted all the problems related to city planning. Instead of criticizing his project from the start, it would be well to set forth the principles upon which the construction of this model city is based. The project is perhaps open to criticism; nevertheless, it deserves close examination.

This is a *contemporary city* of three million inhabitants, not a "city of the future." It is the path leading to the solution of a distressing and threatening problem, that of the *Large City*. The *Large City* is a recent development, from its very beginning an enormous phenomenon which is already playing havoc with the functioning of existing cities. What will

---

"A Plan for a Contemporary City" by Waldemar George. From *L'Amour de l'Art*, 3 (December 1922), pp. 395–98. Copyright Société des Publications Périodiques de l'I.P.D., Paris. Reprinted by permission of the publisher.

° Le Corbusier, *The City of Tomorrow* (London: John Rodker Publisher, 1929), p. xxi.

the situation be in fifty years, twenty years or in ten years? In 1800 Paris, London, Berlin, and New York had populations of 650, 800, 180, and 60 thousand inhabitants respectively; in 1910 they had 3, 7, 3½, and 4½ million! Cities are overcrowded; the inhabitants are packed into houses and crushed in the streets; cars are a menace to pedestrians. Dwellings are infested; one can no longer breathe in a city which has become a stone pit and which is devoid of greenery. Public hygiene is nonexistent; cities live on leftovers from the 18th and even 13th centuries. It is a life fraught with unsanitary conditions, overcrowding, nervous tension, and the impending illness of the masses.

Public officials are debating whether to allow cornices at fifteen or twenty meters above the street, instead of striving to give the city a larger scale in keeping with the vast transformations of economic life. In progressive circles people are belatedly enthusiastic about an obsolete, inconsequential form of city planning practiced in England and Germany; while congested cities are dying we dream of the picturesque, charming streets of old villages—memories from the past! Meanwhile, the ever practical Americans have fashioned a new tool of considerable importance: the skyscraper. They have also made full use of a system possessing enduring value because it is essentially human, *the straight line*—rectangular blocks with streets running parallel to one another. The Old World has for some time been thinking of skyscrapers, but proposing to build them on the outskirts of cities. The skyscraper relieves congestion; they want to relieve congestion where there is no congestion—a fundamental error that has no justification. The confusion of ideas has reached a critical stage; city planning has hardly been born, and it already has the task of resolving one of the most formidable problems of our time. The Cornudet law establishes for the first time in twenty centuries of human history the obligation of every city to have an expansion plan for the future. Where are the technicians who could solve such problems, and where would they have been trained? Today's limited form of city planning is without scope, without goals; it is romantic, and it dreams of picturesque scenes fit for operettas.

At the Salon d'Automne we are presented with a unified solution to the problem of the large city based on the technical analysis of the development and living conditions which characterize the great urban districts. Le Corbusier's conclusions do not herald the coming of the perfect city of tomorrow. For him, there are the underlying primordial and organic causes, there is the course of evolution, there are the techniques which are at our disposal today, and there are the practical and architectural results. The city that Le Corbusier presented *is a result*. The analytical study which led him to his conclusions was presented to the Salon visitors in diagrams, which when deciphered provided an understanding of the logical arrangement of his plan.

Beside the large diorama at the center of the pavilion and the drawings covering a section of the walls, Le Corbusier also exhibited studies of a large villa-apartment [Fig. 8] and a model for a small house intended for mass production [Fig. 6]. He wanted to emphasize thereby that in order to plan an entire city according to revolutionary principles one has to examine the cell—the dwelling, in this case. Le Corbusier devoted himself to the study of the dwelling and to its actual component elements. This was in keeping with new ways of household management resulting from profound changes in contemporary life and particularly from new living habits which have already appeared or are doubtlessly about to appear. The dwelling has to undergo the modifications permitted by progress and required by the new living conditions of our day. . . .

Le Corbusier's city is a large metropolis of three million inhabitants. The principles which govern its layout are unequivocally opposed to current customs and habits of thinking which lead to overcrowded cities. The desired goals are to assure a fast, easy and noiseless traffic flow, to guarantee hygiene and well-being, to facilitate family life, and to insure at last the wholesome and unencumbered growth of the city by taking long-term measures.

The placement of the roadways in an even gridiron pattern of 400 meters does not lead to monotony. On the contrary, due to the distribution of the cruciform-shaped skyscrapers and the apartments with setbacks or with rectangular courtyards, we find that an extraordinary diversity reigns in all parts of the city, a diversity of monumental proportions, which, when combined with standardized methods of building construction, leads to the kind of poetic composition which constitutes the grandure of famous cities. By way of example, let us mention that between two skyscrapers stretch parks as large as the Tuileries, and that around the apartments with setbacks there are parks of 400 by 600 meters . . . providing amenities that no city could have hoped for in the past.

Another conclusion one can draw from Le Corbusier's study is that his city is more moderate in size than the foregoing description would indicate, smaller even than cities of comparable populations, such as Paris, which has an area of eighty square kilometers for every 2,700,000 people; the center of Le Corbusier's city has an area of twenty-three square kilometers for every million inhabitants. It is of utmost importance to keep the city's center limited in size in order to render all the advantages offered by large urban districts directly accessible to its inhabitants.

The problem of transportation is the touchstone of a large city. At this time all large cities are undergoing a perilous crisis for their very survival. The network of major railroads does not come into the heart of the city; nor do the suburban lines. The subways, buses and trolleys make up for this inadequacy to some extent, but at the same time they crowd the streets and make them dangerous. What will happen to the cars that factories cast on the streets by the thousands? Even today they can no longer move in some sections of the city at certain hours. The flood of cars and pedestrians going to work and to the various points of transportation pushes headlong into the incredibly crowded intersections. The use of all these disconnected systems of transportation is a burden on the city and on the public.

Le Corbusier planned only one station consisting of three subterranean levels, a ground level and two upper platforms. On the third sub-level are the four contiguous terminals of the major railroads: east, west, north and south. On the second sub-level are the suburban lines which form loops and serve various regions of the city's outer belt. . . . The north, south, east and west subway lines are on the first sub-level. On the immense ground level we find the vast, systematically organized corridors and passageways leading to all the networks. The first platform consists of the great elevated highway for fast-moving cars; forty meters wide, it is a veritable race track cutting through the entire city without intersections and allowing cars to travel at whirlwind speeds; at times ramps connect the great highway with the rest of the city. This highway absorbs all dangerous traffic and enables cars to move at a velocity totally unknown until now. Finally on the second platform the airport with an area of 20,000 square meters connects, by means of elevators, airplanes to the major railroads and all other systems of transportation. Surrounding this terminal, which is as clear and simple as a well-designed machine, the city offers its vast open spaces constituting 95% of the total area. Thus the movement of passengers and cars is an easy process.

Around the city the green belt, consisting of a vast municipal property, allows further development consistent with the requirements of the plan, eliminating the crushing and immobilizing financial burdens of expropriation. Many cities abroad have regained the land adjoining their boundaries through such means. . . .

This is Le Corbusier's project. We submit it to our readers, who will no doubt be able to appreciate it to the fullest.

LE CORBUSIER AND THE
"PACK-DONKEY'S WAY" (1929)

Cornelius Gurlitt

In 1925 Le Corbusier's work on city planning, *Urbanisme,* appeared in Paris. It was also published in Germany, as was his book on new architecture, *Vers une Architecture.* . . .

Le Corbusier distinguishes between two kinds of cities: those which are based on "the pack-donkey's way" . . . and those which are laid out in a geometric pattern. In his view the rational man goes straight to his goal, whereas the dull-witted donkey does not think, does not exert himself, avoids big stones, and seeks an easy way of climbing hills. According to Le Corbusier the automobile is the expression of rational, technological man, for which he demands level terrain and straight roads. The winding road belongs to the trudging donkey and must disappear from the technologically advanced city!

It would seem to me therefore that technology has wasted its efforts in making a car, where a light motion of the hand on the steering wheel enables one to avoid big stones, a grasp of the gearshift helps to overcome a steep ascent and another prevents a plunge down a precipitous slope. In any event, it is not easier to drive on an absolutely straight road than on a slightly curving one; the driver must always remain alert at the wheel. . . . After all, he is not the only one on the road, but must give way to other cars or pass them—and hence also follow the "pack-donkey's way."

I agree with Le Corbusier that a straight line is the shortest distance between two points. I do not agree that the city street must therefore be straight. For three quarters of a century we have had roads completely based on technology—the railroad lines. They connect two points—the railroad stations of two cities. Some of these lines are straight, where conditions have not prompted the builder to consider a detour more advantageous . . . but some adjust to uneven terrain. . . . The builder chooses between the alternatives of making a tunnel or creating a gentle

"Le Corbusier and the 'Pack-Donkey's Way'" by Cornelius Gurlitt. From *Stadtbaukunst,* IX (January 1929), pp. 198–200.

grade by lengthening the line and building what Le Corbusier calls the "pack-donkey's way." Hence it is the technologist who can accuse Le Corbusier of following the ass's route, for he has not learned to think technologically. . . .

Le Corbusier's plan for the Paris of the future [the Plan Voisin] gives us a good idea of what he is striving for. The center of the city would be torn down and the ground laid bare for new development. Here skyscrapers would be built at great intervals with adjoining residential sections subdivided according to the plan of Washington, D.C. This plan is not Le Corbusier's own invention but was developed at the end of the 18th century. It consists of streets which intersect at right angles and of others which divide the city at forty-five degree angles. This scheme has been praised by modern technologically-oriented city planners in America, but it is no longer popular. At the intersections of four streets star patterns develop, causing serious traffic problems and resulting in corner lots which are unsuitable for building. German city planning, on the other hand, takes into account the need to set aside suitable spaces for public buildings such as churches, schools, theaters, movie houses, stores, post offices, court houses and the like, to be used by the surrounding residents —if for no other reason than to relieve the city of that very monotony which Le Corbusier seems to love and which he hails as the architecture of the future.

The residential houses in his Paris of the future are strictly standardized and lined up in rows like honeycombs, to use Le Corbusier's own frequent expression. I shall not describe the shape of the houses. Their external form is dictated by his ultimate authority, geometry. They dispense with sloping roofs but have peculiar open terraces [Fig. 8]. . . . I shall not consider whether these terraces are suitable for Paris. They certainly would not suit German weather conditions. People there would soon want to convert them into enclosed rooms by adding walls. But to do justice to Le Corbusier, I assume that he intends to banish an uncooperative climate. Technology must overcome it and introduce climate control!

But this is not the only thing which prejudices me against his plan. It is the despotism, no matter how benevolent, which would squeeze the former residents into a single type of housing. Equality is supposed to prevail, meals are to be prepared in communal kitchens and housekeeping governed by common rules. If his plan is officially approved, any alteration of streets and residences would be forbidden by the building inspectors. Those who come after Le Corbusier must simply cease wanting to be modern. They must forego any future innovations. The government shall forbid these, for Le Corbusier demands a law which would enforce the unopposed realization of his plans. The homeowner shall not even have the right to make changes in his own house. I am reminded of the words: "*Property is theft.*" Thus presumably no one should become a property owner; instead the authorities should oversee the upkeep of the buildings.

But as living conditions in the cities change, laws become obsolete. "Reason becomes nonsense, benevolence a plague!" says Goethe. In order to eradicate plagues Le Corbusier proposes not medicine but surgery. Instead of healing the wounds, he would apply the knife to the suffering part of the body. He considers this justified for carrying out his plan, since it is based on "technological analysis and architectonic synthesis." It is "right" and therefore immutable. Whatever thwarts it must be treated with surgery.

The execution of his plan has of course a powerful antagonist—nature. The task of modern technological man is to overcome it. Hence nature must not influence the plan. The terrain of the city must be level. Le Corbusier is little concerned with the unhappy fact that cities have sprung up in mountainous areas also. How the machinations of nature are judged by Le Corbusier can best be seen in his telling image of rivers serving as railroads and freight depots on the water. As the servants' staircase does not lead through the drawing room in a fine house, so the river does not belong in the city. He considers it a servant of the city. Accordingly, London, Paris, Prague, Budapest, Dresden and many other cities seem to him to be botched up by rivers, which break the ground rules of his rectilinear city plan. The railroad station, on the other hand, belongs in the center of the city. Geometry is, after all, Le Corbusier's chief mentor; it must govern art, and the city must be a pure interplay of geometric lines. Yet whose fault is it that the rivers flow through cities in curves—as "paths for donkeys?" The cathedrals and monuments in the center of cities likewise interfere with the rectilinear network of streets. So away with the "venerable carcass!" (*charogne!*) It took centuries before these words of wisdom could be expressed. I fear, however, that Le Corbusier's own plans will sooner fall victim to this dictum—without ever becoming "venerable."

Reading the book was sheer agony. He tries throughout to be witty, to offer us grand images, and to draw conclusions from these by his power of "intuition." But as premises for his conclusions, the images are distorted. One is tempted, in fact challenged, to refute them. I had similar reactions when I read Le Corbusier's financial plan, which was intended to prove the feasibility of his scheme for Paris, the expropriation of the land, the building of skyscrapers and streets, etc. It would cost millions, in fact billions. Those who profited from the venture would have to bear the cost at first. But that might not be easy to accomplish, even if the French government gave Le Corbusier the same mandate which enabled Haussmann to create the Paris of Napoleon III. Here too Le Corbusier finds a solution reminiscent of Columbus' trick with the egg: the center of Paris must be internationalized and the proposed construction done by Americans, English, Japanese and Germans at their own expense. Moreover, it would thereby be protected from barbaric destruction. for the Americans would not permit, and the Germans would beware of, bombing their own property. . . . In exchange France could take the buildings in the large German cities under her protection, since she would erect them at her own expense. Would it not be even wiser to attach portions of a country's army to those of neighboring ones, so that each nation would be afraid of killing its own citizens in a war?

As I read this plan, the thought occurred to me that perhaps it was meant to be ironic. Irony is a witty denial of that which is expressed, without, however, being an affirmation of the opposite. Whenever I came upon facts in the book—of which there are not many—I wondered whether the author was really serious or whether an extremely clever counter-meaning was not to be detected between the lines. Schiller has Wallenstein say:

> If the idea were not so damnably clever,
> One would be tempted to call it downright stupid.

Unfortunately I cannot bring myself to consider the ideas in the book as "damnably clever." After all, I myself stroll along the very street which Le Corbusier calls with kindly condescension the "pack-donkey's way." Therefore he relieves me—polite man that I am—from the temptation of applying Wallenstein's words to his book on city planning. Yet I ask myself whether it was the city planning of the past which followed the ass's way, or this enthusiastic post-industrial apostle of technology.

FROM THE
"CITY FOR 3 MILLION INHABITANTS"
TO THE "PLAN VOISIN" (1968)

Stanislaus von Moos

No matter how objective and scholarly a discussion of Le Corbusier's urbanism might attempt to be, it will necessarily be colored by mixed feelings of admiration and disillusionment. To have been a pioneer and a precursor of modern town planning is no longer an indisputable guarantee of glory. The worldwide impact of the Ville Contemporaine [Fig. 7] and the Plan Voisin upon the thinking of several generations of planners is as obvious as it is embarrassing to the historian: he has to live with the fact that contemporary urbanism has caught up with and indeed partly compromised the dreams of the 1920s. What was then an Olympian vision of a "New World" has become in the fifties and sixties an easy and often fatal policy of urban reform.

However, to lay the shortcomings and failures of recent urban renewal and other large-scale developments at Le Corbusier's doorstep is unfair.[1] It is too simple to judge an idea by the consequences it may have had. To use him as a scapegoat for current urban diseases is to avoid recognizing the real dynamics that shape the urban environment: socioeconomic forces, institutional patterns and ideology. At an early date, Le Corbusier created an imagery for these forces—but he has not brought them to life.

He may be blamed for having accepted these forces as guidelines of action, and for having elevated them to the level of universal and

"From the 'City for 3 Million Inhabitants' to the 'Plan Voisin.'" From Stanislaus von Moos, *Le Corbusier: Elemente einer Synthese* (Frauenfeld and Stuttgart: Verlag Huber & Co., AG., 1968), pp. 179–204. Reprinted by permission of the author and publisher.

[1] For a good presentation and discussion of the principal English and American criticisms of Le Corbusier's urban theory, see Norma Evenson, "Le Corbusier's Critics," in her *Le Corbusier: The Machine and the Grand Design* (New York: George Braziller, 1969), pp. 120–22. The following chapter is based on the revised and enlarged version of my monograph *Le Corbusier—Elemente einer Synthese* (Frauenfeld and Stuttgart: Verlag Huber, 1968), which will be published by MIT Press in 1975. Quotations from Le Corbusier are taken from the original French editions of his works and translated by the author.

natural laws—as indeed he has. At the same time it has to be recognized that the power of creative thought is a matter which lies beyond moral judgment. The act of giving intellectual structure and visual form to facts which would otherwise have remained hidden in the complexity of social and cultural life demands respect, even if this intellectual structure and plastic imagery do not embrace the totality of the problems involved, and even if we cannot concur with the implicit choice of moral, social and political priorities which underlie Le Corbusier's early radical proposals for urban reform.

Thus, two things must be undertaken. First, we have to retrace the outstanding features of that epic and utopian dream of the Radiant City by identifying some stages of its evolution and some of its historic roots. Secondly, we must ask the question what does this dream mean in broader cultural and ideological terms, and which fundamental ideas are expressed and thus consciously or subconsciously propagated through this urbanistic theory and art?

The mechanics of urban life had been one of Charles-Edouard Jeanneret's major concerns since 1910.[2] But again, as in the area of architecture, the leap from study and speculation to creative invention occurred only after 1920. In 1922 Le Corbusier was invited to submit an urbanistic project to the *Salon d'Automne* of that same year. Asked by the architect what he meant by "urbanism," Marcel Temporal, the organizer of the exhibit, explained that he was interested in benches, kiosks, street lamps, signposts and billboards. "Look, why don't you design a fountain for me?" Le Corbusier accepted: "All right, I will make a fountain, but behind it, I will place a city for three million inhabitants."[3]

The project was entitled Ville Contemporaine. It was not to be understood as a utopian project for a distant future, but as the model of a contemporary city: "This is what confers boldness to our dreams: they can be realized."[4] Nevertheless, the Ville Contemporaine was visionary in its outlook and permeated with the idea that in order to change present conditions one must have a clear goal. Obviously this goal could not be attained in a day. Yet Le Corbusier insisted that at least from a technical point of view the project was immediately workable.

He started from scratch, as he had done earlier for the Citrohan house [Fig. 6]. He created a model situation which was to be universally adaptable. "The goal is not to overcome the preexisting state of things but to arrive, through a rigorous theoretical structure, at the formulation of fundamental principles of modern urbanism."[5]

The plans were exhibited at the 1922 *Salon d'Automne* without any

[2] A paper on the town planning of La Chaux-de-Fonds, which was written by Le Corbusier in Munich in 1910, seems to be lost. See Jean Petit, *Le Corbusier lui-même* (Geneva: Rousseau Editeur, 1970), p. 38.
[3] Le Corbusier, *Oeuvre complète 1910–1929*, 6th ed. (Zurich: Les Editions Girsberger, 1956), p. 34.
[4] Le Corbusier, *Urbanisme* (Paris: Les Editions G. Crès et Cie., 1925), p. 135.
[5] *Ibid.*, p. 158.

commentary. As one would expect, they aroused as much indignation as enthusiasm. Much of the discussions that took place during and after the exhibition is summarized in the book *Urbanisme* published in 1925. But there is more: unlike *Vers une Architecture,* which is a journalistic collage of rhetorical assertions, *Urbanisme* offers a thorough documentation and discussion of the facts upon which Le Corbusier's theory is based.[6]

He opens his line of reasoning with general aesthetic and moral postulates borrowed from history. But from the very first pages his remarks reflect that explosive mixture of love and animosity, of enthusiasm and revolt, which characterized his relationship with Paris, its history, and its current dramatic situation. In order to give his theses the strength of imperative postulates, he cites statistics of the demographic explosion and of the problems of transportation in the Parisian region. To this documentation he adds newspaper excerpts testifying to the state of human and social misery in the capital at a time when postwar parades were marching through the great avenues.[7] It was the Paris of dust and of air pollution, the Paris of tuberculosis and of slums, and also the Paris of stagnant customs and of petit-bourgeois conventions which provided the background for his categoric proposals of urban reform.

It is true that the Ville Contemporaine of 1922 was conceived as an abstract model of urban reform and not as a remedy for the specific problems of Paris. Nevertheless, it is as directly dependent upon the situation of Paris as Tony Garnier's Cité Industrielle (1903) was based upon that of Lyon or as Sant'Elia's Città Nuova (1914) was inspired by Milan and its railroad station. Despite its absolute and general character, the Ville Contemporaine is partly to be understood as a response to the immediate situation of Paris after the war and it has its roots in a number of earlier, but not quite as radical proposals for the urbanistic reorganization of the French capital.

The functional program of the Ville responds to the immediate needs of postwar Paris for large-scale housing, office buildings and a new traffic pattern. These needs were more urgent now than ever, but they were not new. Early in the century they had generated a number of projects which, however, were never realized. Most important among these were Eugène Hénard's proposals, entitled *Etudes sur les transformations de Paris,* published in eight fascicules between 1903 and 1906.[8] Hénard (1849–1923), a professor at the Ecole des Beaux-Arts in Paris, had worked since 1882 for the Travaux de Paris, the office in charge

---

6 Cf. Maximilien Gauthier, *Le Corbusier ou l'architecture au service de l'homme* (Paris: Editions Denoël, 1944), pp. 86–107, and Reyner Banham, *Theory and Design in the First Machine Age* (London: The Architectural Press, 1960), pp. 248–56.
7 *Urbanisme,* pp. 97–133.
8 The importance of Hénard as a source for Le Corbusier's urbanistic concepts has been correctly emphasized by Peter Serenyi in his review of the original edition of my monograph on Le Corbusier. See *Journal of the Society of Architectural Historians,* XXX (1971), 255–59. For Hénard see Peter M. Wolf, *Eugène Hénard and the Beginnings of Urbanism in Paris, 1900–1914* (Paris: Centre de Recherche d'Urbanisme, 1968), with complete bibliography.

of municipal architecture. Due to his experience as a municipal architect and to his involvement in the planning of the Paris world fairs of 1889 and 1900, he was the outstanding technical expert in the field of town planning at that time. As the Ville Contemporaine and the Plan Voisin of 1925 demonstrate, Le Corbusier was more than aware of Hénard's work, although of course he was far from Hénard's taste and stylistic outlook. While the need for large open spaces and efficient transportation was clearly anticipated by Hénard, he had embedded these postulates in the fantastic retrospective imagery of Parisian *fin-de-siècle* architecture. On the other hand, Le Corbusier stated the problem of Paris not only in terms of new social requirements and new transportation techniques; he aimed at an urban form consistent with the "spirit of the age."

Next to the grandiose scheme of the Ville Contemporaine Le Corbusier exhibited in 1922 a small sketch proposing an adaptation of the plan to the specific situation of Paris.[9] In 1925, the reorganization of Paris became the great issue. In a sidewing of the *Pavillon de l'Esprit Nouveau* at the *Art-Déco* exhibition[10] he displayed a large diorama of the Ville Contemporaine facing another, similar diorama of what he called the Plan Voisin of Paris. This Plan Voisin brings the "Ville" back to where it originated: to the city of Paris, *oeil de l'Europe*.

The name, Plan Voisin, points to one of the essential features of the project: the fact that it is based upon a new traffic pattern. In the solemn conviction that the present crisis of the French capital, as well as its need for future transformation, were a direct consequence of motorized traffic, Le Corbusier had sought financial support for the *Pavillon de l'Esprit Nouveau*, and the town planning project displayed there, from various automobile firms: Peugeot, Citroën and Voisin. It was Gabriel Voisin who promptly granted him patronage for the project and lent his name to it.

The project is radical indeed. To render Paris habitable, Le Corbusier recommends massive surgery and sets as a preliminary condition of any renewal the total "tabula rasa" between the Seine and Montmartre. Only a few isolated buildings—the Louvre, the Palais Royal and the Place Vendôme (of which he was particularly fond), the Place de la Concorde, the arc de Triomphe, plus a few selected churches and town houses—would be spared. The architect declares that in this way "the historical past, a universal patrimony, is respected. More than that, it is saved." [11] Yet he adds, more modestly: "The Plan Voisin does not claim to provide

[9] *Urbanisme*, p. 265.

[10] For a general discussion of the *Esprit Nouveau* Pavilion in the context of this exhibition, see von Moos, *Le Corbusier*, pp. 96–99.

[11] *Urbanisme*, p. 272. Le Corbusier proposes here that the important monuments of the past should be treated as *objets trouvés*, or—to quote his own term—as *objets à réaction poétique* within the vast open spaces of the new, green city. A similarly selective and "ironical" approach to the urban past has been suggested by Frank Lloyd Wright in *An Organic Architecture. The Architecture of Democracy* (London: Lund, Humphries & Co., Ltd., 1939). The cultural and ideological implications of this approach have been discussed by Manfredo Tafuri, *Teorie e storia dell'architettura*, 2nd ed. (Bari: Editori Laterza, 1970), pp. 68ff.

a complete solution to the problems facing the center of Paris." [12] Its prime intention obviously was to move the urbanistic discussion from the level of small and uncoordinated renovations to a level in keeping with the times,[13] where housing, business accommodation and traffic are aspects of one great problem: urbanism. Nobody regrets that this monstrous, Promethean project was never executed. But everybody will admit that it exerted, decades later, a lasting influence upon large-scale planning throughout the world, and thus a brief survey of its dominant characteristics is appropriate.

THE TOWERS

In 1921, Le Corbusier had already published his first ideas of a tower city in *l'Esprit Nouveau*.[14] Laid out along a cross-shaped plan, the towers were to reach a height of sixty stories (that is to say about 825 feet), and to be placed at a distance of 800 feet from each other. He comments that the idea had been suggested to him by Auguste Perret, but when Perret's first drawings were published in August 1922, the difference between the two concepts turned out to be striking.[15] In terms of style, Perret's towers are conventional skyscrapers, differing from those of New York or Chicago only in that they are visually separated and standing free in open space like posts alongside the road. While this urbanistic setting corresponds to Le Corbusier's concept, the style must have appeared obsolete to him, and he condemned Perret's project altogether,[16] including the only really progressive aspect of the proposal, namely the elevated bridges connecting the towers.

It is clear that in Le Corbusier's view, Perret's solution was not "pure." In order to be "pure," the skyscraper needed a cruciform plan, straightforward cubic elevations and fully glazed surfaces. And to provide good lighting of the interiors, these surfaces were to be *à redents*, i.e., organized in terms of bays and recesses which enabled maximum sight and lighting. Neither the cruciform shape nor the bays were Corbusier's invention—he may have been aware of Sullivan's cruciform skyscraper projects and the frequent use of bays in Chicago around 1890 [17] —but the rigid elementary geometry of this type *was* new, and it was

12 *Urbanisme*, p. 273.
13 *Ibid.*
14 *L'Esprit Nouveau*, 4 (January, 1921), pp. 465ff.
15 Cf. Jean Labadié, "Les cathédrales de la cité moderne," *L'Illustration*, August, 1922, pp. 131–35.
16 Le Corbusier, *Vers une Architecture* (Paris: Les Editions G. Crès et Cie., 1923), p. 44. . . . For Perret's towers of 1922 and 1925 (the latter based on Le Corbusier's cruciform skyscrapers) see Le Corbusier, *Almanach d'architecture moderne* (Paris: Les Editions G. Crès et Cie., 1926), p. 187.
17 Cf. *Urbanisme* and *L'art décoratif d'aujourd'hui* (Paris: Les Editions G. Crès et Cie., 1925), where Le Corbusier published several photographs of early American skyscrapers—none however by Sullivan.

closer to the aesthetics of machines or grainsilos than to anything which had been proposed in the field of architecture before 1920.

Thus, the cruciform skyscraper (for offices) and high-density apart-ment-blocks (for dwellings) appeared the only possible rational solution to the overwhelming evidence of facts. These facts were not new. Over-crowding, social chaos and traffic congestion had been the characteristic diseases of large cities since the beginning of industrialization. But while the traditional remedy of planners ever since Ebenezer Howard had been decentralization and spread,[18] Le Corbusier proposed concentration and increased densities. He shared with the Garden City Movement the pro-found belief in the necessity of greenery and open space for the well-being of urban man. But Paris had imbued him with an equally strong belief in urban density as the premise of cultural progress, and he thus rejected the reformist trends toward limitless expansion and multiplica-tion of individual homes. Le Corbusier argued that even if the highly concentrated metropolis no longer works, it should not simply be dis-solved, as advocated with such success by the exponents of the Garden City Movement or by Frank Lloyd Wright in his Broadacre City. Indeed, Wright's city of the future has since become the American "sub-suburban present,"[19] and this was precisely what Le Corbusier wanted to avoid. If the modern metropolis does not work anymore, it should be brought back under architectural control and equipped with proper tools. It should remain a cultural and architectural "whole," clearly distinct from the rural surroundings.

Hence he pursued two goals, which seem to be mutually exclusive: to increase the density of the urban fabric, to reaffirm the supremacy of its business center, and yet at the same time to bring greenery and nature back to urban life. In his description of the Ville Contemporaine,[20] the two goals appear as aspects of one and the same postulate. On the one hand, after a quick sociological analysis of urban populations, Le Cor-busier aims for an increase of their density; on the other, he aims for a multiplication of green spaces.

NATURE AND SPACE

At the foot of the apartment houses and office towers in the Ville Contemporaine, there are vast open spaces. The sum total of the city's soil must be transformed into a vast recreation zone: 95 percent of the soil in the business district and 85 percent in the dwelling area were to be

---

[18] Ebenezer Howard, *The Garden Cities of Tomorrow* (London: S. Sonnenschein & Co., Ltd., 1902). For the influence of the English Garden City Movement on Le Corbusier's early work see Brian Brace Taylor, *Le Corbusier at Pessac* (Cambridge, Mass.: Carpenter Center for the Visual Arts, Harvard University, 1972), pp. 4–5.

[19] See Lewis Mumford, "Megapolis as Anti-City," *Architectural Record,* December, 1962, p. 101.

[20] *Urbanisme*, pp. 157–69.

turned into public parks.[21] Thus it was a matter of restoring without delay the "conditions of nature" in the city.

Why this obsession with parks and greenery? The answer lies partly in the context of Paris. In order to give one's proposals credibility in the eyes of the public, it is necessary to legitimize them in terms of widely shared ideals. Le Corbusier was very well aware of that. His insistence upon the necessity of large public parks is a direct response to the traditional rhetoric of progressive planners and politicians in Paris. To conceive of the city as one vast recreation zone meant not only to be socially minded, but also to be in keeping with the city's splendid past: it meant bringing the work of the French kings and emperors to its grandiose fulfillment. The Tuileries, the Jardins du Luxembourg, etc., time and again reproduced in Le Corbusier's books, are constantly called upon as points of reference for his plans.[22]

He spices his argumentation with more personal touches. Recalling his trip to the Orient he quotes a Turkish maxim: "Where one builds, one plants trees"—and he adds sarcastically: "We root them up." [23] Plants and greenery appear to him as the biological guarantee of sound urban living. Parks are the "lungs" of the city, its respiratory system. But he pushes his point further: the city itself becomes one great "lung." For him, respiration is not merely a physiological phenomenon; it is a process that involves all his sensitivity and imagination. More than his lungs, his eyes want to "breathe," as it were. He argues of course on biological grounds, but ultimately the overwhelming presence of plants and trees in his ideal city is a matter of cultural idealism rather than physical well-being. It is an aspect of his almost mystical belief in nature, deeply rooted in his mind ever since the early years in La Chaux-de-Fonds.

But while his early studies were characterized by a sympathy for the laws governing organic growth in plants, leaves, flowers, trees, he now developed a hunger for grandiose vistas and the sensation of limitless space. He may have had this sensation on the Jura heights; now, in Paris, it was the Eiffel tower which provided the inspiration:

> "When I ascend, I experience that feeling of serenity; the moment becomes joyful—solemn too. Step by step, as the horizon rises higher, it seems that the mind is projected into wider trajectories: when everything becomes physically broader, when one's lungs inhale more vehemently, when the eye takes in vast horizons, the spirit is animated with nimble vigor; optimism reigns." [24]

This love of panoramic views, this craving for vast horizons, became so compelling that Le Corbusier soon lost sight of the starting point of his belief: the reestablishment of natural conditions in the modern city.

[21] *Ibid.*, p. 165.
[22] *Ibid.*, pp. 192f. and *passim.*
[23] *Ibid.*, pp. 60 and 71.
[24] *Ibid.*, p. 176.

Indeed, eight hundred feet above ground, one no longer perceives the rustling of the leaves at the foot of the towers. Both the green vegetation and the grayish urban carapace grow faint; they are no more than a pleasant decorative carpet. Nature appears under the grandiose (although by no means vital) form of distant perspectives and infinite spaces. One may ask why the occupants of the business center must have parks at the foot of the skyscrapers, when the system of communication and transportation is perfected to the point where no one is likely to linger in the parks which cover 95 percent of the grounds in the center of the city, except perhaps for a quick picnic during the lunch hour when the weather is fair.

In the residential areas the large parks had a more plausible function. Here the height of the buildings reaches no more than six stories of duplex apartments; the contact with nature is thus maintained. The apartment houses are either planned around vast interior courtyards or arranged in a linear pattern of setbacks (*redents*). This latter form is, once again, directly based upon an idea by Hénard; even the name, *rue à redents,* is borrowed from him.[25] The sequence of projections and recessions along the streets had a double function: to insure a maximum of open view to each dwelling and to bring diversity and rhythm to the image of the city.

Compared with the business center these residential quarters have measure and scale. But thirty years later, when the great urban renewal projects in the U.S. were drawn up, architects had forgotten Le Corbusier's villa-blocks (Immeubles Villas [Fig. 8]) as well as the *Esprit Nouveau* Pavilion, only to return to his cruciform shaped office towers which now became the perverted model for social housing.

THE AXES AND THE MYTH
OF SPEED

With a grand possessive gesture, Le Corbusier's city is inscribed into the landscape. Its axes reach out toward the four corners of the horizon. The spirit of Versailles is reborn here; and so is Baron Haussmann's grandiose vision, partly realized in his reorganization of Paris at the time of Napoleon III.

For Le Corbusier the rigor of the axis constituted an essential principle, both moral and aesthetic. "Man walks in a straight line because he has a goal and knows where he is going." [26] The straight line is the line of man, the curved line that of the donkey. Le Corbusier rejected the romantic and picturesque idea of basing urban design on the random forms resulting from the growth of medieval cities; in his opinion this

[25] See Peter M. Wolf, *Eugène Hénard,* fig. 23. Hénard's term however is *boulevard à redans.* The first version of *rue à redents* has been published by Le Corbusier in *L'Esprit Nouveau,* p. 469, which was then reproduced in *Vers une Architecture.*
[26] *Urbanisme,* p. 3.

was the principal error of Camillo Sitte, "an intelligent and sensitive Viennese who simply stated the problem badly." [27]

In his eyes, the chessboard or gridiron plan was the only correct way of approaching the problem of city planning, and this point can indeed be substantiated by historic evidence. Thus we find in *Urbanisme* the layouts of a large number of orthogonal cities, from the thirteenth century *bastides* in the south of France, to the plans of American colonial cities of the sixteenth, seventeenth, and eighteenth centuries, including L'Enfant's plan of Washington, D.C.[28] One gridiron plan however does not appear among the documents published in *Urbanisme*, although it must have played a major role in the determination of Le Corbusier's urbanistic preferences: the plan of his native town of La Chaux-de-Fonds. The town had been heavily damaged by a fire in 1794, and it was then rebuilt according to a "plan américain" with a grand axis in the middle, the Avenue Léopold-Robert, where, incidentally young Charles-Edouard Jeanneret had spent a part of his youth.

Ultimately Le Corbusier's obsession with monumental axes was not based upon an abstract theoretical postulate, but upon an urban experience which had to be preserved. It comes as no surprise that the Baron Haussman was the subject of his admiration as well as of his constant criticism: in Le Corbusier's eyes, the great axial thoroughfares which Haussmann pierced in the Parisian maze from 1853 to 1868 were the answer to an imperative necessity, even though he did not sympathize with Napoleon III's utilization of the boulevards and avenues for parades and military displays.[29]

Time and again he uses Haussmann's approach to the renewal of Paris as the background for his own argumentation. In 1937, for instance, Le Corbusier pointed out that in Baron Haussmann's city, "tradition . . . required that all straight avenues should be climaxed by a set piece: the Opéra at the end of the avenue of the same name, the church of Saint-Augustin at the end of the boulevard Malesherbes." [30] Instead, Le Corbusier wanted traffic arteries that run through the entire city without interruptions, such as the Champs-Elysées, which terminates at the Place de la Concorde.[31] In short, for Le Corbusier, the straight axis was no longer a mere formal principle; it was justified only as a tool of modern

27 *Quand les cathédrales étaient blanches* (Paris: Gonthier, 1965), p. 58 (first edition 1937). However, as Maurice Besset has shown in *Qui était Le Corbusier?* (Geneva: Editions d'Art Albert Skira, 1968), p. 151, Le Corbusier's conception of the city as a picturesque sequence of grandiose vistas was deeply influenced by Sitte. This is well documented in almost all of his early urbanistic studies. His contempt for Sitte's theory may partly be the result of the total deformation it had undergone in the French version of *Der Städtebau*. Cf. George R. Collins and Christiane Crasemann Collins, *Camillo Sitte and the Birth of Modern City Planning* (London: Phaidon Press Ltd., 1965), pp. 63–72, 145.

28 *Urbanisme*, pp. 5–11, 77–86.

29 *Ibid.*, p. 255. For his later comments on Haussmann, see *La ville radieuse* (Boulgne-sur-Seine: Editions de L'Architecture d'Aujourd'hui, 1935), p. 209.

30 *Quand les cathédrales étaient blanches* (Paris: Gonthier, 1965), p. 59.

31 *Ibid.*, p. 60.

traffic. No wonder that, in 1936, he admired the ten-mile long avenues of Manhattan, symbols of an efficient traffic pattern determining the entire physiognomy of a metropolis.

In order to articulate the system of the axes in the Ville Contemporaine and in the Plan Voisin, Le Corbusier returned, however, to the most classical means. The main axis of the "Ville" is a superhighway laid out between two triumphal arches. A closer look at the obelisks, columns, monumental domes along the main traffic arteries as well as the general layout reveals a composition worthy of any Beaux-Arts student.

Once again, the ideals of the classical tradition are intermingled with those of the machine age. One has to consider here the quasi-magical character that Le Corbusier ascribed to speed. "The city that has speed has success," he claims.[32] This sounds like a futurist slogan; and indeed Sant'Elias' projects of about a decade earlier were based upon a similar worship of *velocità*. However, it seems doubtful whether the Città Nuova was an actual source for the Ville Contemporaine. Le Corbusier hardly ever refers to the Italians, but on the other hand he was familiar with the rhetoric of French automobile advertisements. In *Urbanisme,* he quotes an article by one of the directors of the Peugeot plant, Philippe Girardet, who saw in the automobile the vigorous and brilliant confirmation of an age-old dream of humanity. Girardet describes man as one of the slowest animals in creation: "a sort of caterpillar dragging himself with difficulty on the surface of the terrestrial crust. Most creatures move more quickly than this biped so ill-constructed for speed, and if we imagined a race among all the creatures of the globe, man would certainly be among the 'also rans' and would probably tie with the sheep." [33] It was, of course, motorized traffic that ultimately allowed him to triumph over this deplorable condition.

For Le Corbusier, speed and motorization are factors in the "lyricism of modern times," a lyricism which is too Olympian to be judged on utilitarian grounds. One of the sketches of the Ville Contemporaine shows how the urban superhighway connects the two triumphal gates; outside of the city, where a highway would be justified, the urban axis reverts into a simple country road.

DIFFERENTIATION OF TRAFFIC LINES: THE DEATH OF THE STREET

Again, the situation of Paris forms the background for Le Corbusier's redefinition of the urban street. The traditional complexity of its functions seems obsolete to him in the age of automobile traffic. The increase of urban density and the sudden advent of motorization have turned

[32] *Urbanisme,* p. 169.
[33] "Le règne de la vitesse," *Mercure de France* (1923), quoted in *Urbanisme,* p. 182.

the street into a scene of paralyzing chaos and constant danger. So far, the argument is convincing. But for Le Corbusier, the question is not so much to analyze the crisis of the traditional urban street as to justify its radical disappearance in the Ville Contemporaine. Thus the argumentation becomes resolutely polemic when, in an article published in *l'Intransigeant* of May, 1929, he shoots red bullets at that secular element of the city, the *rue corridor*: "It is the street of the pedestrian of a thousand years ago, it is a relic of the centuries; it is a nonfunctioning, an obsolete organ. The street wears us out. It is altogether disgusting! Then why does it still exist?" [34]

Since 1924 he publicized his redefinition of the street in terms of the modern superhighway: it is a "machine for circulating" he insists, "a circulatory apparatus . . . a kind of factory in length." [35] Hence the superhighway as the central axis of his urbanistic schemes. Hence the constant urge for separating automobile traffic from pedestrian circulation, and of layering the different levels of mechanical transportation according to function, range and speed. This latter concern is not new. The idea of a city efficiently served by a vascular system of streets, canals and tunnels is as old as scientific speculation about the city as an "organic" whole; it was one of Leonardo da Vinci's hobby-horses, as a number of famous sketches show. [36] In the 19th century the differentiation of urban traffic lines became a frequent concern in progressive town planning proposals. Around 1860, Tony Moilin, a French country doctor, proposed the construction of a city in which the streets and the trains would be arranged on different levels. [37] Whether or not Le Corbusier or, before him, Sant 'Elia knew of this project is a question of secondary importance. However, it is certain that the widely publicized urban utopias and reform projects promulgated around 1900 gave first place to the idea of the separation of traffic lines. Long before 1900, the great capitals—Paris, Berlin, London, New York, Chicago—had built their subway systems and elevated railways. In Paris, it was again Eugène Hénard who had suggested as early as 1903 a number of important urban changes in order to cope with the increasing dangers of traffic. His *carrefour à giration*, probably the first traffic roundabout in the modern sense, was designed for horse-drawn carriages; it was published by Le Corbusier in *Urbanisme* and obviously served as an inspiration for the great central station in the heart of the Ville Contemporaine. [38] While Hénard had proposed two

[34] *Oeuvre complète 1910–1929*, pp. 112f.

[35] *Urbanisme,* p. 113.

[36] The most famous are in the Institut de France, *Ms. B.*, fol. 36 r., fol. 16 r., fol. 37 v. These sketches have often intrigued modern architects and planners. For their discussion see Alberto Sartoris, *Léonard architecte* (Paris: A. Tallone, 1952).

[37] Reyner Banham, *Theory and Design in the First Machine Age*, p. 132.

[38] Cf. Peter M. Wolf, *Eugène Hénard*, pp. 49–60. Hénard's plan is illustrated on p. 111 of *Urbanisme*. For the American background, Le Corbusier seems to have used books such as Werner Hegemann, *Amerikanische Architektur und Stadtbaukunst* (Berlin: Ernst Wasmuth, 1925). An illustration on p. 53 of this book reappears on p. 144 of *Urbanisme*.

levels of circulation—vehicles on the surface and pedestrians underneath—Le Corbusier suggests no fewer than seven superimposed layers.
At the lowest levels, the terminals for the main lines; above, the suburban
lines; then the subway; above that, all pedestrian circulation; then the
throughways for rapid motor traffic; and last, at the top, the airport.
This last idea was indeed the most fantastic aspect of the project, the
only one which has remained fantastic up to this day. But who is able
to predict whether someday the technique of vertical takeoff may indeed
bring large jetliners right into the center of great cities? . . .

SOCIAL AND ECONOMIC
ASPECTS

As to the social and economic aspects of the scheme, Le Corbusier
is well aware of which card to play. He leaves no stone unturned in
order to prove the great virtues of the Ville Contemporaine as a guarantor
of business profits and social peace. "Paris, the capital of France, must
build up in this twentieth century its position of command," [39] he announces. And the whole urbanistic imagery of the Ville Contemporaine
as well as of the Plan Voisin—the huge, 800-foot-high, steel and glass
office towers, lined up on the flat land between the superhighways like
figures on a chessboard—is indeed a glorification of big business and of
centralized state control. "But where is the money coming from?" [40]
Le Corbusier was enough of a businessman himself not to be embarrassed
by such a question; his closest friends from the Swiss colony in Paris
were bankers after all. "To urbanize means to valorize," he proclaims.
"To urbanize is not to spend money, but to earn money, to make
money." [41] How? The key word is density: the greater the density of
land use, the greater the real estate value. And again the reassurance:
the colossal towers are not "revolutionary," they are a means of multiplying business profits.

The Plan Voisin thus characterizes itself as the ideal city of capitalism, and not of French big business alone; foreign capital should have
its share in it too. This distribution of land among French, German and
American trusts would, Le Corbusier argues, minimize the danger of
possible air attack.[42] Around 1925 the proposal may have sounded strange
at best, but it appears today as an extremely realistic anticipation of
what actually has become a primary factor of urban downtown development in Western Europe since World War II: the overpowering role of
foreign capital and its silent but efficient "entente" with official planning
policy. In economic terms, if not in those of urban imagery and planning

[39] *Urbanisme,* p. 270.
[40] *Ibid.,* pp. 275ff.
[41] *Oeuvre complète 1910–1929,* p. 111.
[42] *Urbanisme,* p. 280.

procedure, the Quartier de la Défense north of Neuilly and other recent large-scale surgery inside Paris are based on the very forces with which Le Corbusier had hoped to put his Plan Voisin into action. However, compared with any of Le Corbusier's numerous proposals, recent business complexes such as the new Montparnasse skyscraper are piecemeal work, arrogant in scale, poorly designed and badly coordinated with the urban infrastructure and traffic pattern which played such a decisive role in the Plan Voisin and its later and more reasonable modifications.

These later modifications gradually did away with the bulky cruciform towers and suggested a smaller number of tall, Y-shaped skyscrapers to be built increasingly far from the existing center.[43] But it was the cruciform towers of 1922 which caught the imagination of two generations of planners. For example, the cruciform Place Ville Marie tower in Montreal is an office building, and thus in agreement with the function assigned to this form in Le Corbusier's early Parisian plans. Yet a multitude of large-scale, low-cost housing schemes in the U.S. adopted the cruciform shape with well-known, often more than questionable results. What has remained of the utopia of 1922 is nothing but an aesthetic formula translated into the massiveness of compact brick or masonry walls, as opposed to the reflecting glass Le Corbusier had envisaged. Furthermore, the surrounding parks degenerated rapidly either into parking lots or worse, into deserted wastelands inviting delinquency and crime.[44]

This background is likely to obscure the appropriate understanding of the social and political philosophy of the Ville Contemporaine and the Plan Voisin. They were not conceived as a mere formal exercise, but as a remedy against overcrowding, social disorder and political unrest. The housing situation in Paris was deplorable for the poor living in the center of the city, and this has hardly changed since. Plumbing, heating and electricity were scarce if not lacking altogether. Le Corbusier approaches these problems from above; he addresses himself not to the poor, but to those in command. Thus he recommends his solution not as a pretext for revolution, but as a means of avoiding it: "Architecture or Revolution. Revolution can be avoided." [45] How? Through the solution of the housing problem, which has always been perceived by the bourgeoisie as the most important, if not as the only real problem of the proletariat.

With the keen insight of a La Bruyère, he exposes in *Urbanisme* the petty distractions by which the average Parisian consoles himself on an evening in Montmartre or Montparnasse, away from the dirt and squalor of his small, badly aired and unheated apartment.[46] For Le Cor-

[43] Cf. the various volumes of the *Oeuvre complète* and Norma Evenson, *op. cit.*, figs. 16–25.

[44] For examples see Vincent Scully, *American Architecture and Urbanism* (New York: Frederick A. Praeger Publishers, 1971), pp. 166–69.

[45] *Vers une Architecture*, p. 243.

[46] *Urbanisme*, pp. 203–12.

busier, this is a mean and indecent definition of "freedom." For him, there is only one solution: "freedom through order," an order which secures an ample and flawlessly hygienic apartment for every person.[47] People, he argues, have a right to live in comfortable apartments; after working hours in the factory or office, they should be granted the pleasure of sweet reveries in the midst of nature; they should know the "essential joys" of leisure. What he promises is a weekend paradise, however a paradise where it would be easier to play a game of tennis in the parks surrounding the "villa super-blocks" than to find a café in which to have a glass of wine with friends.

It is easy enough to ridicule the ideology, but more difficult to refute it. The housing crisis was real in Paris after World War I and it called for technical and administrative action of some sort. However, the philanthropic and humanitarian idealism of Le Corbusier may sound naïve today. It is compromised by the failure of many Corbusier-based attempts to create well-being and happiness by means of large-scale physical planning alone. Moreover, we have reached a point where not only the failure, but also the apparent success of such planning principles have become a subject of concern, at least for a generation which can no longer equate human progress with the adoption of Western middle-class standards by the so-called "underprivileged." Indeed the whole philosophy of Le Corbusier's Ville Contemporaine implicitly offers a strategy for such an alignment, a strategy whose potential was hardly understood at the time, however. It is a bourgeois utopia of social order and harmony based on middle-class virtues, business ethics and modern technology; in short, a brilliant and optimistic ideological prefiguration of post-World War II reality throughout the industrialized world. . . .

[47] The ideology of collective happiness which underlies Le Corbusier's approach has been the subject of numerous and often perceptive comments. See for instance, Pierre Francastel, *Art et téchnique* (Paris: Éditions de Minuit, 1956), p. 42.

THE CITY OF DIALECTIC (1969)

Kenneth Frampton

In spite of its 1933 dedication to those in authority, Le Corbusier's book *La Ville Radieuse*, subtitled "elements of a doctrine of urbanism to be used as a basis of our machine age civilization," and published for the first time in English, as *The Radiant City*, in 1967, can be of but marginal interest to those now charged with city and regional planning. Thirty-six years after its initial appearance, however, it stands as a document of the greatest cultural importance, for not only does it illuminate the infinitely complex nature of its author's thought, but it also remains as a warning to our benighted present, rife as it is with both absurd affluence and abject poverty. Unlike *Vers une Architecture* its style is neither aphoristic nor didactic and lacking the oracular touch, it has yet to become popular. Little of its text has the necessary density and terseness to serve, out of context, as an ideological quote. In common with other works by Le Corbusier it is a diffuse and polemical book; rhetorical in its reiterations; revelatory in its illustrations. Its structure which is clearly tabulated in the first few pages bears only an elliptical relation to its actual content which, through recapitulation and transposition, reveals itself as resting on a number of separate but related dialectical themes. These themes are occasionally declared by the author as sub-headings or sub-sections within the main chapters. Thus in the introductory chapter we encounter an initial discussion of a recurrent theme; the issue of useful as opposed to useless consumer goods, while later under a crucial sub-section entitled LAWS we are pedantically instructed as to the cosmic importance of the male/female correlation. This kind of polarized theme occurs with such frequency as to suggest that the *Ville Radieuse* may be regarded fruitfully as a "city" of dialectic.

What then was the multiple argument of the *Ville Radieuse* as set out in the years 1930 to 1933? Certainly as an "ideal" city in its most general form it was consciously opposed to what Le Corbusier regarded as the "premachine-age utopia" [1] of the garden city. As illustrated in the 17 plates first assembled under the book's initial title, as *Réponse à Moscou*, it was a demonstration of urbanization rather than disurbaniza- tion, which was then favoured in Soviet Russia as the orthodox Marxist line on city and regional planning.

In Le Corbusier's own words "to urbanize the town and to urbanize the country" rather than to disurbanize both, was seen by him as the correct technical approach to the immediate future. This was his stand at the Brussels CIAM congress of 1930, where the Ville Radieuse was first publicly exhibited. The pro-*res publica* city of concentration (1000 persons per hectare), was set by him against the anti-urban garden city of dispersal. This opposition was ironically re-inforced by the criticism and the counter criticism which he exchanged with both Marxist and bourgeois camps. While he denounced the American suburb as "the organized slavery of capitalist society," [2] as leading to isolated individual- ism and to the destruction of the collective spirit and, by virtue of an inherent increase in commutation time, as being an actual attack upon human freedom, he also saw Soviet disurbanization as being an un- economic and inhuman technique of urban colonization. For, he wrote "the USSR is also intent on dismantling its great cities, just as our own city authorities are all dreaming of sending us out into their fields (their garden cities) to scrabble earth around a lot of hypothetical onions and to live out Jean Jacques' eighteenth century fantasies (without the wit)." [3]

For this, of course, he was denounced by Soviet critics, such as the linear city theorist Miluitin, as being a propagator of capitalism. The provocative text which he appended to his *Réponse à Moscou*, to the effect that, "the cornerstone of all modern urbanization is absolute respect for the freedom of the individual," [4] was hardly well received in Soviet circles. It is clear that he did not mean by such freedom a state of perpetual pluralist anarchy. What he had in mind was human biological and spiritual freedom, subject only to the sanctions of universal social and cosmic law and to the dictates of a *plan* collectively conceived and administered. He was for a despotism of facts (i.e. technique) rather than that of men. He was for the concentration of "capital" and for a control of its power by a syndicalist society. Thus despite the title page disclaimer that "plans are not politics," the *Ville Radieuse* envisaged a system of technical and social organization, with specific political im- plications. These Le Corbusier consciously set out in Chapter 5 of his book, entitled *Prélude*—after the magazine in which the material had first appeared.

Prélude was the monthly organ of the Central Committee for Regionalist and Syndicalist Action; edited by Hubert Lagardelle, Dr.

[1] Le Corbusier, *The Radiant City* (New York: The Orion Press, 1967), p. 94.
[2] *Ibid.*, p. 38.
[3] *Ibid.*, p. 136.
[4] *Ibid.*, p. 90.

Pierre Winter, François de Pierrefeu and Le Corbusier, and subtitled "thèmes préparatoires à l'action," it was the successor to the magazine *Plans*, put out by the same group during 1930–31. Le Corbusier's association with this group, continuing into the 40s (*La Maison des Hommes*) testifies to his close affinities with the great French regional-syndicalist tradition.

Tony Garnier had of course based his "ideal" city on the tenets of this tradition and thus both the Cité Industrielle and the Ville Radieuse are to be seen as having common roots in nineteenth century Regional-Syndicalism and in Utopian Socialism (i.e., in a complex to be delineated in the works of Proudhon, Pelloutier, St. Simon, Fourier and Considérant). In a diagram curiously evocative of the ground plan of Garnier's assembly building in the Cité Industrielle, Le Corbusier sketches out his "natural hierarchy" of authority in which power is to be vested in the collective voice of the *unions* who send their representatives to an *inter-union* assembly, from which the *extra-union* supreme leadership (i.e. the cabinet or the municipium at a more local level) is eventually drawn. Clearly Le Corbusier meant something of wider connotations than the English word "trade" (translation for *métier*) when he wrote: "All men work, practice a trade. All men are capable of making judgments about things concerning their own trades. Men's trades must therefore form the foundation for our edifice of authority and power and for our hierarchy of responsibility. . . . On the next level, the qualified deputations of each trade meet at an inter-union conference where the main problems of economic interdependence are hammered out and a state of balance achieved. All of which means that the supreme authority is freed from all problems stemming from technical insufficiencies. It is at liberty to concentrate on the country's higher purposes. For it is in the works of this supreme authority that the whole philosophy of a civilization will be expressed: its direction and purpose." [5] In this pyramidal structure, the mutual education of society is combined with the act of government. To avoid the extremes of either despotism or anarchy, *control* is shown as exercised up and *information* as feeding down.

Despite his assertion at the close of *Vers une Architecture* that "revolution can be avoided," this mode of government was equally inaccessible to both Capitalists and Bolsheviks alike. Yet his three main DECISIONS set out in Chapter 4, as indispensable pre-conditions to the establishment of a planned economy, even today, seem "revolutionary" enough. As they appear in the text these are:

1. "To undertake a wholesale reorganization of land tenure in the country as a whole and in the cities in particular." He adds: "The lawyers say that this means calling all the beliefs by which we live into question. I have expressed myself more clearly still; requisitioning of land for public good." [6]

---

[5] Le Corbusier, *The Radiant City*, pp. 192–93.
[6] *Ibid.*, p. 148.

2. "To take an inventory of our cities' populations: differentiation, classification, reassignment, transplantation, intervention, etc." [7]

3. "To establish a plan for producing permissible goods; to forbid with stoic firmness all useless products. To employ the forces liberated by this means in the rebuilding of the city and the whole country." [8]

Le Corbusier was well aware that this represented a simplistic view of the inherent economic structure of modern industrial society and its decision making processes, for in his address to the Brussels CIAM congress on disurbanization, he said: "Let's not get into politics and sociology here. . . . We are not competent to discuss these intricate questions. . . . I repeat: here we should make known . . . the possibilities afforded by modern techniques and the need for a new kind of architecture and city planning," and later on, "hope in the present era . . . restitution of freedom which has been lost. . . . Modern society is better prepared than its predecessor for collective disciplines. Disciplines which are beneficial so long as they tend towards individual freedom." [9]

In spite of his evident concern for the proper correlation of *individual* and *collective,* to many outside of the extreme left, his disclaimer that he was not a Marxist was disregarded. Yet the fact remains that the regional syndicalists were neither of the right nor the left. As a 1933 front page to *Prélude,* reprinted in *La Ville Radieuse,* makes clear: "Right . . . Left. We pose the question, are there some Frenchmen who think like us that this political division of philosophical origin is a sentimental usage totally unsuitable to 1933?"—"Capitalism . . . Marxism. There again, are these words the only vocabulary to be employed?"

Regional-Syndicalism meant for Le Corbusier (from the Swiss Jura) [10] and his colleagues, the important notion of "participation." With this concept they postulated the disappearance of the "proletariat," so indispensable to Marxist ideology. It was out of respect for this Fourierist social concept of "harmony and collaboration" as opposed to the mores of a "cruel and ruthless civilization of money" or to those of man "coldly stockpiled on the interest of some anonymous trust," [11] that Le Corbusier became attached to the achievements of Holland. . . .

The infrastructure layout of the Ville Radieuse was a direct development of ideas first postulated by Le Corbusier and Pierre Jeanneret in their Ville Contemporaine. It was in this project, for instance, that the 400 metre square road grid, based on the average distance between Parisian metro stops was first adopted; together with the notion of totally separating vehicular and pedestrian traffic; a system of separation that was never as successfully resolved as the plans would at first suggest. Both these devices were more subtly developed in the Ville Radieuse as was the town plan as a whole. The concentricity of the Ville Contemporaine

[7] Le Corbusier, *The Radiant City,* p. 149.
[8] *Ibid.,* p. 152.
[9] *Ibid.,* p. 37.
[10] *Ibid.,* p. 70.
[11] *Ibid.,* p. 69.

was in any case later rejected by its author, in 1933, as a biological defect, unconducive to growth. The Ville Radieuse suffered from no such defect, for apart from its administrative centre (its head) and its cultural core (its heart) each of its remaining zones, that is, its residential and industrial areas, were designed to expand independently of each other, in a linear sequence. Again one may detect in this allowance for linear expansion, the presence of Russian influence.

The Ville Radieuse residential blocks themselves, the blocks *à redent,* were to be more variably disposed in relation to the 400 metre grid, than had been the case in the Ville Contemporaine. Integral to this improved layout was the distribution of schools and sports facilities together with the general system of access, parking and service. Anticipating Louis Kahn's terminology of the 50s, the elevated roads themselves were regarded as "rivers" or "viaducts"; while the similarly elevated "autoports," serving the residential units, were considered to be "harbours." This natural analogy to "moving" canals and "stagnant" inlets was first observed by Le Corbusier from Saint Exupéry's aircraft when flying over South America in 1929.

At an altogether larger scale, the biological attributes of linear expansion were to impart to the Ville Radieuse model certain regional planning implications, the full consequences of which were not fully worked out by Le Corbusier until his ASCORAL book of 1944, *Les Trois Etablissements Humains.* Le Corbusier's 1937 plan for Paris (based on his 1925 Voisin plan), envisaged a linear growth for Paris, in which the various elements of the Ville Radieuse would be fairly freely disposed along a new highway axis, running parallel, to the north of the old triumphal route linking Versailles to the centre. This axis would eventually be deflected to link into the national autoroute network.

From 1930 onwards the basic elements of the Ville Radieuse were to undergo development and transformation. . . .

CHANDIGARH (1969)

Norma Evenson

In spite of his fame as a theoretical urban designer, Le Corbusier might well have concluded his career without ever participating directly in a successful urban plan were it not for two gentlemen from India who, in November, 1950, approached him with regard to the development of a new capital for the province of Punjab. Although the proposal seemed in many ways unpromising, Le Corbusier, after some hesitation, agreed to join the project, and the remote provincial town of Chandigarh now remains his only realized plan [Fig. 28].

Le Corbusier was engaged primarily as an architect, rather than as a planner. A master plan for the Punjab capital had already been designed by the New York firm of Mayer, Whittlesey and Glass, and Le Corbusier's services were sought for the architectural realization of this scheme. It was natural, however, in view of his long involvement with urban design, that Le Corbusier would seek to modify the existing plan some-what when he began its execution.

Le Corbusier was the dominant member of a group of designers engaged in Chandigarh, including his cousin, Pierre Jeanneret, and the British architects Maxwell Fry and Jane Drew. In the division of labor, Le Corbusier was to concentrate his efforts on the overall ordering of the master plan and the design of major architectural monuments, leaving the detailed development of the urban fabric, including housing design, to his colleagues.

Chandigarh had been conceived in a time of crisis following the partition of India, during which the province of Punjab had been divided, with the capital city of Lahore going to Pakistan. The decision to construct the new city was motivated partly by necessity, but represented also the desire to respond to political uncertainty with a symbolic gesture of strength and creativity. The colonial yoke had been discarded, and

---

"Chandigarh." From Norma Evenson, *Le Corbusier: The Machine and the Grand Design* (New York: George Braziller, Inc., 1969), pp. 97–106. Reprinted by permission of the author and publisher.

the opportunity had arrived for India to demonstrate that she could stand alone, that she could command her own destiny and govern her own house, and that against the brutality of nature and the vastness of her continent she could impress an ordered, yet viable pattern of human life. Viewing the new city as a focal point of national importance, Prime Minister Nehru had said, "Let this be a new town, symbolic of the freedom of India, unfettered by the traditions of the past . . . an expression of the nation's faith in the future." [1]

Although the Chandigarh project was meant to symbolize India's independence, a lack of trained local technicians had necessitated the importation of foreign planners. The plan as it had been developed by the Mayer firm represented in many ways a synthesis of Western urban design theory, incorporating a system of residential neighborhood units containing schools, housing, small commerce and parkland, a system of pedestrian and motor separation, and discrete zoning of major activities. At the upper edge of the city a complex of government buildings was projected, while a commercial district was sited toward the center, and an industrial area placed at one side.

The initial planners had to a degree been dominated by the Garden City predilection for low-density, somewhat picturesque design, and Le Corbusier, although retaining many general features of the original scheme, began his modifications by classicizing and geometricizing the plan, straightening major streets and transforming the slightly irregular superblocks into rectangles. He sought to give the city a large-scale unified design appropriate to its monumental character, establishing within the new rectilinear outlines a cross-axial configuration of major boulevards focusing on the commercial center, with the capitol complex culminating in the northeastern axis toward the mountains.

Referring to the Chandigarh project, Le Corbusier once stated, "I have conceived a capital for the Punjab, a completely new town, standing on a plain at the foot of the Himalaya. As architect I had a free hand but very little money.

"This gave great scope for ideas, invention and imagination. But the program provided by the authority is banal and unimaginative, both for the housing and for the institutional elements of the town. Nowhere yet have the fundamental problems of town planning been put, the problems of economy, sociology and ethics, the conquest of which will make man the master of his civilization." [2]

In addition to whatever programmatic limitations the project embodied, Chandigarh also presented Le Corbusier with a set of technical and social conditions far removed from the industrialized society for which he had always projected his schemes. The means for large-scale mechanized transport did not exist; a shortage of steel coupled with

---

[1] Quoted in L. R. Nair, *Why Chandigarh?* (Simla: Publicity Department, Punjab Government, 1950), p. 6.

[2] Le Corbusier, *Oeuvre complète 1946–52* (Zurich: Les Editions Girsberger, 1953), p. 11.

inadequate technical services made high-rise building unfeasible, while the climate and semirural way of life mitigated against apartment housing.

Although plunged into an unfamiliar environment, and compelled to work in conditions unfavorable to his previous predilections, Le Corbusier found in India perhaps the most receptive patronage he had ever known. His unwavering confidence was reassuring to the Indians, while the largeness of his vision and the grandness of his concepts seemed to harmonize appropriately with their aspirations for the new capital. Although he had frequently found government officials less than sympathetic, his personal relations with the Indian administrators of Chandigarh seem altogether successful; and Prime Minister Nehru, who took great interest in the project, became a warm friend. It was once observed that "India understands idea men and treats them well—perhaps better than any other country—and Le Corbusier benefits from this." [3]

After a lifetime of seeking to master the demands of the machine age, Le Corbusier found himself trying to come to terms with an environment still largely untouched by industrialism. Describing his Indian experience, he once wrote: "In modern life, today so distracting, Le Corbusier finds in India a friendly terrain: this old tradition where man is face to face with nature, with her violence also. Friendly contacts with nature, the animals, the creatures, sleeping under the stars, a land far removed from the stupidity of certain comforts . . . so often questionable. Le Corbusier has found in this land the opportunity to apply all his energy in the search for solutions which surpass ordinary architecture. It concerns a truly human problem freed of all conformity." [4]

In general, the conception of Chandigarh represented a relaxation of the rigid geometry which had dominated Le Corbusier's earlier designs, embodying an interweaving of geometric and picturesquely ordered elements. The determination of proportions in the civic design as well as in the architecture involved use of the Modulor, a system of proportioning which he had evolved during World War II and patented as an invention in 1947, but related also to traditional classical ordering. The basic unit of the city, the residential sector, was formed on the golden rectangle, with dimensions of 800 x 1,200 meters (½ x ¾ miles).

The measurement of 800 meters, which recurs in the planning of the capitol complex and elsewhere, may be found also in the monumental composition which Le Corbusier admired in his native Paris. In Paris, it is 800 meters from the Louvre to the Place de la Concorde, and another 800 meters from the Place de la Concorde to the Place Clemenceau, while the Madeleine and the Chambre des Députés terminate opposite ends of an 800-meter axis passing through the Place de la Concorde. In Chandigarh, the distance along the monumental avenue between the commercial

[3] Christopher Rand, "City on a Tilting Plain," *The New Yorker*, XXXI (April 30, 1955), 42.
[4] Le Corbusier, paper delivered at a press conference at the Palais de la Découverte, March 18, 1953.

center and the capitol complex duplicates that between the Etoile and the Place de la Concorde. Although it is not unnatural that Le Corbusier, in ordering a totally new urban pattern, might be inspired by the dimensions of a familiar and beloved city, the monumental effectiveness of the Indian capital may be vitiated through lack of a correspondingly scaled urban architecture.

In developing the plan of Chandigarh, Le Corbusier employed a scheme of traffic separation which he termed "the 7V's" (*les Sept Voies*), a system which he had previously projected for Bogotá and South Marseilles. Some degree of traffic separation had always been present in Le Corbusier's schemes, and the 7V's represented an attempt to develop a fully organized, universally applicable system dividing traffic into a series of seven categories comprising a hierarchy of circulation ranging from arterial roads to apartment house corridors.

The specific organization of the 7V system in Chandigarh is as follows: The V1 represents regional roads leading into the city from the outside, while the V2 designation refers to the two major cross-axial boulevards of the city. One of these provides the ceremonial avenue linking the central district with the capitol complex, while the other forms a cultural-commercial axis. Surrounding the residential sectors and establishing the grid pattern of the city are the V3 streets intended for fast motor traffic. Frontage development along these streets is prohibited, the sectors being designed to focus inwardly. Bisecting the long side of each sector is a bazaar street—the V4—following a slightly irregular path and permitting a variety of slow-moving traffic. This street, intended to provide for neighborhood shopping needs, carries shops only on the south side, to ensure shade for pedestrians and also to eliminate excessive street crossing. The V5 is a loop road intersecting the V4 and serving as the main distributor of traffic within the sector, while V6 lanes give additional access to houses. A strip of parkland containing schools extends through each sector, providing continuous bands of open space throughout the city, and including the V7 pedestrian paths.

Applying his favorite biological analogy to the road system, Le Corbusier stated, "The 7V's act in the town plan as the blood stream, the lymph system and the respiratory system act in biology. In biology these systems are quite rational, they are different from each other, there is no confusion between them, yet they are in harmony. They create order. It is God who has placed them in the world; it is for us to learn from them when we are organizing the ground which lies beneath our feet." [5]

The abundant provisions for motor traffic in Chandigarh represented anticipation of future mechanization, rather than a system adapted to existing conditions, although the wide mixtures of traffic characteristic of Indian cities, ranging from trucks and automobiles to bicycles and bullock carts, justified an elaborate system of separation. The success of the Chandigarh system, however, can only be evaluated when traffic

[5] Quoted in Rand, *op. cit.*, p. 50.

volumes, especially of motor traffic, have risen sufficiently to test the resources of the plan.

Both technical and social conditions determined that Chandigarh be predominantly a low-rise city, although in preliminary drawings, Le Corbusier indicated a desire for the inclusion of some high-rise building both in the capitol complex and the central business district. The architectural composition of the city reflected Le Corbusier's long-standing preference for a controlled environment—for a simplification of building types and a disciplined unity of building form. Government housing followed a pattern of standardized designs, while private housing was architecturally controlled. Neighborhood shops were built to specified designs, and in the central business district, a potentially competitive and varied architecture was forestalled by Le Corbusier's predetermined plan.

As ultimately developed by Le Corbusier, the central business district was architecturally unified by means of a standardized four-story, concrete frame building. Its height was determined by the lack of elevators —the size of building which most owners might be able to afford—and the possibility of earthquakes. Although interiors could be developed according to the builder's wishes, the exterior treatment was required to follow a prescribed design providing exterior verandas, that of the ground floor serving as a continuous 3.6-meter-wide pedestrian shelter.

The largest building projected for the complex was a ten-story slab housing the post and telegraph building and providing the focal point of a central square. Although the central business district was designed as a pedestrian area, with motor access restricted to the periphery, the dimensioning of circulation areas and open spaces seems excessive, and generally inappropriate both to the climate and the scale of the surrounding building. The design effort may have involved an attempt to balance the symbolically important capitol complex with another ensemble of monumental dimensions, but, lacking either symbolic purpose or compelling architecture, the business district may be deemed a questionable success both visually and functionally.

It was to the capitol complex, the symbolic focal point of the city, that Le Corbusier devoted his most intensive efforts. This provincial government center, containing the High Court [Fig. 30], Legislative Assembly [Fig. 29], Secretariat [Fig. 29], and (initially) the Governor's Palace, was sited at the upper edge of the city, surrounded by open land [Fig. 28].

Within a stretch of open plain, in sight of the Himalayas which close the landscape to the north, Le Corbusier conceived a grandly scaled ensemble, basically ordered by a plan involving 800 and 400 meter squares, but depending for visual cohesion on an interplay of massive building forms seen against the distant mountains and within a configuration of excavated earth mounds and reflecting pools. The scale of the complex is vast, in keeping with the surrounding landscape, an area designed for sweeping visual impact, rather than ease of physical communication. In designing this complex, Le Corbusier reported,

"There was anxiety and anguish in taking decisions on that vast, limitless ground. A pathetic soliloquy! I had to appreciate and to decide alone. The problem was no longer one of reasoning but of sensation. Chandigarh is not a city of lords, princes or kings confined within walls, crowded in by neighbors. It was a matter of occupying a plain. The geometrical event was, in truth, a sculpture of the intellect. . . . It was a battle of space, fought within the mind. Arithmetic, texturique, geometrics: it would all be there when the whole was finished. For the moment, oxen, cows and goats, driven by peasants, crossed the sun-scorched fields." [6]

The capitol area as a whole was conceived as a pedestrian plaza, motor traffic being channeled into sunken trenches leading to parking areas. The generating motif of the complex was a slightly asymmetrical cross axis, one arm of which comprises a pedestrian promenade penetrating the area and extending the line of the monumental boulevard leading from the commercial center. The long slab of the Secretariat bounds the space to the left, and stands adjacent to the Legislative Assembly, while the High Court and Legislature terminate the cross axis on either side of a 450-meter esplanade. The center of the area is marked by a series of monuments devised to illustrate Le Corbusier's theories of city planning, while outlined against the hills at the outer edge of the complex was projected a Museum of Knowledge (on a site set originally for the Governor's Palace) and a symbolic sculptural monument designed by Le Corbusier in the form of a great open hand about 26 meters high.

The monuments were reportedly suggested by Jane Drew who advised Le Corbusier to "set up in the heart of the Capitol the signs which symbolise the basis of your philosophy and by which you arrived at your understanding of the art of city design. These signs should be known— they are the key to the creation of Chandigarh." [7]

Included would be a symbolic representation of the Modulor and the Harmonic Spiral representing the Modulor series of proportions. Additional monuments were designed to represent the Twenty-four Solar Hours "which rule men's activity," and the path of the sun between two solstices, "this sun, which governs men—friend or enemy," [8] while the Tower of Shade would demonstrate principles of sun protection. Near the approach to the Museum of Knowledge a monument was projected to the martyrs of the Indian partition. The Open Hand—sometimes referred to by the architect as the Monument of Chandigarh—was conceived by him in Paris in 1948 and "during the years that followed, it occupied my mind, finding its first existence in Chandigarh." [9] The symbolism, he claimed, arose "spontaneously, or more exactly, as the result of reflections and spiritual struggles arising from the feelings of anguish and disharmony which separate mankind, and so often create enemies. . . . Little by

[6] Le Corbusier, *Modulor 2* (Cambridge, Mass.: Harvard University Press, 1958), p. 215.

[7] Quoted in Le Corbusier, *Oeuvre complète 1946–52*, p. 157.

[8] Le Corbusier, "The Monuments," *Marg*, XV (December, 1961), insert between pp. 10–11.

[9] Le Corbusier, *Modulor 2*, p. 254.

little the open hand appeared as a possibility in great architectural compositions." [10]

Although some might question the suitability of including in the capitol complex what are in effect monuments to Le Corbusier himself, many have found their symbolism wholly appropriate. An Indian engineer wrote to Le Corbusier, "We have a word Ram Bharosa, which indicates deep faith in the ultimate—faith born of the surrender of the will to the Ultimate Source of Knowledge, service without reward and much more. I live in that faith and feel happy in the vision of the new city which is so safe and so secure in its creation in your hands. We are humble people. No guns to brandish, no atomic energy to kill. Your philosophy of 'open hand' will appeal to India and what we are taking from your open hand, I pray, may become a source of new inspiration in our architectural and city planning. We may on our side, when you come here next, be able to show you the spiritual heights to which some of the individuals have attained. Ours is a philosophy of open hand. Maybe Chandigarh becomes the new center of thought." [11]

Although some observers have been overwhelmed by the sweeping scale of the Chandigarh capitol complex, its architectural embodiment has been widely regarded as one of the most masterful achievements in modern building. Almost primordial in their evocative strength, the symbolic civic structures, through their massive plasticity of form, and bold use of exposed concrete, were influential in liberating postwar architecture from the formal restrictions of the International Style, reinforcing Le Corbusier's position as an innovative leader of modern design. For devotees of architecture, the Chandigarh capitol complex has become a place of pilgrimage, as much a part of the Indian itinerary as the Taj Mahal.

More importantly, Le Corbusier's efforts served to revitalize the modern concept of monumental building. Chandigarh was the product of political crisis, embodying the desire of a new nation, poor, technically undeveloped, and torn with inner dissension, to create a city symbolic of permanence and order, a focal point for the incipient nationalist spirit. As Le Corbusier had sought to redefine the master plan of the city to achieve a suitably monumental scale, so he struggled to give the capitol complex the imprint of unity and power appropriate to its symbolic function.

The Secretariat [Fig. 29], a long concrete slab, combines with the earth mounds to define the complex, becoming itself like a natural barrier—a man-made cliff providing a backdrop for the smaller structures. In keeping with its essentially utilitarian function, the Secretariat stands apart from the main plaza of the capitol upon which face the great entrance porticos of the High Court and Assembly buildings. Throughout the building ensemble is a subtle and harmonic interplay of diversity and unity: the High Court [Fig. 30] classically contained in outline, but

[10] Le Corbusier, *Oeuvre complète 1946–52*, p. 159.
[11] The statement was written by P. L. Varma, Chief Engineer of Punjab.

split by a brilliantly painted portico, balanced by the Assembly [Fig. 29], its roofline pierced from within by the dramatically sculptural forms of the interior chambers, and carrying an external, free-standing portico like a giant *brise-soleil*. The space of the plaza is vast, yet retains, albeit tenuously, a sense of place, partially enclosed by earth mounds, yet open to the mountains.

Although for much of his career, Le Corbusier's visionary architecture had symbolized a world of economic affluence, technical virtuosity, and mechanical comfort, he triumphantly culminated his career within a set of restraints both harsher and spiritually richer. As India herself stood alone and threatened when Chandigarh was planned, so the capitol structures seem to stand alone within a hostile world. They are not comfortable buildings, nor do they stand in a comfortable place. Nor do they speak of a comfortable life, or of a life taken for granted, but of a life maintained through effort and tenacity.

Disciplined by climate, poverty, and primitive technology, the buildings of the capitol complex rise from the earth, asserting the presence of man against the vast sweep of plain and the distant mountains. There is no shelter here. Battered by rains and dust storms, scorched by a brutal sun and buffeted by winds, these structures have been laboriously built by the toil of many men. They are meant to last. Like the classical builders he so admired, Le Corbusier countered the uncertainty of fate with a certainty of vision, establishing a bold and powerful testament for the future, whatever destiny it brings.

As he became more and more absorbed in the monumental architecture of Chandigarh, however, he tended to disassociate himself from the overall planning of the city, leaving primary responsibility for developing the urban design to the Capital Project Office directed by Pierre Jeanneret. During the years in which the city took form, Le Corbusier worked in Paris, visiting Chandigarh only periodically, while Pierre Jeanneret remained on the site directing construction as the Chief Architect and Planner of Punjab.

Le Corbusier's contribution to the design of the residential sectors consisted of a schematic outline providing a generalized pattern of street layout, parkland and bazaar placement. Within these sectors, the predominant visual character was determined by a prescribed program of thirteen categories of government housing, the initial housing-types having been developed by Maxwell Fry, Jane Drew, and Pierre Jeanneret. So significant is this hierarchic pattern of housing in the overall appearance of the city that there seem virtually to be two Chandigarhs, that of Le Corbusier embodied in the monumental foci, and that of Pierre Jeanneret comprising the bulk of the building.

The master plan of Chandigarh implied the creation of a dual scale of urban design, a monumental scale allied to the capital function and seen in the wide boulevards and major building complexes, and a smaller, domestic, pedestrian-oriented scale within the neighborhood sectors. The most pronounced design failure of the city lies in the development of these residential districts, where a loose and monotonous pattern of building placement, excessive, unmaintained open space, and overscaled streets accord poorly with the prevailing lack of motors, and a climate characterized by dust storms, searing hot winds, and scorching sun. Although the standardized bazaar streets provided premises for relatively prosperous shop owners, no facilities were included in the scheme for the small peddlers and artisans so much a part of Indian town life.

Chandigarh embodied an attempt to apply Western conceptions of urban design to the Indian environment, with the result that the city lacks not only the spatial variety and visual interest, but the functional viability of a traditional Indian town. Indian vernacular building, employing narrow streets and a relatively dense pattern of inward-oriented courtyard houses, represents a far more sophisticated method of coming to terms with a tropical climate, a predominantly pedestrian environment, and a need for privacy than is evidenced in the misplaced Garden City ambience of Chandigarh.

By and large, the development of the Punjab capital reveals an unimaginative application of urban design formula, rather than a sensitive awareness of the lively qualities of town life and the aesthetics of a non-motorized urban environment. It may be noted, however, that the looseness of scale encountered in Chandigarh characterized much postwar design, and in Britain, where the climate and degree of mechanization would justify a more open urban pattern than in India, the first new towns were frequently criticized for their lack of compactness and urbanity.

In view of Le Corbusier's long concern with urban design it may seem strange that, having at last been given the opportunity to realize a city plan, he would largely abdicate responsibility for its development. Just as his earliest schematic designs had placed emphasis on the large-scale generalized aspects of the city, making little attempt at developing the more intimate texture, so in Chandigarh Le Corbusier restricted his planning efforts to delineating the major outlines of the master plan, and the creation of monumental complexes. He may have found the programmatic and technical restrictions of the project too hampering to justify a total involvement on his part. He had been unwilling to abandon Paris for an uninterrupted residence in India, and may have felt that his associates, residing on the site, would be better qualified to establish the residential pattern. He may also have sensed that his talents and predilections were primarily those of a monumental architect, and thus chose to dedicate himself to the sphere in which he excelled.

Just how the small-scale fabric of Chandigarh might have evolved at Le Corbusier's hand is uncertain. It could be argued that his fondness for Baroque expansiveness combined with his long-term obsession with the industrialized city had rendered him unsympathetic to the functional workings and aesthetic subtlety of the traditional Indian environment. Yet there is evidence that Le Corbusier was not insensitive to the indigenous building practices of hot, dry climates. In his North African travels he had admired and sketched Arab towns and houses, observing the dense ground coverage, the narrow streets, the buildings with blank external walls and sheltered internal courtyards. "While the street is a channel of violent movement," he noted, "your houses know nothing of it: they have closed the walls which face the street. It is within the walls that life blooms." Although his schematic designs consistently advocated an open urban pattern, in Algiers he praised the "pure and efficient stratification of the Casbah," pointing out that "among these terraces which form the roof of the city, not an inch is wasted." [12]

It is difficult, therefore, to predict with certainty what Le Corbusier might have produced in Chandigarh, had he elected to study local conditions and develop detailed sector layout and housing design. As the city now exists, it owes to him only its skeletal outlines, while the flesh and substance have been created by others. Nevertheless, Chandigarh remains the only realized scheme which can be directly attributed to Le Corbusier.

[12] Le Corbusier, *The Radiant City* (New York: The Orion Press, 1967), p. 230.

Biographical Data

<table>
<tr>
<td>1887–1918</td>
<td>The Formative Years. Le Corbusier was born on October 6, 1887, in La Chaux-de-Fonds, Switzerland. Between 1900 and 1905 he attended the School of Art of La Chaux-de-Fonds. In 1907 he went to Italy, Hungary and Austria. In Vienna he worked in the office of Joseph Hoffmann. In 1908 he went to Paris, where he worked for Auguste Perret. In the fall of 1909 he returned to La Chaux-de-Fonds where he remained until April, 1910. He then left for Germany to study the artistic conditions there; he also spent some time in the office of Peter Behrens in Berlin. During the summer and fall of 1911 he visited Turkey and Greece, and was especially impressed by Istanbul, Mount Athos and Athens. Between 1912 and 1914 he taught at the School of Art of La Chaux-de-Fonds. Between 1905 and 1916 he built five houses and a theater in his native town and one house in Le Locle, near La Chaux-de-Fonds. In October 1916 he settled in Paris.</td>
</tr>
<tr>
<td>1918–1922</td>
<td>A New Beginning. In December 1918 he exhibited his first paintings with Amédée Ozenfant at the Galerie Thomas and published Après le Cubisme. In October, 1920, he published the first issue of L'Esprit Nouveau. Between 1919 and 1922 he created his four seminal projects: the Monol and Citrohan Houses, the Villa-Apartment Blocks and the Contemporary City for Three Million Inhabitants. In 1922 his cousin, Pierre Jeanneret, joined him in a partnership which lasted until 1940.</td>
</tr>
<tr>
<td>1922–1930</td>
<td>New Realizations. During this period he published his most significant theoretical and polemical books on painting, the decorative arts, architecture and city planning. He also created his visually and intellectually most searching buildings to date.</td>
</tr>
<tr>
<td>1930–1945</td>
<td>Reassessment. In 1930 he married Yvonne Gallis and became a French citizen. After 1930 he undertook a new direction in architecture and city planning by modifying his attitude toward materials, formal composition and nature. During this period he traveled widely. In 1931 he went to Algiers, Morocco and Spain. He also visited Moscow for the third time. In 1933 he saw the Greek Islands. His first visit to the U.S.</td>
</tr>
</table>

took place during the winter of 1935–36. In the summer of 1936 he made his second trip to Rio de Janeiro (the first was in 1929). Between 1941 and 1945 he lived mostly in occupied Paris.

1945–1965   *Fulfillment.* During this period he created his most significant buildings and established himself as one of the foremost architects the world has known. He died on August 27, 1965, in Roquebrune–Cap Martin on the French Riviera.

Notes on the Editor and Contributors

Reyner Banham (1922–   ). English critic and historian of architecture. Professor at the School of Environmental Studies, University College, London, since 1969. Author of many pioneering books and articles on the theory and history of modern architecture.

Walter Curt Behrendt (1884–1945). German historian of architecture and city planning. Worked for the Department of Housing and the Department of Public Buildings in Berlin from 1919 to 1933. Came to U.S. in 1934, and was professor of city planning and housing at Dartmouth College.

Philippe Boudon. French architect associated with the Atelier de Recherche et d'Etudes d'Aménagement in Paris.

Peter Collins. Canadian critic and historian of architecture. Professor at McGill University in Montreal. With his book *Concrete—The Vision of a New Architecture* (1959) he established himself as an authority on the rationalist tradition in French architecture.

Alan Colquhoun (1921–   ). English architect and critic. Educated at Edinburgh and at the Architectural Association in London. Has a private practice in London.

Norma Evenson (1928–   ). American historian of architecture and city planning. Professor at the University of California, Berkeley. Her Yale University doctoral dissertation on Chandigarh published in 1966 is the first extensive historical study on a major aspect of Le Corbusier's work.

Kenneth Frampton (1930–   ). English architect, critic and historian. Fellow of the Institute for Architecture and Urban Studies, New York, and Associate Professor at Columbia University. Has written widely on modern architecture and city planning.

Maximilien Gauthier (1893–   ). French journalist, author and art critic. Has written biographies of Dürer, Géricault, Daumier and Le Corbusier, among others.

Sigfried Giedion (1888–1968). Swiss historian of architecture and city planning. Trained under Wölfflin, he applied methods used for the interpretation of earlier historical periods to the 20th century. Participated in and wrote about the emergence of modern architecture.

Cornelius Gurlitt (1850–1938). German historian of art, architecture and city planning. Between 1893 and 1920 was professor at the Technische Hochschule in Dresden; was editor of *Stadtbaukunst.* Was a pioneer in the historical reappraisal of the Baroque period. The subjects of his many books and over 400 articles range from the Middle Ages to the 20th century.

Stanislaus von Moos (1940–   ). Swiss historian of art, architecture and city planning. Lecturer at Harvard University. Founder and editor of *Archithese*. Author of books and many articles on Renaissance and modern architecture. Published the first historical study of Le Corbusier's entire artistic career.

Marcello Piacentini (1881–1960). Italian architect and city planner. Editor of *Architettura* between 1922 and 1940. His most progressivist buildings were designed in the 1910s, but subsequently he became more conservative. Was the chief architect of the University of Rome (1932–35).

Steen Eiler Rasmussen (1898–   ). Danish architect and city planner. Professor of architecture at the Royal Academy of Fine Arts, Copenhagen (1938–1968). Author of numerous books on architecture and city planning.

Colin Rowe. English architect, critic and historian. Since 1962 professor of architecture at Cornell University. Was a pioneer in recognizing Le Corbusier's indebtedness to past historical styles.

Peter Serenyi (1931–   ). American historian of art and architecture, born in Hungary and educated in his native country, Austria, and the United States. Teaches at Northeastern University in Boston.

James Stirling (1926–   ). English architect and critic. Visiting teacher at the Architectural Association, London. His many important buildings include the Engineering Laboratories at Leicester University (1959–63) and the Florey Building at Queens College, Oxford University (1967–71). Has taught at Cambridge University and Yale University.

Brian Brace Taylor (1943–   ). American historian of architecture. On the staff of *L'Architecture d'Aujourd'hui* in Paris. Educated at Amherst College and Harvard University (Ph.D., 1974).

Karel Teige (1900–1951). Czech architect, author and critic. Editor of *Stavba* between 1923 and 1931. Organized several avant-garde groups in Prague: Society for Economic and Cultural Ties with New Russia, Union of Socialist Architects, etc. Was a member of the Prague Surrealist Group. Author of many books and articles on modern architecture and theory.

Paul Turner (1939–   ). American historian of architecture. Has taught at Stanford University since 1971. Educated at Union College and Harvard University (Ph.D., 1971).

Waldemar George, pseud. (1893–1970). French critic, editor and historian born in Poland as George Jarocinski. Editor of *L'Amour de l'Art* (1919–1926), *Formes* 1929–34), *Art et Industrie* (1946–55), and after 1956 *Prisme des Arts*. Author of many books on modern artists and art.

Paul Westheim (1886–1963). German author, historian and critic. Editor of *Das Kunstblatt*. His numerous books include *Klassizismus in Frankreich* (1922) and *Für und wider; Kritische Anmerkungen zur Kunst der Gegenwart* (1923).

Rudolf Wittkower (1901–1971). Historian of art and architecture. Member of the Bibliotheca Hertziana in Rome (1923–33). Taught at the Warburg Institute in London (1934–1956). Chairman of the Department of Art History and Archaeology at Columbia University (1956–1968). Named Avalon Professor in the Humanities at Columbia in 1968. Author of many pioneering works on Renaissance and Baroque art and architecture.

Selected Bibliography

Personality

BARDET, GASTON, "Charles-Edouard contre Le Corbusier, essai de psycho-analyse," in *Revue Méditerranée*, 5 (1948), 513–30.

GIRSBERGER, HANS, "Le Corbusier and his 'Oeuvre Complète,' " in *International Asbestos Cement Review*, 41 (January 1966), 3–6.

HELLMAN, GEOFFREY, "From Within to Without," in *The New Yorker*, 23 (26 April 1947), 31–36; 23 (3 May 1947), 36–40.

HOFER, PAUL, "Griff in die Doppelwelt: Notizen zur Person Le Corbusiers," in his *Fundplätze Bauplätze*, pp. 155–60. Basel: Birkhäuser Verlag, 1970.

JARDOT, MAURICE, "Sketch for a portrait," in Le Corbusier, *Creation is a Patient Search*. New York: Praeger, 1960, pp. 9–14.

JENCKS, CHARLES, "Charles Jeanneret-Le Corbusier," in *Arena*, 82 (1967), 299–306.

MALRAUX, ANDRÉ, *Oraisons funèbres*. Paris: Gallimard, 1971.

POSENER, JULIUS, "Le Corbusier," in *Baumeister*, 65 (1968), 544, 548, 550–52.

Drawing, Painting, Sculpture

ALLOWAY, LAWRENCE, "Le Corbusier and some London exhibitions," in *Art International*, 3, no. 1–2 (1959), 29–30, 53.

BERGOT, FRANÇOISE, "Le Corbusier. Expression graphique et picturale," in *Aujourd'hui*, no. 51 (1965), 102–7.

GASSER, HANS ULRICH, "The Painter, Le Corbusier," in *Architects' Year Book*, 6 (1955), 35–44.

GREEN, CHRISTOPHER, "Léger and L'Esprit Nouveau, 1912–1928," in J. Golding and C. Green, *Léger and Purist Paris*. London: The Tate Gallery, 1970, pp. 25–82.

HOHL, REINHOLD, *Le Corbusier, peintre*. Bâle: Galerie Beyeler, 1971.

KURTZ, STEPHEN A., "Public Planning, Private Painting," in *Art News*, 71 (April 1972), 37–41, 73–74.

MOOS, STANISLAUS VON, "Cartesian curves," in *Architectural Design*, 42 (1972), 237–39.

————, "Der Purismus und die Malerei Le Corbusiers," in *Werk*, 53 (1966), 413–20.

OZENFANT, AMÉDÉE, "Extraits des Mémoires," in *Aujourd'hui*, no. 51 (1965), 14–15.

PAPADAKI, STAMO, ed. *Le Corbusier—Architect, Painter, Writer*. New York: The Macmillan Company, 1948.

RAYNAL, MAURICE, "Ozenfant & Jeanneret," in *L'Esprit Nouveau*, 7 (1921), 807–32.

RECASEUS, JOSÉ DE, "Psicogenesis de la pintura de Le Corbusier," in *Proa* (Bogota), no. 8 (1947), 14–18.

SAMONÀ, ALBERTO, "La lezione di Le Corbusier," in *Communità*, 17 (March 1963), 78–86.

SAVINA, JOSEPH, "Sculpture de Le Corbusier-Savina," in *Aujourd'hui*, no. 51 (1965), 96–101.

SEKLER, MARY PATRICIA MAY, "The Early Drawings of Charles-Edouard Jeanneret (Le Corbusier) 1902–1908." Unpublished Ph.D. dissertation, Harvard University, 1973.

Architecture

ALAZARD, JULES and JEAN-PIERRE HEBERT, *De la fenêtre au pan de verre dans l'oeuvre de Le Corbusier*. Paris: Dunod, 1961.

ALFORD, JOHN, "Creativity and Intelligibility in Le Corbusier's Chapel at Ronchamp," in *The Journal of Aesthetics & Art Criticism*, 14 (1958), 293–305.

————, "Modern Architecture and the Symbolism of Creative Process," in *College Art Journal*, 14 (1955), 102–23.

ALLISON, PETER, "Le Corbusier 'Architect or Revolutionary?' " in *Architectural Association Quarterly*, 3, no. 2 (1971), 10–20.

BANHAM, REYNER, "Ateliers d'Artistes: Paris Studio Houses and the Modern Movement," in *The Architectural Review*, 120 (1956), 75–83.

BOYD, ROBIN, "The search for pleasingness," in *Progressive Architecture*, 38 (April 1957), 193–205.

CARON, JULIEN, "Une villa de Le Corbusier 1916," in *L'Esprit Nouveau*, 6 (1921), 679–704.

CHAVANNE, ETIENNE and MICHEL LAVILLE, "Les premières constructions de Le Corbusier," in *Werk*, 50 (1963), 483–88.

CHICER, R., "Le Corbusier und Pierre Jeanneret—Haus des H. Cook," in *Sovremenaya Arkhitektura*, 3, no. 3 (1928), 97–102. (In Russian)

CHOMBART DE LAUWE, PAUL-HENRY, *Famille et Habitation*. Paris: Centre National de la Recherche Scientifique, 1967.

CHOWDHURY, V. E., "Recent Works of Pierre Jeanneret," in *Progressive Architecture*, 44 (February 1964), 148–53.

COCAGNAC, A.-M., "Un projet d'église paroissiale de Le Corbusier," in *L'Art Sacré*, no. 3–4 (1964), 2–24.

CORDIER, GILBERT, "Architectonic reflexions on the written work of F. L. Wright and C. E. Le Corbusier," in *Review of the international union of architects*, 12 (1971), 34–51. (Also in French)

COURTHION, PIERRE, "Le Pavillon Suisse dans la Cité Universitaire, Paris," in *Oeuvres* (May, 1934), 7–11.

CURJEL, HANS, "Produktgestaltung im Frankreich der zwanziger Jahre," in *Werk*, 52 (February 1965), 57–65.

EASTON, KENNETH et al., "Le Corbusier's Unité d'Habitation," in *The Architectural Review*, 109 (1951), 292–300.

ETCHELLS, FREDERICK, "Le Corbusier: A Pioneer of Modern European Architecture," in *Creative Art*, 3 (September 1928), 156–63.

FRAMPTON, KENNETH, "The humanist v. the utilitarian ideal," in *Architectural Design*, 38 (1968), 134–36.

FRY, MAXWELL et al., "Le Corbusier—his impact on four generations," in *Journal of the Royal Institute of British Architects*, 72 (1965), 497–500.

FURNER, A. STANLEY, "The Modern Movement in Architecture," in *South African Architectural Record*, 10 (1925), 87–89; 11 (1926), 6–8.

GHYKA, MATILA, "Le Corbusier's Modulor and the Concept of the Golden Mean," in *The Architectural Review*, 103 (1948), 39–42.

GIEDION, SIGFRIED, "Ein Mietsblock Le Corbusiers in Genf," in *Monatshefte für Baukunst und Städtebau*, 16 (1932), 491–98.

———, "Le Corbusier et l'architecture contemporaine," in *Cahiers d'Art*, 5 (1930), 205–11.

———, "Le Corbusier und der Nachwuchs," in his *Bauen in Frankreich, Eisen, Eisenbeton*. Berlin: Klinkhardt & Biermann, 1928, pp. 83–106.

———, "Swiss Pavilion: Le Corbusier and Pierre Jeanneret," in *The Architectural Record*, 75 (1934), 400–403.

GUTHEIM, FREDERICK, "The New Le Corbusier," in *Architectural Record*, 118 (1955), 180–87.

HANSON, NORMAN, "Architecture and the new aesthetic," in *South African Architectural Record*, 21 (1936), 375–79.

HERBERT, GILBERT, "Le Corbusier and the Origins of Modern Architecture in South Africa," in *Architectural Association Quarterly*, 4 (1972), 16–30.

HITCHCOCK, HENRY-RUSSELL, "Le Corbusier and the United States," in *Zodiac*, 16 (1966), 6–23.

———, "Modern Architecture: II. The New Pioneers," in *The Architectural Record*, 63 (1928), 453–60.

———, "The New Pioneers: France," in his *Modern Architecture, Romanticism and Reintegration*. New York: Payson & Clarke Ltd., 1929, pp. 163–71.

HOWARD, SEYMOUR, "Living with Corbu," in *Progressive Architecture*, 51 (November 1970), 90–97.

JACOBUS, JOHN M., JR., "Fantasy and the International Style," in *Arts and Architecture*, 75 (February 1958), 14–15, 30.

JORDY, WILLIAM H., "The Symbolic Essence of Modern European Architecture of the Twenties and Its Continuing Influence," in *Journal of the Society of Architectural Historians*, 22 (1963), 177–87.

JULLIAN DE LA FUENTE, GUILLERMO, "*The Venice Hospital Project of Le Corbusier*." In *Architecture at Rice*, no. 23. Houston: School of Architecture, Rice University, 1968.

"*Le Corbusier—Entwurf für das Zentrossojus-Haus,*" in *Sovremenaya Arkhitektura*, 3, no. 6 (1928), 177–81. (In Russian)

MANGIAROTTI, ANGELO AND BRUNO MORASSUTTI, "In una villa di Le Corbusier," in *Domus*, no. 368 (1960), 9–22.

MARTIENSSEN, REX, "The Contemporary House," in *South African Architectural Record*, 19 (1934), 267–70.

MARTIN, CAMILLE, "Le concours pour l'édification d'un Palais de la Société des Nations à Genève," in *Das Werk*, 14 (1927), 163–71.

MAZZARIOL, GIUSEPPE, "Le Corbusier a Venezia" (with English translation), in *Zodiac*, 16 (1966), 88–93.

MEIER, RICHARD, "Les Heures Claires," in *Le Corbusier Villa Savoye*, Global Architecture, No. 12, ed., Yukio Futagawa. Tokyo: A.D.A. Edita Tokyo Co., Ltd., 1972, pp. 2–7.

MILLON, HENRY A., "Rudolf Wittkower, *Architectural Principles in the Age of Humanism*: Its Influence on the Development and Interpretation of Modern Architecture," in *Journal of the Society of Architectural Historians*, 31 (1972), 83–91.

MOOS, STANISLAUS VON, Review of Colin Rowe and Robert Slutzky, *Transparenz*, and Paul Hofer, *Fundplätze, Bauplätze*, in *Zeitschrift für Schweizerische Archäologie und Kunstgeschichte*, 27 (1970), 237–38, 240–43.

MÜLLER-REPPEN, W., *Le Corbusier's Wohnheit 'Typ Berlin.'* Berlin: Heilsberger Dreieck Grundstück AG., 1958.

NELSON, GEORGE, "Architects of Europe Today 5—Le Corbusier, France," in *Pencil Points*, 16 (1935), 368–74.

OSBORN, F. J., "Concerning Le Corbusier," in *Town and Country Planning*, 20 (1952), 311–16, 359–63.

PEVSNER, NIKOLAUS, "Time and Le Corbusier," in *The Architectural Review*, 125 (1959), 158–65.

PLATZ, GUSTAV ADOLF, "Die neue Baukunst in Frankreich," in his *Die Baukunst der Neuesten Zeit*, Berlin: Propyläen Verlag, 1930, pp. 97–119.

POSENER, JULIUS, Häring, Scharoun, Mies, and Le Corbusier," in his *From Schinkel to the Bauhaus*. New York: George Wittenborn Inc., 1972, pp. 33–41.

RAGGHIANTI, C. L., "Le Corbusier à Firenze" (with English and French translations), in *Zodiac*, 12 (1963), 4–17, 219–37.

RITTER, JOHN, "World Parliament—The League of Nations Competition," in *The Architectural Review*, 136 (1964), 17–23.

ROBERTSON, HOWARD, "Some Recent French Developments in Domestic Architecture," in *The Architectural Review*, 61 (1927), 2–7.

ROERIG, UTE, "Architektur und Natur. Zur Architekturtheorie im 20. Jahrhundert," in *Zeitschrift für Ästhetik und Allgemeine Kunstwissenschaft*, 15, no. 2 (1970), 200–236.

ROGERS, ERNESTO, "Il metodo di Le Corbusier e la forma della 'Chapelle de Ronchamp'" (with English and French translations), in *Casabella*, no. 207 (1955), 2–6.

———, "Villa, Townhouse, and Unité: The Utopian Spectrum," in *Four Great Makers of Modern Architecture*, ed., Richard A. Miller. New York: Da Capo Press, 1970, pp. 205–15.

ROTH, ALFRED, "Maison de vacances: Les Mathes," in his *Nouvelle Architecture*. Zurich: Les Editions Girsberger, 1940, pp. 19–24.

———, *Zwei Wohnhäuser von Le Corbusier und Pierre Jeanneret*. Stuttgart: Akad. Verlag Dr. Fr. Wedekind & Co., 1928.

ROWE, COLIN, "Dominican Monastery of La Tourette, Eveux-sur-Arbresle, Lyons," in *The Architectural Review*, 129 (1961), 400–410.

————, "Mannerism and Modern Architecture," in *The Architectural Review*, 107 (1950), 289–99.

————, and ROBERT SLUTZKY, "Transparency: Literal and Phenomenal," in *Perspecta*, 8 (1963), 45–54.

————, ROBERT SLUTZKY, and BERNHARD HOESLI, *Transparenz*. Basel: Birkhäuser Verlag, 1968.

SABATOU, J. P., "Immeuble à Paris," in *L'Architecture d'Aujourd'hui*, 5 (September 1934), 41–52.

SCHAFER, ROGER, "Marseille: A housing consultant's look at Le Corbusier's Unité d'Habitation after two decades of use," in *Architecture plus*, 2 (1974), 86–91.

SEGAUD, MARION, and HENRI RAYMOND, "Un espace architectural le Corbusier," in *Cahiers du centre d'études architecturales*, 11 (1970), 6–50.

SHAND, P. MORTON, "Flat of the Parc de Princes, Paris by Le Corbusier and Jeanneret," in *The Architectural Review*, 77 (1935), 73–76.

STEWART, DAVID, "Le Corbusier's Theory of Architecture and *L'Esprit Nouveau*." Unpublished Ph.D. dissertation, Courtauld Institute, London University, 1972.

SUMMERSON, JOHN, "Architecture, Painting and Le Corbusier," in his *Heavenly Mansions*. London: Cresset Press, 1949, pp. 177–94.

TURNER, PAUL V, "The Education of Le Corbusier: A Study of the Development of Le Corbusier's Thought, 1900–1920." Unpublished Ph.D. dissertation, Harvard University, 1971.

WATT, ALEXANDER, "Fantasy on the Roofs of Paris: Structure by Le Corbusier, decoration by Carlos de Beistegui," in *The Architectural Review*, 79 (1936), 155–59.

WEINERT, HERMANN KARL, "Le poème électronique," in *Antares* (Mainz), (1959), 3–19.

WITTKOWER, RUDOLF, "Systems of Proportion," in *Architects' Year Book*, 5 (1953), 9–18.

WOODS, SHADRACH, "Why Revisit 'Le Pavillon Suisse'?" in *The Architectural Forum*, 122 (June 1965), 59–63.

City Planning and Architecture

ADSHEAD, S. D., "Camillo Sitte and Le Corbusier," in *Town Planning Review*, 14 (November 1930), 85–94.

ANAND, MULK RAJ, "Postscript: The building of Chandigarh," in *The Architectural Review*, 150 (1971), 389–92.

ANTHONY, HARRY ANTONIADES, "Le Corbusier: His Ideas for Cities," in *Journal of the American Institute of Planners*, 32 (January 1966), 279–88.

BENOIT LEVY, GEORGES, "A French Garden Hamlet," in *The Town Planning Review*, 7 (1918), 251–52.

BROLIN, BRENT C., "Chandigarh was planned by experts, but something has gone wrong," in *Smithsonian*, 3 (June 1972), 56–63.

CHAVANCE, RENÉ, "Réflexions sur l'oeuvre et les idées de Le Corbusier," in *Art et Décoration*, 65, no. 4 (1936), 129–36.

CHOWDHURY, EULIE, "Le Corbusier in Chandigarh: creator and generator," in *Architectural Design*, 35 (1965), 504–13.

COGNIAT, RAYMOND, "Une conception nouvelle de l'Urbanisme," in *L'Architecture*, 36, no. 15 (1923), 224–30.

COLLINS, GEORGE R., "Linear Planning Throughout the World," in *Journal of the Society of Architectural Historians*, 18 (1959), 74–93.

CORBOZ, ANDRÉ, "Encore Pessac," in *Archithese*, no. 1 (1972), 27–36.

CORREA, CHARLES, "The Assembly, Chandigarh," in *The Architectural Review*, 135 (1964), 405–12.

DREW, JANE, "Chandigarh Capital City Project," in *Architects' Year Book*, 5 (1953), 56–66.

EDWARDS, TRYSTAN, "The Dead City," in *The Architectural Review*, 66 (1929), 135–38.

EVENSON, NORMA, *Chandigarh*. Berkeley, Calif.: University of California Press, 1966.

FISHMAN, ROBERT L., "Ideal Cities: The Social Thought of Ebenezer Howard, Frank Lloyd Wright and Le Corbusier." Unpublished Ph.D. dissertation, Harvard University, 1974.

FRY, E. MAXWELL, "Chandigarh: The Capital of the Punjab," in *Journal of the Royal Institute of British Architects*, 62 (1955), 87–94.

GALANTAY, ERWIN, "Corbu's Tightrope," in *Progressive Architecture*, 48 (1967), 198, 200, 206.

GIEDION, SIGFRIED, "CIAM at Sea—The Background of the Fourth (Athens) Congress," in *Architects' Year Book*, 3 (1949), 36–39.

GINZBURG, MOSES, "Letter to Le Corbusier," in Anatole Kopp, *Town and Revolution*. London: Thames and Hudson Ltd., 1970, pp. 253–54.

GOLDFINGER, ERNÖ, "Pessac de Le Corbusier," in *L'Architecture d'Aujourd'hui*, no. 148 (1970), xix.

HANSON, NORMAN, "Letter to the Editors," in *South African Architectural Record*, 27 (1942), 298–99.

HILBERSEIMER, LUDWIG, *Groszstadt Architektur*. Stuttgart: Verlag Julius Hoffmann, 1927.

HOFER, PAUL, "Le Corbusier und die Stadt," in *Bauen und Wohnen*, 15 (1961), 67–72.

HOFFMANN, HUBERT, "Chandigarh, die Stadt Le Corbusiers," in *Bauen und Wohnen*, 27 (1972), 419–22.

HOWE, GEORGE, "Master Plans for Master Politicians," in *Magazine of Art*, 39 (February 1946), 66–68.

JAMESON, CONRAD, "Le Corbusier's Pessac: A Sociological Evaluation," in *Architectural Association Quarterly*, 4, no. 3 (1972), 51–56.

KANTOROVICH, ROY, "The Modern Theorists of Planning; Le Corbusier and Frank Lloyd Wright etc.," in *South African Architectural Record*, 27 (1942), 6–15.

MOOS, STANISLAUS VON, "Anatomie d'une ville, Chandigarh ville morte?" in *L'Architecture d'Aujourd'hui*, no. 146 (1969), 54–61.

———, "Corbusiana—zum Stand der Corbusier-Kritik," in *Bauwelt*, 63 (1972), 8–9, 56.

Mumford, Lewis, "Yesterday's City of Tomorrow," in *Architectural Record,* 132 (1962), 139–44.

Nicoletti, Manfredi, "Flash Gordon and the Twentieth Century Utopia," in *The Architectural Review,* 140 (1966), 87–91.

Piccinato, Giorgio, "Metodologia di Le Corbusier," in *Casabella,* no. 274 (1963), 16–25.

Pokorny, Jan and Elisabeth Hird, "Zlin, Czechoslovakia," in *Architectural Record,* 102 (1947), 68–75.

Romain, Paul, "La Ville Radieuse," in *Les chantiers nord-africains* (May, 1931), 473–82.

Serenyi, Peter, "Le Corbusier's Art and Thought: 1918–1935." Unpublished Ph.D. dissertation, Washington University, 1968.

———, Review of M. Besset, *Who Was Le Corbusier?;* S. von Moos, *Le Corbusier, Elemente einer Synthese;* Ph. Boudon, *Pessac de Le Corbusier;* N. Evenson, *Le Corbusier: The Machine and the Grand Design,* in *Journal of the Society of Architectural Historians,* 30 (1971), 255–59.

Stillman, Seymour, "Comparing Wright and Le Corbusier," in *Journal of the American Institute of Architects,* 9 (1948), 171–78, 226–33.

Tafuri, Manfredo, "La crisi dell utopia: Le Corbusier ad Algeri," in his *Progetto e utopia.* Rome: G. Laterza, 1973, pp. 115–37.

Taylor, Brian Brace, "Le Corbusier's Prototype Mass-Housing: 1914–1928." Unpublished Ph.D. dissertation, Harvard University, 1974.

Toxiri, Anna Maria, "Le Corbusier teorico," in *Commentari,* 16 (1965), 268–81.

Troedsson, Carl Birger, "Two Standpoints Towards Modern Architecture: Wright and Le Corbusier," in *Transactions of Chalmers University of Technology* (Gothenburg, Sweden), no. 113 (1951), 3–22.

Vidler, Anthony, "The Idea of Unity and Le Corbusier's Urban Form," in *Architects' Year Book,* 15 (1968), 225–37.

Wittkower, Rudolf, "Camillo Sitte's *Art of Building Cities* in an American Translation," in *Town Planning Review,* 19, no. 3–4 (1947), 164–69.

List of Illustrations